Walking with Jesus

Developing a Daily Personal Time with Your Savior

Marcel Sanchez

Walking with Jesus

Cover and interior designed by Brenda Ulloa, Brenda@IBBchurch.org

IBB Church
17701 NW 57th Avenue
Miami, FL 33055
305.620.5111
www.IBBChurch.org

Introduction

It is by far one of the biggest challenges faced by believers worldwide. It does not matter whether you are married or single, young or old, educated or uneducated, rich or poor. This struggle does not make any distinctions. It is common to all believers. "What is this great challenge?" you might ask. This struggle, we all face is to start and develop a daily personal time with the Savior, to grow in our love for God, our knowledge of His Word, and to receive spiritual nourishment. It is the struggle to set aside time every day to be alone with the Savior. Spiritual replenishment is not automatic and it is never easy. You have to work at it moment-by-moment.

Don't miss this next statement: God is at work in your life. He is doing a good work in you. This work started at the moment of your salvation, and continues until you meet with Christ in glory. The Apostle Paul wrote, *"And I am sure of this, that he who began a good work in you will bring it to completion at the day of Jesus Christ"* (Philippians 1:6, ESV). While serving time in prison, the Apostle Paul reminded his friends in Philippi of an encouraging reality: What God starts in your life, He always finishes. God intends to finish the good work He started in your life. This is thrilling.

Your daily personal time with God is a part of this good work. It serves to perfect your faith, and to conform you to the image of the Lord Jesus Christ. It is how you refresh your spirit and transform your soul. Your daily personal time with God is what God uses to change your thinking and align your thoughts with the mind of Christ. It's what God primarily uses to change your attitude, adjust your behavior, and transform the way you speak with others. It's what fuels your spirit. It is necessary for your spiritual maturity to flourish. It is at the heart of an abiding life (John 15). You can't grow spiritually without it. It is absolutely essential to your faith.

Although this may be a significant struggle for you right now, it can also become your greatest opportunity to experience God in a completely new way. Personal struggles can often be converted into spiritual breakthroughs. Are you ready for a spiritual breakthrough? Are you ready to dig deeper into God's Word and live in greater obedience? Do you long for God to use you in a powerful way to change the lives of those around you? If so, it begins with allowing His Word to transform you from the inside out as you follow His commands with all of your heart, all of your mind, all of your soul, and all of your strength.

This daily devotional is designed for you to read five days a week for an entire year. It purposely leaves out two days for you to do something different such as review the entire week, memorize key scriptures, have an extended time of prayer, participate in a small group or attend a live worship service. Please don't rush through each devotional. Let God's Word sink deep within your heart. Allow God's Word to work in you and change you from the inside out. Prayerfully reflect on the progression as we unfold the book of John section-by-section, and include other important scriptures for you to meditate on. Each devotional is followed by a three-fold plan for personal reflection:

READ

Reading the scriptures is very important. Reading parallel passages is very helpful to further understand the section being studied. I encourage you to read each parallel scripture out loud at least twice. Think through the relationship between the daily devotional being read and the parallel scriptures provided. Ask yourself, "How does one compliment the other?"

REFLECT

This section helps you analyze the Scripture from multiple angles with a sharp focus on personal application. It is designed to help you discover more about the text through the use of questions and observations. You will learn more about God's characteristics, and the unique ways that He works through His Son, Jesus. Finally, personal application is highlighted to help you start applying these truths in your life right away.

RESPOND

As we grow in our personal time with the Savior, we have to be willing and ready to respond to His inner promptings. This involves asking the Lord, "What do I need to change, and how do I begin making these changes?" In other words, our response requires a plan of action. Every change takes a step of action. The question we have to ask is, "What is my next step in obeying God's Word?" This is often where spiritual breakthrough takes place—through our obedience to the Living Word of God—as the Spirit of God uses the Word of God to transform our heart for God.

My prayer is that you would experience more of God's presence and power working in and through your life as you seek Him more each and every day. May you serve Him more as He reveals His love and His good work in your life day-by-day, and moment-by-moment.

Marcel Sanchez
www.MarcelSanchez.com

How Do I Become A Christian?

Are you a Christian? How do you know? There are many misconceptions about how a person becomes a Christian. With more information available and accessible in our world than ever before in history, it is no wonder why someone can be confused or even misguided by what they have read or have been taught by others.

Here are a few examples of very sincere, but misguided assumptions about the Christian faith: "I am a Christian if I go to church regularly. I am a Christian if I help others. I am a Christian if I give money to the church or to the poor. I am a Christian if I read the Bible. If my parents are Christians, it automatically makes me a Christian. Since I believe in God, I am a Christian. I am a Christian because I am a good person."

The Christian life is about a living relationship with a person, Jesus Christ. Loving, knowing and serving Him is what the Christian life is all about. Jesus is the Christian life. Since God is relational, the Christian life is relational as well. When you begin a relationship with Jesus, you begin a relationship with the Father. Are you ready to begin a vibrant relationship with a God who loves you, and died on a cross to give you eternal life? If so, here are four key words to guide you and help you begin the Christian life: *Love, separation, provision, and connection.*

1. Love: God loves YOU! Recognize that He loves you just the way you are, unconditionally. He loved you before you were born. His desire is for you to know Him. God wants you to find complete spiritual satisfaction by starting a living relationship with His Son, Jesus Christ.

GOD LOVES YOU: *"For God so loved the world that He gave His only begotten Son, that whoever believes in Him should not perish but have everlasting life" (John 3:16).*

2. Separation: Know and admit that your **SIN** has separated you from God. Knowingly or unknowingly, you've broken at least one of God's 10 Commandments, His standard for perfection. Right now, you stand guilty before God for your sin.

Your SIN separates you from God: *"For all have sinned and fall short of the glory of God" (Romans 3:23).*

Your personal goodness or ability to help others can't solve the separation problem. There is NOTHING you can do to pay the penalty of your sins. Morality, religion, generosity, or good works do not satisfy God's holy standard. The writer of Proverbs reminds us: "*There is a way that seems right to a man, but its end is the way of death*" (Proverbs 14:12).

3. Provision: Jesus died on the cross to pay the penalty of your sins. He is God's **ONLY** solution to your sin problem. Jesus died on the cross to connect you to God. He was buried, and on the third day He rose from the grave. Jesus was your substitute, and His death paid the penalty of your sins.

JESUS DIED TO CONNECT YOU TO GOD:

Peter wrote, "*For Christ also suffered once for sins, the just for the unjust, that He might bring us to God*" (1 Peter 3:18).

Jesus said, "*I am the way, the truth, and the life. No one comes to the Father except through Me. (John 14:6)*

4. Connection: Connection involves believing, confessing, and receiving. You connect with God through FAITH, by believing in Jesus' finished work on the cross and confessing your sins directly to Him through prayer. You receive Jesus by personal invitation. The Apostle John wrote, "*But as many as received Him, to them He gave the right to become children of God, to those who believe in His name*" (John 1:12).

John promises us "*If we confess our sins, He [Jesus] is faithful and just to forgive us our sins and to cleanse us from all unrighteousness*" (1 John 1:9)

Paul wrote, "*If you confess with your mouth the Lord Jesus and believe in your heart that God has raised Him from the dead, you will be saved*" (Romans 10:9).

Starting the Christian Life: You begin the Christian life through a prayer of faith. Here is a sample prayer to repeat out loud to the Lord if that is your heart's desire and you are ready to do so:

Lord God, I thank You for Your great love for me. Today I understand how much You love me. I know that I have sinned against You, and broken Your commandments. I'm truly sorry. I ask You, Lord Jesus, to forgive me for all my sins. Cleanse my heart and make all things new. Jesus, I believe that You died on the cross to pay for my sins. I believe that You were buried and on the third day, you rose again from the grave. Today I invite you into my heart and receive you as Lord and Savior. Amen.

A Timeless God and Savior

"In the beginning was the Word" (John 1:1).

Imagine not having to worry about setting your alarm clock or being on time for your next appointment. Picture what your life would be like if you lived without any time limitations whatsoever. What would you do differently if your life were not governed by the laws of time? What new adventures would you plan? It's hard to even imagine, isn't it?

We only have 24 hours each day to get everything done. We simply have to make the best use of each moment to advance God's plan of reconciling all men to Himself through Jesus Christ: *"The Lord is not slow to fulfill his promise as some count slowness, but is patient toward you, not wishing that any should perish, but that all should reach repentance" (2 Peter 3:9).*

Now imagine being alive before time, as we understand time, ever existed. Think about what would happen if you lived in a perfect environment, one that never aged or was subject to negative environmental factors. Can you picture the beauty of such a place? Prior to His arrival on earth, Jesus lived in such an environment. Did you know that Jesus Christ is the Eternal Word of God? *"Jesus said, 'I am the Alpha and the Omega,' says the Lord God, 'who is and who was and who is to come, the Almighty' " (Revelation 1:8).* God is one, but exists in three distinct persons: Father, Son and Holy Spirit. *"Hear, O Israel: The LORD our God, the LORD is one" (Deuteronomy 6:4, ESV).* They each function in perfect relational and spiritual harmony. The Word of God is the spoken representation of God's person (John 1:1).

Although a distinct person, Jesus shares His divine attributes with the Father. *"While we wait for the blessed hope—the glorious appearing of our great God and Savior, Jesus Christ" (Titus 2:13, NIV).* Jesus is the exact representation of God Himself (Colossians 1:15-20). The Holy Spirit also shares in this divine nature. He exists as a separate person and serves a unique purpose within the divine trinity. The Spirit is also eternal in nature.

Read: Open your Bible and read Colossians 1:15-20.

Reflect: Prayerfully consider the following: Why would Jesus be able to hold your life together when challenges arrive without any warning? List three characteristics regarding the person of Jesus. When it comes to allowing God's Word to rule in every area of your life, which areas do you find yourself still resisting?

Respond: As a result of these truths, what might need to change in my attitude, beliefs, and actions? What steps do I need to take outwardly?

Creating Something Out of Nothing

"In the beginning, God created the heavens and the earth" (Genesis 1:1).

The Jewish teachers interchangeably connected the *"word of God"* with the God of Israel. They used this phrase to point their people to the One True God. Throughout the Old Testament, God's creative power is described as the *"word of God."* This is the power that makes something out of nothing. It is the power that brought all forms of matter into existence, and provided the perfect form and ecosystem for its survival. It is the power that created life. And this *"word"* is the force, the power, that sustains life and provides the necessary structure and environment for that life to prosper. God is amazing. Our God is a powerful God!

As a believer in Christ Jesus, you are the result of God's magnificent creative power. He provided you with a new Spirit—His Spirit—when you accepted His Son into your heart, and confessed your sins to Him. Here is the promise: *"But to all who did receive him, who believed in his name, he gave the right to become children of God" (John 1:12).* You now belong to God.

John would later write, *"If we say we have no sin, we deceive ourselves, and the truth is not in us. If we confess our sins, he is faithful and just to forgive us our sins and to cleanse us from all unrighteousness. If we say we have not sinned, we make him a liar, and his word is not in us" (1 John 1:8-11).* Jesus replaced what was dead and decaying with what is eternally alive and thriving. He moved in and now permanently lives within you. You no longer have to try to control every detail of your life. Let Jesus lead, and start following Him.

You can now rest in the perfect work of Jesus Christ crucified on the cross at Calvary. Just as God expressed Himself and created life through the Word, Jesus Christ, He wants to express who He is and create more life through your life. He wants others to experience His great love for them through you. He wants His love to be obvious to those around you. He wants to use you as an instrument of His grace in bringing people into a greater knowledge and love for His Son—the Living Word, the One who was present in the beginning. Let His unlimited power flow through you.

Read: Open your Bible and read Genesis 1:1-31.

Reflect: Prayerfully consider the following: What patterns do you find as you study God's creation? Since you are created in the image of God, what does this statement say about the value God places on your life?

Respond: As a result of these truths, what might need to change in my attitude, beliefs, and actions? What steps do I need to take outwardly?

Keeping it Real

*"In the beginning was the Word, and the Word was with God,
and the Word was God" (John 1:1).*

The Kingdom of God is eternal. Jesus Himself had no beginning, and has no end. Before this world was created, He ruled and shared the glory of Heaven's throne with the Father and the Holy Spirit in eternity past. Although Jesus is a distinct person from God the Father, He always shared God's qualities and His divine nature. The author of Hebrews writes, *"He is the radiance of the glory of God and the exact imprint of his nature, and he upholds the universe by the word of his power. After making purification for sins, he sat down at the right hand of the Majesty on high, having become as much superior to angels as the name he has inherited is more excellent than theirs"* (Hebrews 1:3-4). Imagine experiencing the glory of God forever and ever.

The Apostle John wrote, *"The life appeared; we have seen it and testify to it, and we proclaim to you the eternal life, which was with the Father and has appeared to us"* (1 John 1:2). Jesus enjoyed a divine fellowship with the Father, a shared relationship that was spiritually fruitful, relationally profound, and perfectly aligned. This communion was both unique and transparent. It went far beyond anything that we could possibly create on our own. This powerful relationship produced a unique splendor that radiated throughout all of Heaven. Now we have the opportunity to experience God's Kingdom everyday as we allow His presence to flow through our lives. Nothing can compare with God's eternal presence.

Before enduring the cross, Jesus prayed, *"And now, Father, glorify me in your own presence with the glory that I had with you before the world existed"* (John 17:5, ESV). In another translation it reads, *"Now, Father, bring me into the glory we shared before the world began"* (John 17:5, NLT). Jesus longed to reunite Himself with the glory of the Father to once again experience the majesty and beauty of their fellowship in Heaven. This idea of a shared relationship is available and extended to every believer. The more you experience God's presence, the better. What new habits do you need to create to improve your relationship with God and with others around you?

Read: Open your Bible and read Hebrews 1:3, and Philippians 2:6.

Reflect: Consider the following: Do you enjoy your relationship with God? What is it that you enjoy the most? Since God is a ruler of an Eternal Kingdom, what encouragement does that provide for your life?

Respond: As a result of these truths, what might need to change in my attitude, beliefs, and actions? What steps do I need to take outwardly?

Starting Point

"He was in the beginning with God" (John 1:2).

Have you ever arrived late to a good movie? You may have prepaid your tickets online, but local traffic, and possibly your small children, obstructed every effort to arrive on time. When you ask the person sitting next to you, "How much did I miss?" They look at you and smile, "Oh, only about thirty minutes." By this time you're disappointed and very frustrated. You're not sure where the story is headed or what key parts were missed because you were not present in the opening scene. You missed the starting point of the entire movie. Why? You were not present in the opening scene. Jesus has always existed. He is the starting point of life.

The title *"I AM"* was used in the Old Testament to refer to the God of the Hebrews. During one of his teachings, Jesus responded, *"I tell you the truth…before Abraham was born, I am!" (John 8:58, NIV).* In other words, Jesus unapologetically declared that He was the eternal God over all of creation! This assertion infuriated the religious leaders of the day. Why? Simply put, it placed Jesus in the same divine category as the God of Israel.

It meant that Jesus already existed in eternity past with the Father and Holy Spirit. If Jesus was the great *"I am"* it meant that He is eternal and shares God's divine nature. What these leaders failed to understand was that before time ever existed, before the movie of this world started playing, Jesus was already living. Jesus was present in the opening scene and they were not. Isaiah wrote, *"For to us a child is born, to us a son is given; and the government shall be upon his shoulder, and his name shall be called 'Wonderful Counselor, Mighty God, Everlasting Father, Prince of Peace' " (Isaiah 9:6).*

Jesus was an active part of eternity before our world began. Why? Jesus is the starting point of life. One day everyone will bow and recognize Jesus as Lord of all things. The Living Word of God will return to earth, destroy all evil and reign supreme over His creation. John describes our great God and Savior powerfully when he writes, *"He is clothed with a robe dipped in blood, and His name is called The Word of God" (Revelation 19:13, NASB).*

Read: Open your Bible and read John 8:48-59.

Reflect: Prayerfully consider the following: What activities are you involved in that bring glory to God? What two friends need to hear more regarding who Jesus is and what He has done to pay for our sins?

Respond: As a result of these truths, what might need to change in my attitude, beliefs, and actions? What steps do I need to take outwardly?

A Special Purpose

"But you are a chosen generation, a royal priesthood, a holy nation, His own special people, that you may proclaim the praises of Him who called you out of darkness into His marvelous light; who once were not a people but are now the people of God, who had not obtained mercy but now have obtained mercy."
(1 Peter 2:9-10, ESV)

Right from the start, God chose you for a very special purpose. In His infinite wisdom, God selected you to be His ambassador, His personal representative here on earth. He removed you from a life without an eternal purpose to carry out His master plan of leading all people to Himself. As a believer in Christ, you are a chosen vessel of God. In Christ, you have been distinctly set apart to fulfill a specific purpose. Paul wrote, *"I thank my God in all my remembrance of you, always in every prayer of mine for you all making my prayer with joy, because of your partnership in the gospel from the first day until now. And I am sure of this, that he who began a good work in you will bring it to completion at the day of Jesus Christ" (Philippians 1:3-6).*

God has a unique plan for your life. This plan was crafted well before you ever existed. It is a plan that brings true satisfaction and personal fulfillment by living through the starting point of life—Jesus. You may find it hard to believe, but you have been personally chosen by God to be a part of His royal family. Right now, you are royalty. You are a child of the King!

There is no higher calling for your life. If God has chosen you to be His child, there is no higher status. No position can compare with being an heir to the King. You are no longer a slave to your past or a slave to sin. You are a slave of Christ. He is your Savior and Lord. Darkness has no power over your life. Nothing hidden or visible can separate you from your new position. In Christ Jesus, you are permanently secure! You belong to the King! Paul wrote, *"Yet in all these things we are more than conquerors through Him who loved us. For I am persuaded that neither death nor life, nor angels nor principalities nor powers, nor things present nor things to come, nor height nor depth, nor any other created thing, shall be able to separate us from the love of God which is in Christ Jesus our Lord" (Romans 8:37-39).*

Read: Open your Bible and read 1 Peter 2:9-10.

Reflect: Prayerfully consider the following: What can I do today to make God's name known to others? What skills or resources can I use to minister to others? What can I do right now to live for God's purposes?

Respond: As a result of these truths, what might need to change in my attitude, beliefs, and actions? What steps do I need to take outwardly?

Still Searching

"You do not delight in sacrifice, or I would bring it; you do not take pleasure in burnt offerings. The sacrifices of God are a broken spirit; a broken and contrite heart, O God, you will not despise" (Psalm 51:16-17, NIV).

Have you ever lost something of great personal value? If so, how long did you continue searching for what was lost? The more we value something the more we pursue it. Have you ever considered what God values? Since God never loses anything, what could He possibly need to find? We know that God's desire is to live in a shared relationship with His people. This idea serves to remind us of God's great love for authentic fellowship. God is looking for people who recognize their spiritual emptiness. He wants to fill this emptiness with His perfect presence. God is still searching.

God is not looking for spiritual puppets, but He is searching for empty vessels. An empty vessel in the hands of an Almighty God is powerful. He is not looking for great performers, but He is searching for the right heart to carry out His great work. God is pursuing those who want to follow His ways, and worship Him in spirit and in truth. Consider this: *"For the eyes of the Lord run to and fro throughout the whole earth, to give strong support to those whose heart is blameless toward him" (2 Chronicles 16:9).*

Today, as you read this devotional, is your heart broken and empty before the Lord? When you sin, does it trouble you deeply and bring you to sorrowful repentance? Repentance means a change of direction. If you are not allowing God to deal with your sin, you are not broken. If this is the case, don't expect a rich spiritual experience. Personal holiness precedes authentic fellowship. Are you willing to live a life of personal holiness?

Paul pleaded with the believers in Rome, *"Therefore, I urge you, brothers, in view of God's mercy, to offer your bodies as living sacrifices, holy and pleasing to God—this is your spiritual act of worship" (Romans 12:1, NIV).* Your sin should point you to the Savior. First, remove the things from your life that continue to lead you into sin. Second, get ready to love and worship God like never before. God is still searching to fill hearts that are broken and empty. If today you are unforgiving and resentful, your heart remains full.

Read: Open your Bible and read 2 Chronicles 16:9, and Psalm 51:1-19.

Reflect: Prayerfully consider the following: How can I demonstrate a broken and empty heart before God? What would that look like?

Respond: As a result of these truths, what might need to change in my attitude, beliefs, and actions? What steps do I need to take outwardly?

The Master Designer

"All things were made through Him, and without Him nothing was made that was made" (John 1:3).

Some of the most entertaining shows online and on television have to do with professional cake making: designing and preparing gourmet cakes for special events. These shows enter into the world of professional cake design. Depending on the complexity of the client's order, a cake can take anywhere from four hours to more than sixteen hours to design, bake and build. You learn the secrets to what keeps a cake together and how they endure refrigeration challenges, travel, and unexpected surprises.

Some professional bakers design a beautiful cake, but in the end do not satisfy the client. Why? In some cases, because the cake does not hold together until the very end. When it arrives at the event, an important section falls apart. When the weight of the cake is too much for the support structure to endure, the cake slowly falls apart from the inside out. Jesus is the master designer of life, *"By the word of the LORD the heavens were made, and by the breath of his mouth all their host" (Psalm 33:6, ESV).* Jesus Christ is the architect of life. He is the One who created all things for life to exist. Everything and everyone you see is the result of His work.

Since the master designer has created us, we all have eternal value in God's eyes. Everything was created by Jesus, and for Jesus. In Him, all things exist, move, and have their place. Jesus is the source of life. He is Lord of all. Jesus is our sustainer. Jesus personalized the reality of eternity when He decided to leave His glory in Heaven and live among us: *"And the Word became flesh and dwelt among us, and we have seen his glory, glory as of the only Son from the Father, full of grace and truth" (John 1:14).* Jesus came as the physical manifestation of God's spoken Word. He is the Living Word. Jesus represented the revelation of God's Word in the Old Testament.

Can you imagine looking into the face of Jesus and knowing that He was the One responsible for everything you've studied from God's word? What a powerful thought. Remember to thank the Lord Jesus for His magnificent creation. Remember to point others to God through the visible work of His hands. What a great work He has done!

Read: Open your Bible and read Psalm 33:6, and John 1:14.

Reflect: Prayerfully consider the following: What part of God's creation can I share with others today to point them to Jesus?

Respond: As a result of these truths, what might need to change in my attitude, beliefs, and actions? What steps do I need to take outwardly?

A Perfect Design

"For you formed my inward parts; you knitted me together in my mother's womb" (Psalm 139:13, ESV).

Have you ever worked on a difficult project for several weeks? Whether a project from your professor, employer, or customer, perhaps it stretched you personally, and required more time than you originally planned. You were responsible for the design and the delivery of the project. In the end, though, everyone was delighted because all of your work was intentionally and perfectly designed for the desired outcome. You have also been perfectly designed by the Lord to accomplish His purposes for your life. You are not a mistake. You were intentionally created by God to display His qualities to those who do not know Him and to bring honor and glory to His name. Before you took your first breath, God already knew you.

You are who you are by divine design. You are not an accident. God does not make mistakes: *"For we are his workmanship, created in Christ Jesus for good works, which God prepared beforehand, that we should walk in them"* (Ephesians 2:10). God has carved out a good plan for your life. In Christ Jesus, you have all of the resources necessary for this plan to be realized. You were perfectly designed by God to accomplish His purposes for your life. No matter what breaks down around you, Jesus has the power to keep you together. He provides the strength needed to endure every challenge, from the inside out and from the outside in. Since Jesus is the designer and sustainer of your life, He is the One who holds you together.

God's perfect work in your life is a direct result of His perfect design for your life. He wants to use your experiences, both good and bad, to display His unlimited power. He wants to use your education to teach and encourage others. He wants to use your talents, gifts, and abilities to skillfully serve His church. God wants to use your finances and material things to demonstrate His heart of generosity. God made you by His perfect design. He has designed all that you are to be all that He wants you to be. He knows exactly how you function best. He wants to use your life for His will, and He knows just where to place you. You can trust God completely with your life. His master design is perfect for your life.

Read: Open your Bible and read Psalm 139:1-24.

Reflect: Prayerfully consider the following: Am I afraid to let God use every part of my life? If so, why do I have such a hard time trusting God?

Respond: As a result of these truths, what might need to change in my attitude, beliefs, and actions? What steps do I need to take outwardly?

14

Embracing the Life

"In Him was life, and the life was the light of men" (John 1:4).

Do you remember, as a child, when you first realized the light in the refrigerator did not always remain on while the door was closed? You knew the bulb shined brightly when the refrigerator was open, but you had doubts about whether or not it stayed on when the door was closed. If you were the curious type, you may have wrestled with this thought for days and asked, "How long does this light last? What happens to the food when it's dark? Do scary creatures walk around inside?" The Apostle John spends considerable time contrasting life and death and light and darkness. He wants his readers to know explicitly that Jesus is the life, the light of the world. Jesus is not only the source of life, but also the distributor of life. His presence on Earth served in part to shine light into the darkness. Jesus is the light of the world. Through the power of His presence, Jesus distributed life into a world filled with darkness, pain, and hopelessness.

Jesus, the light of life, was the true light. There were no gimmicks or empty promises. Jesus delivered on His every word. He brought freedom from spiritual bondage, healing for the brokenhearted, and rest for those who were tired of figuring life out on their own. Jesus said, *"As long as I am in the world, I am the light of the world" (John 9:5).* The life of Jesus is to be accepted and embraced. Jesus said, *"I am the light of the world. He who follows Me shall not walk in darkness, but have the light of life" (John 8:12).*

Jesus' life was exactly what people needed 2,000 years ago, and it is exactly what people need today to break free from their world of sin, brokenness, and despair. *"In him was life, and the life was the light of men. The light shines in the darkness, and the darkness has not overcome it" (John 1:4-5).* If you are a believer, you now have the light of life living within you. Embrace the light and live in the light! Leave the darkness alone. Remember, in Christ, you are the salt and light of the earth. Jesus said, *"You are the light of the world. A city set on a hill cannot be hidden. Nor do people light a lamp and put it under a basket, but on a stand, and it gives light to all in the house. In the same way, let your light shine before others, so that they may see your good works and give glory to your Father who is in heaven" (Matthew 5:14-16).*

Read: Open your Bible and read John 12:46.

Reflect: Prayerfully consider the following: Is any part of my life drifting closer to the darkness? What can I do to stop this pattern right now?

Respond: As a result of these truths, what might need to change in my attitude, beliefs, and actions? What steps do I need to take outwardly?

Replaced to Shine

"In the same way, let your light shine before others, so that they may see your good works and give glory to your Father who is in heaven" (Matthew 5:16).

Imagine living a life without hope, without peace, and without God. Now imagine knowing someone living with the power of God inside them. We were all once without God's perfect presence living within us. But what if you are the one who has the life of God in you? Don't you think now is the best time to start shining your light and telling others about the gift of life in Jesus? Paul wrote, *"Besides this you know the time, that the hour has come for you to wake from sleep. For salvation is nearer to us now than when we first believed. The night is far-gone; the day is at hand. So then let us cast off the works of darkness and put on the armor of light" (Romans 13:11-12).*

When you connect with others in conversation, don't just talk about baseball, the new cable show or the latest news flash. Plead with them to embrace the life. Plead with them to consider God's mercy, forgiveness and unchanging love. When you connect with people, make sure you intentionally connect them to the light of life. God not only wants us to trust Him for our salvation, but also to live for Him through our daily sanctification. You don't have time to continue flirting with sin. You don't have time to invest in the things that have no eternal value. You only have time to shine! Your old life has been replaced to shine. God's counting on you to shine the life of His Son through your life. He's counting on you to replace your old desires with His desires. He's counting on you to shine.

Your real life, your total fulfillment and satisfaction, is found in Jesus (John 15:1). His life in you is the light of this world. His life in you is the hope for those who live in spiritual bondage. Jesus is the power of God for salvation to those who are eternally lost. This is the message that must visibly shine through our lives every day. Others can embrace the power of life as you allow God's light to shine through your life. People desperately need to see the light of life. You have the light of life permanently living within you. *"For you died, and your life is now hidden with Christ in God" (Colossians 3:3, NIV).* Your life has been replaced with Christ's life. Why? So you can freely live for God and express His love to others.

Read: Open your Bible and read Matthew 5:14-16.

Reflect: Prayerfully consider the following: Where can my light begin to shine brighter? What old patterns of ungodly behavior need replacing?

Respond: As a result of these truths, what might need to change in my attitude, beliefs, and actions? What steps do I need to take outwardly?

Spiritual Blindness

"And the light shines in the darkness, and the darkness did not comprehend it"
(John 1:5).

Without a doubt, you've been here on more than one occasion. You begin sharing what God has done in your life with an unbeliever. You tell them about Jesus. You explain their inability to reach God on their own merit, and how Jesus died on the cross for their sins. You plead with them about the importance of turning away from their life of sin and surrendering their life to Jesus. Your effort, however, seems totally useless. Jesus said, *"And this is the judgment: the light has come into the world, and people loved the darkness rather than the light because their works were evil"* (John 3:19).

No matter what you tell them, they are simply not interested. They really don't care about spiritual things. They believe everything will work out just fine in the end. Before God brought you into His family by grace through faith in Jesus Christ, you were spiritually blind. Because of your sin nature, you were born this way. Not only did you live in darkness, you were darkness. You were alive to sin, and dead to God. Regardless of your educational background, you did not have the spiritual capacity to understand the things of God. Why? These realities are spiritual in nature.

Spiritual realities are understood and applied as God awakens our spirit when He shines His light of life in our hearts. For this reason, God is the One who receives all of the credit for our spiritual understanding. God is the one who receives all honor and glory for our salvation. Paul wrote, *"These things we also speak, not in words which man's wisdom teaches but which the Holy Spirit teaches, comparing spiritual things with spiritual. But the natural man does not receive the things of the Spirit of God, for they are foolishness to him; nor can he know them, because they are spiritually discerned"* (1 Corinthians 2:13-14). If Jesus Christ is your Savior, you are no longer spiritually blind.

Don't get discouraged when you share God's love with others and they laugh in your face. Don't get upset when people reject Jesus. Refuse to argue with those who are spiritually antagonistic. Remember, these individuals are spiritually blind. They can't see spiritual realities as you do. Why? They are unable to see God's ways because they are spiritually blind.

Read: Open your Bible and read 2 Corinthians 4:4-6.

Reflect: Prayerfully consider the following: Who is the one responsible for spiritual blindness? What specifically can't they see and why?

Respond: As a result of these truths, what might need to change in my attitude, beliefs, and actions? What steps do I need to take outwardly?

Get Up and Go

"And I said, 'What shall I do, Lord?' And the Lord said to me, 'Rise, and go into Damascus, and there you will be told all that is appointed for you to do' "
(Acts 22:10).

Have you ever experienced a dramatic encounter that radically changed your life? The Apostle Paul experienced a dramatic encounter with our Lord. In the prime of Paul's life, he was recognized as a top religious, educational, political, and social leader (Philippians 3:1-9). He was well respected, but spiritually bankrupt. Paul was known for hunting down and persecuting Christians. He did not understand the Christian faith. Paul was determined to overcome this new teaching by eliminating their growing influence. His actions seemed rational, patriotic, and righteous. He was determined to destroy the Christian faith, regardless of the cost.

When Paul was speaking to a large crowd in *Acts 22:6-11*, he explained how God's light shined into his life, *"Now as he went on his way, he approached Damascus, and suddenly a light from heaven shone around him" (Acts 9:3).* He asked the Lord, *"What shall I do?"* God told him to *"get up"* and *"go to Damascus."* God removes us from the darkness to lead us further into the light. God had a plan for Paul's life. Paul was ready to pursue God's plan. Light is designed to reveal. When God's light shines in our hearts, it reveals the truth about our spiritual condition, the reality of our sin. We forget sometimes that God's light is always shining though us. We don't always respond in the Spirit, but the light continues to shine and expose the true condition of our heart. If we allow God's light to eliminate all sin, our willingness to go and serve Him can increase.

As you look inside your heart today, what darkness is God trying to remove? What areas of the flesh constantly pull you back into the darkness? As you pray for your friends who don't know Christ, what areas of darkness are holding them back? What is the enemy using to keep them from the light? Take additional time to pray through these things. Remember, you were designed to live in the light. Paul wrote, *"Indeed, I count everything as loss because of the surpassing worth of knowing Christ Jesus my Lord" (Philippians 3:8).* Know Christ, then get up and go serve Him.

Read: Open your Bible and read Acts 22:6-11.

Reflect: Prayerfully consider the following: When was the last time I asked God, "What do you want me to do to advance your kingdom?"

Respond: As a result of these truths, what might need to change in my attitude, beliefs, and actions? What steps do I need to take outwardly?

Sent to Proclaim

"There was a man sent from God, whose name was John. He came as a witness, to bear witness about the light, that all might believe through him. He was not the light, but came to bear witness about the light" (John 1:6-8).

After many months of preparation, the moment has finally arrived. The guests all made it early to this highly anticipated ceremony. The wedding planner synchronized every detail with complete beauty and grace. The Pastor finished his message after the bride and groom exchanged their vows. They look deep into each other's eyes and display radiant smiles. The crowd gets ready to stand to their feet and the wedding party gets ready to celebrate. This is a moment that they will cherish forever.

It is the moment everyone has been waiting for—the proclamation, the public announcement of husband and wife. The Pastor raises his voice and boldly declares, "I now pronounce you husband and wife." He looks at the groom and says with a large smile, "You may now kiss your wife!"

After 400 years of revelatory silence and much anticipation, God began to speak through His servant John the Baptist. John was a bold and adventurous individual. Although he was a prophet, John the Baptist was not a religious scholar, a political hero, or a shrewd entrepreneur. John was given a simple mission: be a witness to the Light of Life—Jesus Christ.

His purpose consisted in giving evidence to all men that Jesus was the Christ, the promised Messiah. The prophet Isaiah declared, *"The people who walk in darkness will see a great light. For those who live in a land of deep darkness, a light will shine" (Isaiah 9:2, NLT).* John's reason for living was to prepare the way for Jesus and boldly proclaim who He was: the Light of Life. John was a simple man with a simple task: He was sent to proclaim.

In the same way, you were sent by God to proclaim the good news of Jesus Christ. God chose you to tell others about His great love. He wants all people to know about Jesus' substitutionary work of redemption on the cross for their sins, and the power of His resurrection for eternal life. Your mission is simple, but significant. You were sent by God to proclaim.

Read: Open your Bible and read John 3:25-28.

Reflect: Prayerfully consider the following: Is my life attracting others to Jesus? What can I do to increase my witness for the Lord Jesus?

Respond: As a result of these truths, what might need to change in my attitude, beliefs, and actions? What steps do I need to take outwardly?

Revealing the Darkness

*"I, the LORD, have called You in righteousness, and will hold Your hand;
I will keep You and give You as a covenant to the people, as a light to the
Gentiles, to open blind eyes, to bring out prisoners from the prison,
those who sit in darkness from the prison house" (Isaiah 42:6-7).*

A lamp fulfills its purpose when it provides light. It doesn't do anyone any good to have a five foot lamp in the middle of a crowded dark room and not turn it on. Leaving it off can pose a serious risk to those who are in the room. Lamps are designed to shine light. This is their purpose for existing. They expose the darkness while illuminating their surroundings.

Jesus came to expose and destroy the works of darkness. He was intentional about bringing the works of Satan out in the open. Those men and women who were in need of physical healing, Jesus restored. Those who were imprisoned by sin, Jesus released from their bondage. To those who were without hope, Jesus provided hope. And to those who needed salvation, Jesus offered His life. Jesus conquered the works of darkness.

Regarding the promised Messiah, the prophet Isaiah writes, *"It is too small a thing for you to be my servant to restore the tribes of Jacob and bring back those of Israel I have kept. I will also make you a light for the Gentiles, that you may bring my salvation to the ends of the earth" (Isaiah 49:6, NIV).* God wanted the darkness exposed and destroyed within every people group through Jesus' mission. You have an important role to play in the success of this mission.

From the start, God's plan was to redeem the nations (Genesis 12:1-3). Think of the great bondage, pain, and suffering people find themselves in as a result of sin: spiritual darkness. Sometimes, it is the sin of others that places them in this world of self-destruction. This is very painful to watch.

Jesus came to destroy the power of sin. He came to infuse the light of life into the darkness of your life. God does not want you to live in oppression. He does not want you to be a prisoner to sin. God wants you to be free. He wants you to find true freedom. God reveals the darkness in your life to bring you to the Light of Life, Jesus Christ.

Read: Open your Bible and read John 5:31-32, 35.

Reflect: Prayerfully consider the following: Am I focused on helping others escape the darkness? How can I shine better for Jesus?

Respond: As a result of these truths, what might need to change in my attitude, beliefs, and actions? What steps do I need to take outwardly?

From Disorder to Order

"The LORD is my light and my salvation; whom shall I fear? The LORD is the strength of my life; of whom shall I be afraid?" (Psalm 27:1)

There is nothing better than having the right light in a dark place. When the need arises to find a small object in your dark attic, and the flashlight is running out of power, you're in big trouble. But when a friend extends a large electric lamp connected to an unlimited power source, you're in great shape to find even the smallest of objects. When the right kind of light arrives on the scene, even the darkest corners of life are fully exposed.

The darkness cannot escape the power of the light. The power of the light reveals what is obscure and hidden from the naked eye. It clarifies, and unfolds what is difficult for most of us to see. Light provides many good things. Light brings order to disorder. It gives shape to the shapeless, and fills what is empty. Light will always overpower and eliminate the darkness.

From the time the Earth was created, utter chaos and darkness were transformed into great beauty through the power of God's light. Envision the original power of God's light as we look back to creation. Picture yourself sitting in a chair watching these events unfold before your eyes:

"In the beginning God created the heavens and the earth. The earth was without form, and void; and darkness was on the face of the deep. And the Spirit of God was hovering over the face of the waters. Then God said, 'Let there be light'; and there was light. And God saw the light, that it was good; and God divided the light from the darkness. God called the light Day, and the darkness He called Night. So the evening and the morning were the first day" (Genesis 1:1-5).

Light is one of God's characteristics. The distinctiveness of light reflects the very nature of Almighty God. The Psalmist declares, *"He wraps himself in light as with a garment" (Psalm 104:2).* And Isaiah tells us, *"The light of Israel will become a fire, and his Holy One a flame" (Isaiah 10:17).* God wants to reveal Himself to mankind. He wants people to understand who He is, and who they become when He enters into their life. God is light.

Read: Open your Bible and read John 3:19-21.

Reflect: Prayerfully consider the following: What has God changed from disorder to order in my life recently? Did I freely cooperate with God to make this change, or did I put up a fight to try and stop the change? Why?

Respond: As a result of these truths, what might need to change in my attitude, beliefs, and actions? What steps do I need to take outwardly?

26

Walk as Children of Light

*"The one who is the true light, who gives light to everyone,
was coming into the world" (John 1:9, NLT).*

Jesus is the True Light. He gives light to everyone. The world was in complete darkness until Jesus arrived on the scene. Although many claimed to be the True Light, this title has been reserved exclusively for the Lord Jesus. As you can imagine, many have rejected the True Light.

God reveals Himself in a variety of ways: His wisdom is revealed through creation; His love and mercy is displayed on the cross; and His power is demonstrated through the resurrection of His Son, Jesus. It is really no secret. God's ways are clear, but people still choose to reject the truth and live in complete darkness. People enjoy living in the darkness.

"For the wrath of God is revealed from heaven against all ungodliness and unrighteousness of men, who suppress the truth in unrighteousness, because what may be known of God is manifest in them, for God has shown it to them. For since the creation of the world His invisible attributes are clearly seen, being understood by the things that are made, even His eternal power and Godhead, so that they are without excuse" (Romans 1:19-20).

Jesus is the One who brings all people out of darkness (Isaiah 60:1-3). Consider this for just a moment: Jesus is the only one who can break the chains of darkness in the lives of those you know. Can you picture the number of relationships He can restore and the deep emotional wounds He can entirely heal and transform? *"For God, who said, 'Let light shine out of darkness,' has shone in our hearts to give the light of the knowledge of the glory of God in the face of Jesus Christ" (2 Corinthians 4:6, ESV).*

Jesus is the one people need to know and experience. The Apostle Paul wrote, *"For you were once darkness, but now you are light in the Lord. Walk as children of light" (Ephesians 5:8).* The light of God shines through you. Therefore, walk in the Light! There is only one True Light. Jesus is the True Light. Keep walking faithfully in God's ways. Don't get distracted by the darkness. Let the True Light of Jesus shine through your life today!

Read: Open your Bible and read Romans 1:19-20.

Reflect: Prayerfully consider the following: Am I responding in faith as I hear God's truth? Is there an area of truth I am choosing to ignore? Do I struggle with lying? What's keeping me from walking in the light?

Respond: As a result of these truths, what might need to change in my attitude, beliefs, and actions? What steps do I need to take outwardly?

Unknown and Rejected

"He was in the world, and the world was made through him, yet the world did not know him. He came to his own, and his own people did not receive him" (John 1:10-11).

Has this ever happened to you? You are working on a difficult group project. Those whom you are counting on to help decide to check out along the way. Now you are all by yourself, without help, and without much time left before the deadline. The need to sleep is displaced by the need to finish on time. You decide to spend the entire night working on the project to make sure everything is just right. When you turn in the project, the professor asks, "How much did you personally contribute?"

You tell him the simple truth, "I did all of the work." Suddenly, your "partners" reject you by refusing to talk with you again. Although your intentions were good, it does not matter. Even though your strategy involved including everyone, they deliberately chose not to participate. If you have ever felt the pain of rejection, you know how much it hurts. If you follow Jesus, rejection from others is inevitable.

Jesus is the one who created all things: *"Yet for us there is one God, the Father, of whom are all things, and we for Him; and one Lord Jesus Christ, through whom are all things, and through whom we live"* (1 Corinthians 8:6). It is hard to understand, and even harder to believe. Even though Jesus created all things, He was despised and rejected by His own people.

This was not new territory for the Lord. The prophets struggled with this same rejection and rebellion throughout the entire Old Testament as they proclaimed the word of the Lord to the children of Israel. Isaiah declared, *"I have stretched out My hands all day long to a rebellious people, who walk in a way that is not good, according to their own thoughts"* (Isaiah 65:2). Can you picture the deep disappointment in God's heart? He sent His people a good prophet to point them in the right direction, but they rejected him.

God sent many others to communicate His word and the result was still the same—rejection, rejection, and more rejection. Jesus was unknown and rejected by His own people. He was despised by His own creation.

Read: Open your Bible and read Jeremiah 7:25-27.

Reflect: Prayerfully consider the following: How did God describe the people in Jeremiah 7:25-27? What did they do? What did they not do?

Respond: As a result of these truths, what might need to change in my attitude, beliefs, and actions? What steps do I need to take outwardly?

Relentless Rejection

"He is despised and rejected by men, a man of sorrows and acquainted with grief. And we hid, as it were, our faces from Him; He was despised, and we did not esteem Him. Surely He has borne our griefs and carried our sorrows; yet we esteemed Him stricken, smitten by God, and afflicted. But He was wounded for our transgressions, He was bruised for our iniquities; the chastisement for our peace was upon Him, and by His stripes we are healed. All we like sheep have gone astray; we have turned, every one, to his own way; and the Lord has laid on Him the iniquity of us all" (Isaiah 53:3-6).

Are you ready for rejection? If not, prepare yourself! Every follower of Jesus will experience rejection at one time or another. Jesus shared the Parable of the Ten Minas with a group of elite religious leaders in Luke 19 to express the reality of His rejection in light of the prophetic writings.

Jesus was angered and grieved over the hardness of their hearts. He used this parable to remind them of the judgment to come for those who reject the Messiah (Luke 19:14). Even after Jesus performed many signs and wonders, there was a relentless rejection of the message of salvation.

The Apostle John would later write, *"But although He had done so many signs before them, they did not believe in Him, that the word of Isaiah the prophet might be fulfilled, which he spoke: 'Lord, who has believed our report? And to whom has the arm of the Lord been revealed?' " (John 12:37-38).* If people rejected Jesus openly, what do you think they will do to you?

"For those who dwell in Jerusalem, and their rulers, because they did not know Him, nor even the voices of the Prophets, which are read every Sabbath, have fulfilled them in condemning Him. And though they found no cause for death in Him, they asked Pilate that He should be put to death" (Acts 13:27-28).

Jesus was rejected for you. It was a rejection that paved the way for your salvation. If people rejected Jesus, they will certainly do the same to you. Do not get discouraged when people reject you for following Jesus. In fact, if everyone loves you, there may be a problem! When you radiate the light of Jesus, not everyone wants that light to reveal the reality of their heart.

Read: Open your Bible and read Isaiah 53:1-12.

Reflect: Prayerfully consider the following: How would you describe the price Jesus paid for being rejected for your salvation? What was the cost?

Respond: As a result of these truths, what might need to change in my attitude, beliefs, and actions? What steps do I need to take outwardly?

Born of God

"But to all who did receive him, who believed in his name, he gave the right to become children of God, who were born, not of blood nor of the will of the flesh nor of the will of man, but of God" (John 1:12-13).

The phrase, "Who's your daddy?" was made popular several years ago in a sports movie that involved a high school football team. In the film, a young, prideful athlete could no longer count on the influence of his father to play football. He was forced to grow up. The coach made it clear that he was now the authority figure. The athlete would have to submit to his rules.

When you accept Jesus as Savior, your spiritual birth certificate changes. The Holy Spirit seals this divine certificate. You are now a child of the Eternal King. You belong to God, and He is now your Heavenly Father. Direct access to God was made available through your faith in Jesus Christ. You now have the privilege to live for a higher purpose: God's Kingdom.

Since you were born of God, it only makes sense to live for God. Every spiritual birth has a divine purpose. God is now the one who governs your life. When you get up in the morning, ask your King these simple questions: "Lord, what do You want me to do today? What do I need to adjust on my schedule? Who should I speak with today about Jesus?"

In every kingdom, the will of the king must prevail for the kingdom to prosper. For this to happen, everyone under the rule of the king must submit to his leadership. Since you were born of God it only makes sense to submit every part of your life to God. This includes personal dreams, family planning, career aspirations, personal finances, planned activities, etc.

Here is what most people forget: Completely submitting your life to God is the best move you can make. You will find your greatest fulfillment in life as you live purposefully through Jesus Christ. Your total surrender will lead to your total satisfaction, because in God's Kingdom, submission brings freedom. You are now free to live as God designed you to live. Start living! Since you were born of God it only makes sense to live for God's purposes. Align your life with God's perfect will. You were born of God.

Read: Open your Bible and read Romans 12:1-2.

Reflect: Prayerfully consider the following: What part of my life do I need to submit to God's rule? Why have I delayed this submission?

Respond: As a result of these truths, what might need to change in my attitude, beliefs, and actions? What steps do I need to take outwardly?

God on Earth

"And the Word became flesh and dwelt among us, and we have seen his glory, of the only Son from the Father, full of grace and truth" (John 1:14).

Filmmakers have perfected the element of surprise. With advanced technology, they can create special effects to get audiences to laugh, cry, or even scream. When Jesus arrived on earth there was an element of surprise. People were not expecting the Messiah to arrive quietly. They were waiting for the Messiah to establish His eternal throne and rule.

No doubt the disciples were also waiting for a spectacular demonstration of political power. They even argued about which disciples would have positions of authority in this new Kingdom. They totally missed the point. John later reflected profoundly on what really happened: God came near. Jesus became one of us, and the disciples experienced all of it.

Does it really matter what our title is if God is present in our lives? Does it really matter how much money we make or how many things we can acquire if the presence of God lives within us? Each of the disciples experienced the majestic glory of God. They literally lived with Jesus.

The disciples spent time eating, talking, and watching the Creator of life in action. They witnessed His healing touch and learned from His teachings. It did not matter if they were near the ocean or on top of a mountain. The key was that God was present among them. He was close and available.

Don't forget what's important in life. Regardless of where you find yourself on the "corporate ladder," there is so much more to life. Making time to talk with God and listen to His voice are essential elements of the faith. Reading God's Word and letting Him make the necessary adjustments in your life can be painful, but necessary. God prunes you to grow you.

In Christ Jesus we find the glory of God. We reflect this glory when our lives match our identity. Your identity is found in a person, Jesus, not in a position. Be encouraged! Even at this very moment, God is near you. He understands what you are experiencing. Cling to Him right now in prayer.

Read: Open your Bible and read John 15:4-5.

Reflect: Prayerfully consider the following: How can I make more time to get closer to Jesus? Am I seeking approval from people, or from God? Do people see God's love, mercy, and justice living through me?

Respond: As a result of these truths, what might need to change in my attitude, beliefs, and actions? What steps do I need to take outwardly?

Grace and Truth

"(John bore witness about him, and cried out, 'This was he of whom I said, He who comes after me ranks before me, because he was before me.') For from his fullness we have all received, grace upon grace. For the law was given through Moses; grace and truth came through Jesus Christ. No one has ever seen God; the only God, who is at the Father's side, he has made him known"
(John 1:15-18).

What would people say are your two best characteristics? Maybe they would say that you are "cheerful," or "loving and gentle." For others, it may be "adventurous and fearless," or "quiet and kind." But think about the implications of someone being described by *"grace and truth."*

These two qualities are very powerful for us to consider. Jesus is the complete embodiment of grace and truth. He is the source of grace, and the source of truth. The richness of these two qualities flows directly from our Savior. The more we know Jesus, the more grace and truth can flow through our lives. Is your desire to grow more in grace and truth?

Essentially, grace is God's favor. It is the overflow of God's unlimited kindness to all people. Grace is not something we deserve. When God chooses to grant favor, it is entirely His doing. Grace is not something we earn, nor is it something that we can buy. God's grace towards us is fully expressed through Jesus. Jesus is the living example of God's grace.

Truth has to do with what is real. We don't always like the truth, and we may not always want to accept it. The mother who says, "My child is an angel," even after seeing her son captured on video destroying school property, is not accepting the truth. Whether or not we like it, truth has to do with the way things really are. Truth can be tested. It is irrefutable. Jesus is the fullness of truth. He is also the fullness of grace.

We know that our lives are properly aligned with God when grace and truth flow freely. Instead of swift judgment when others sin, grace should be our first response. Grace should serve as our filter. Truth is equally important. We need to know the realities of the way things are. Truth does not sacrifice grace, and grace does not sacrifice the truth.

Read: Open your Bible and read Ephesians 2:8-9.

Reflect: Consider the following: Am I extending the same grace to others as God has extended to me? Is there a truth that I am ignoring?

Respond: As a result of these truths, what might need to change in my attitude, beliefs, and actions? What steps do I need to take outwardly?

I am Not

"And this is the testimony of John, when the Jews sent priests and Levites from Jerusalem to ask him, 'Who are you?' He confessed, and did not deny, but confessed, 'I am not the Christ.' And they asked him, 'What then? Are you Elijah?' He said, 'I am not.' 'Are you the Prophet?' And he answered, 'No' "
(John 1:19-21).

Have you ever had someone mistake you for another person? You may closely resemble a family member, or a friend from their past. They walk up to you and ask, "Aren't you _____?" You say, "I am not." If they feel confident, they many ask you again. At that time you would respond, "I am not," while smiling graciously.

No doubt some were confused about John the Baptist. They knew he was a prophet from God. His message was direct and convicting. Could he be the Messiah? They also knew that the prophet Elijah was supposed to return someday, and John lived in the wilderness and ate strange things like Elijah used to do. Maybe John was really Elijah in disguise!

Sometimes the best way to help people understand who you are is to describe who you are not. So John says clearly, "I am not the Christ." As for the prophet Elijah who will return before the second coming of Christ, John made that clear as well: he was not Elijah. *"The Prophet"* in this passage points to the Messiah, Jesus. Again, John's answer is clear. He is not the Christ, he is not Elijah, and he is not the Prophet.

It is good for us to know who we are not. Since Satan wants to enslave us to our past, it is important for us to remind ourselves of who we are not. It also helps to know who we are no longer trying to be. Consider reading these five statements out loud to serve as a good reminder:

1. "I am not the same person today as I was before accepting Jesus."
2. "I am not a slave to sin. I am now a slave of the Lord Jesus."
3. "I am not a liar. I won't lie or try to manipulate others to get my way."
4. "I am not trying to be famous. I want Jesus to shine through my life."
5. "I am not a product of my past. In Christ, I am a product of the cross."

Read: Open your Bible and read Romans 11:25-27.

Reflect: Prayerfully consider the following: Have I allowed my heart to be "partially" hardened? Am I trying to be someone who I am not? Which reminder would I say is a challenge for me to verbalize and practice?

Respond: As a result of these truths, what might need to change in my attitude, beliefs, and actions? What steps do I need to take outwardly?

One Voice and One Purpose

"So they said to him, 'Who are you? We need to give an answer to those who sent us. What do you say about yourself?' He said, 'I am the voice of one crying out in the wilderness, 'Make straight the way of the Lord,' as the prophet Isaiah said' " (John 1:22-23).

Have you been around people who absolutely love to talk? You ask them a simple question, and the answer they give you is nothing short of a mini-book. If you are in a hurry, their response may force you to be late. There are times when it is important to get right to the point. Many have said, "Clarity is the window to opportunity." Let us be clear about who we are.

The religious leaders asked John two questions: *"Who are you?" and "What do you say about yourself?"* John's answer must have surprised these men. John humbly referred to himself as *"the voice."* The voice? What a bizarre response. John was a man of great humility. He did not focus on his position; he focused on his purpose. He was the voice that God would use to prepare for the arrival of the Messiah. John summarized the purpose of his life in one sentence. What about you? Could you do the same?

We are often asked the question, "What do you do?" Our normal response is to identify our title along with the company we work for. If we are studying, we might identify ourselves as a student at a particular school. Think about the two penetrating questions asked of John. If we removed your title, or your current level of study, what statement would best describe your life's singular purpose? Would it be God-focused?

Paul provides an example in *Philippians 3:13-14, "Brothers, I do not consider that I have made it my own. But one thing I do: forgetting what lies behind and straining forward to what lies ahead, I press on toward the goal for the prize of the upward call of God in Christ Jesus."* The phrase, *"But one thing I do"* is a powerful statement. Paul refused to live in the past. He refused to believe that his past would control the outcome of his future in Christ.

Paul made every effort to focus his life on the spiritual reward set aside for those who make it their goal to become like Christ. He used all of his strength to advance the gospel while reflecting the character of his Lord.

Read: Open your Bible and read Philippians 3:12-21.

Reflect: Prayerfully consider the following: How would I summarize God's purpose for my life in one statement? What would it require of me?

Respond: As a result of these truths, what might need to change in my attitude, beliefs, and actions? What steps do I need to take outwardly?

What's Your Motive?

"They asked him, 'Then why are you baptizing, if you are neither the Christ, nor Elijah, nor the Prophet?' John answered them, 'I baptize with water, but among you stands one you do not know, even he who comes after me, the strap of whose sandal I am not worthy to untie.' These things took place in Bethany across the Jordan, where John was baptizing" (John 1:25-28).

Have you ever clearly answered a question and those who are listening still don't have a clue what you are talking about? John the Baptist could relate. His response to those who questioned him was very clear. The religious agents sent by the Pharisees probably expected a more elaborate answer. But, John kept things simple. He kept his focus on the Lord Jesus.

John's opponents continued their line of hard questioning. They were direct and to the point. If you were in John's shoes, how would you respond? Consider the following questions: Why do you obey God? What's the motive behind your activity? Why do you pray? Why do you read your Bible and go to church? Why do you give the first ten percent of your income to the church? Why do you serve God through your gifts?

These are questions that require introspection. They force us to think through the core motivation for our ministry. Are we obeying God to gain a higher social status, make more money or, increase our power? Once again, John points these agents of religion to the Savior; he was simply doing his part to provide a way for the Messiah to shine. John was trying to decrease his popularity in order to increase the ministry of his Messiah.

We return to our question: Why do you obey God? Is the goal of your obedience to provide a way for Jesus to shine and touch others through your life? I certainly hope so. If it is, then we have to take steps to get the focus off of ourselves and onto our Lord. This is not necessarily an easy thing to do. Our culture promotes self-centeredness and selfishness. Let the words of the Apostle Paul be your constant prayer:

"I have been crucified with Christ. It is no longer I who live, but Christ who lives in me. And the life I now live in the flesh I live by faith in the Son of God, who loved me and gave himself for me" (Galatians 2:20).

Read: Open your Bible and read Galatians 2:20.

Reflect: Prayerfully consider the following: Is the life of Jesus visible in my attitude and in my actions? What new steps of faith do I need to begin?

Respond: As a result of these truths, what might need to change in my attitude, beliefs, and actions? What steps do I need to take outwardly?

The Lamb of God

"The next day he saw Jesus coming toward him, and said, 'Behold, the Lamb of God, who takes away the sin of the world! This is he of whom I said, After me comes a man who ranks before me, because he was before me. I myself did not know him, but for this purpose I came baptizing with water, that he might be revealed to Israel" (John 1:29-31).

When technology companies announce that they are bringing a new product into the market, they try to create anticipation and excitement from the moment the product is announced to the media until the day it is available for purchase. The amount of time spent discussing the product and how it will be used is truly amazing. It can be a thrilling experience.

Back in John's day, everyone was well aware of the Messiah's arrival and what it would mean to Israel. But, there was a problem. The people wanted the benefits and glory of His Second Coming before accepting the reality of His suffering during His first arrival. This is nothing new for us. We often want the benefits before working through the difficult realities.

Jesus' first arrival was not about establishing a kingdom to rule over the nations. His first visit had to do with destroying the power of sin, the penalty of sin, and ultimately the presence of sin. Jesus came to destroy the works of darkness by becoming a sacrificial lamb. He did not come to rule, but to serve. He came to seek out and save those who were lost.

Jesus' sacrifice on the cross served to provide payment for our sins. It perfectly satisfied God's legal and holy requirement. Because of the precious blood of the Lamb of God, we no longer have to carry the weight and hopelessness of our sins. Jesus carried all of our sins on the cross. He made full payment for all of them—past, present, and future sins.

Consider the depth of God's love for you. His primary purpose for coming to Earth was to provide a way for you to have direct access to the Father. He deliberately endured the pain and agony of the cross. As an innocent lamb, His intention was to permanently deal with your sin problem. He knew your limitations. The Lamb of God suffered and died in your place.

Read: Open your Bible and read 1 Timothy 2:5.

Reflect: Prayerfully consider the following: How grateful am I for what Jesus did for me? Have I accepted Jesus as my Savior? Why or why not?

Respond: As a result of these truths, what might need to change in my attitude, beliefs, and actions? What steps do I need to take outwardly?

The Son of God

"And John bore witness: 'I saw the Spirit descend from heaven like a dove, and it remained on him. I myself did not know him, but he who sent me to baptize with water said to me, 'He on whom you see the Spirit descend and remain, this is he who baptizes with the Holy Spirit.' And I have seen and have borne witness that this is the Son of God' " (John 1:32-34).

It's like solving a great mystery. You find clues along the way and begin piecing each of them together. You ask questions and gather information. Everything starts coming together. It may take hours or even weeks to figure out how everything is connected. But once you find the last clue, everything else suddenly becomes crystal clear. Case solved!

God told John that the Messiah would arrive. John surely must have been thrilled. His entire life's work revolved around preparing people for the Messiah, and making a clear path for His arrival. God told John what to look for to identify the Savior. When John witnessed the promised sign take place right before his eyes, the mystery was solved. John received closure. He was now certain. This was the Messiah, the Son of God.

Can you imagine knowing one of your cousins since you were a child, but never understanding that he was the Messiah? John was not able to know the real Jesus until God revealed it to him. The term, *"Son of God"* points to the deity of Jesus Christ. It points to His divine origin, His eternal existence, and His shared relationship with the Father and Holy Spirit.

The Messiah was destined to rule in righteousness, peace, and joy in the Holy Spirit. His Kingdom would prevail over all evil and would have no end. From this point forward, God would speak to his people through Jesus, the Son of God. It was a powerful moment in the life of John. Here he stood with the King of Kings, the Lord of Lords.

Jesus would now take things to another level. He would begin to baptize and immerse people into God's Kingdom through faith in Him. Through the power of the Holy Spirit, Jesus would change lives. He would do much more than simply foreshadow our salvation. Jesus became our salvation.

Read: Open your Bible and read Hebrews 1:1-9.

Reflect: Prayerfully consider the following: How has knowing Jesus changed your life? What words would best describe His work in you?

Respond: As a result of these truths, what might need to change in my attitude, beliefs, and actions? What steps do I need to take outwardly?

What Are You Seeking?

"The next day again John was standing with two of his disciples, and he looked at Jesus as he walked by and said, 'Behold, the Lamb of God!' The two disciples heard him say this, and they followed Jesus. Jesus turned and saw them following and said to them, 'What are you seeking?' And they said to him, 'Rabbi' (which means Teacher), 'where are you staying?' He said to them, 'Come and you will see.' So they came and saw where he was staying, and they stayed with him that day, for it was about the tenth hour" (John 1:35-39).

"Can I help you?" It is a popular question among retail store employees. They see you walk through the door of their store and ask, "Is there anything in particular I can help you find?" Most of us say, "No, thank you. I want to look around." At least we know who to go to for help if needed.

There are many different reasons why people go to church or join a small group. They begin exploring the Christian life one step at a time, one activity at a time. They may not be able to fully explain their presence, but their growing desire to know God personally is usually a key factor.

Why do you go to church? Why have you joined a small group? Jesus was very direct with John's disciples. He asked, *"What are you seeking?"* Without question, John shared with his disciples the spectacular events that took place the day before. But what they were looking for was the central question. Were these disciples of John looking for the Messiah, or did they want to see another spectacular activity? What were they looking for?

John's disciples wanted to learn more about Jesus. They called Jesus "Rabbi." Jesus was recognized as a teacher. The disciples were willing to learn from the Master Himself. They were ready to listen to His teachings. The disciples simply wanted to know more about Jesus. Conversations on the street don't compare to spending time with someone at their home.

Why the pursuit? Are you hoping to see a spectacular show, or do you really want to better know Jesus? Knowing Jesus intimately and understanding his ways is a process. It is not a mechanical pursuit. It is a relationship. Are your ready to invest the time? What are you seeking?

Read: Open your Bible and read 1 Corinthians 4:5.

Reflect: Prayerfully consider the following: Since God knows your heart, how does that encourage you in your pursuit of knowing Him more?

Respond: As a result of these truths, what might need to change in my attitude, beliefs, and actions? What steps do I need to take outwardly?

Bring Him to Jesus

"One of the two who heard John speak and followed Jesus was Andrew, Simon Peter's brother. He first found his own brother Simon and said to him, 'We have found the Messiah' (which means Christ). He brought him to Jesus. Jesus looked at him and said, 'You are Simon the son of John. You shall be called Cephas' (which means Peter)" (John 1:40-42).

Everyone is waiting in line with you for the doors to open. It's 11:59 PM on Thanksgiving night. Shoppers are ready to attack the isles. You know exactly where to go to quickly get what you need. You have a list memorized in your mind. The question is where do you go first? Knowing that time and quantities are limited, it can be a tough decision indeed.

When you accepted Jesus Christ as Savior, whom did you tell first about your transformation? It may have started with your immediate family, close circle of friends, and co-workers. We usually share good news with those who know us best. We want them to be part of the celebration.

The challenge for us is to make sure we do everything we can to reach everyone we can. Notice Paul's deep conviction: *"To the weak I became weak, that I might win the weak. I have become all things to all people, that by all means I might save some. I do it all for the sake of the gospel, that I may share with them in its blessings" (I Corinthians 9:22-23).* Paul was relentless in his pursuit of bringing men and women to Jesus. It was his singular focus.

You have a key role in bringing people to Jesus. You might object and say, "Well, I'm not a Pastor, an Evangelist, or a Teacher." That may be true, but you are an ambassador for Christ. God is counting on you to make Jesus known to everyone that you possibly can. You are God's voice in a dark and gloomy world. Regardless of your gifts, you are salt and light on this earth. Right now, people desperately need you to bring them to Jesus.

You may not be the one to lead them in prayer to accept Jesus. You may not be the one to answer all of their doubts. However, God has a specific purpose for you, in their process to knowing the Savior. Do your part and let God do His part. Don't be afraid and don't delay. Bring them to Jesus.

Read: Open your Bible and read I Corinthians 9:19-23.

Reflect: Prayerfully consider the following: Paul made personal adjustments to reach all people. How flexible are you in this area?

Respond: As a result of these truths, what might need to change in my attitude, beliefs, and actions? What steps do I need to take outwardly?

Come and See

"The next day Jesus decided to go to Galilee. He found Philip and said to him, 'Follow me.' Now Philip was from Bethsaida, the city of Andrew and Peter. Philip found Nathanael and said to him, 'We have found him of whom Moses in the Law and also the prophets wrote, Jesus of Nazareth, the son of Joseph.' Nathanael said to him, 'Can anything good come out of Nazareth?' Philip said to him, 'Come and see' " (John 1:43-46).

Visiting your local zoo can be a great way to spend time with your family. Some of the animals are very visible during the day while others enjoy hiding from the large crowds. When those in hiding eventually come out, the guests begin shouting and calling their families to "come and see." They want those in their family, both young and old, to see the action, too.

When Jesus began winning disciples, it took careful thought on the part of these men and women to grasp the significance of His presence. Their thoughts must have been, "This is too good to be true." The disciples challenged and encouraged others to see Jesus for themselves. They not only wanted to talk about Jesus, they wanted people to see Him in action.

People want to see real Christians in action. They are tired of the empty promises, the greedy schemes, and the hypocritical lifestyles. When people meet a genuine believer in action, it is a sight to behold. Unfortunately, the bad examples illustrated by believers seem to outpace the good ones.

Make no mistake; your life influences others to follow Jesus or abandon Him altogether. When you lose your job or suffer from health problems, people are watching. When you correct your children or speak with your spouse, others take notice. When the opportunity to help someone is presented to you, your actions will speak louder than your words.

Someone may say to their close relative, "I found someone who says they are a Christian. Come and see." If they do, what would they find that reflects Christ in your place of work? What habits would they be able to observe throughout your week? Would they say that you trust God in every area of your life? Would generosity and sacrificial love be observed?

Read: Open your Bible and read Psalms 1:1-6.

Reflect: Prayerfully consider the following: How can delighting in God's Word strengthen my character? What metaphor describes the change?

Respond: As a result of these truths, what might need to change in my attitude, beliefs, and actions? What steps do I need to take outwardly?

Greater Things

"Jesus saw Nathanael coming toward him and said of him, 'Behold, an Israelite indeed, in whom there is no deceit!' Nathanael said to him, 'How do you know me?' Jesus answered him, 'Before Philip called you, when you were under the fig tree, I saw you.' Nathanael answered him, 'Rabbi, you are the Son of God! You are the King of Israel!' Jesus answered him, 'Because I said to you, 'I saw you under the fig tree,' do you believe? You will see greater things than these.' And he said to him, 'Truly, truly, I say to you, you will see heaven opened, and the angels of God ascending and descending on the Son of Man.' "
(John 1:47-51)

Video cameras are everywhere these days. You find them on traffic lights, government buildings, and in smart phones. Not too long ago, video cameras were not accessible to most people. Now, even small children have video capabilities on their phones. When you think no one is paying attention, out comes a video device to record all of the action.

Jesus is well aware of your most intimate moments. When you think no one is watching, God is watching. When you think no one cares, God cares. When we are by ourselves we are not alone. Did you know that God is omnipresent? He is everywhere all of the time. His presence is not limited. Right now, God sees you. Right now, God lives within you.

We don't know exactly what Nathanael was thinking as he remained under the fig tree. The Bible does not say. Let's add a little sanctified speculation. What if Nathanael was grieving over the loss of a friend? What if he was crying out to God in prayer and agonizing over a difficult situation or asking God to let him meet the promised Messiah? This was a huge moment.

It seems that only God and Nathanael were aware of the details. Jesus encouraged Nathanael, *"You will see greater things than these."* Have you ever experienced a time in your life when you felt God's absence? You start doubting God's great power and His provision. Suddenly, God shows up in a totally unexpected way. These moments serve as a reminder that He is fully aware of your needs. Don't allow your circumstances to discourage your heart. You will see greater things! God is with you!

Read: Open your Bible and read Matthew 6:25-33.

Reflect: Prayerfully consider the following: What things should I not spend time worrying about? What should be my life's chief priority?

Respond: As a result of these truths, what might need to change in my attitude, beliefs, and actions? What steps do I need to take outwardly?

Do Whatever He Tells You

"On the third day there was a wedding at Cana in Galilee, and the mother of Jesus was there. Jesus also was invited to the wedding with his disciples. When the wine ran out, the mother of Jesus said to him, 'They have no wine.' And Jesus said to her, 'Woman, what does this have to do with me? My hour has not yet come.' His mother said to the servants, 'Do whatever he tells you.' "
(John 2:1-5)

Weddings are designed for celebration. The guests come to encourage the family with gifts, laughter, and support. One can usually find an abundance of food, dancing, and smiles. Weddings are memorable events. When unexpected problems emerge, they must be resolved quickly. There was a huge problem at the wedding in Cana: the wine suddenly ran out.

For the family, this was an embarrassing problem. Wedding guests expect the best wine at the start of the wedding, and the common wine towards the end. Not having any wine to offer the guests is not part of the plan. It is a big mistake that needed much more than a quick fix; it required a miracle. Mary came to Jesus to find such a solution.

In the second coming of Christ, wine and celebration will be in abundance (Jeremiah 31:12). The first coming of Christ had a different focus. Perhaps Mary already accepted Jesus as the promised Messiah. Unaware of this divine timeline, Mary directed the problem to Jesus. Jesus responded, *"My hour has not yet come."* The time of blessing and abundance, when wine would flow freely, was certain, but not yet fulfilled (Amos 9:13-14).

Somehow, Mary knew that Jesus would take care of the problem. She confidently instructed the servants, *"Do whatever he tells you."* Think through the challenges you face right now. Regardless of the problem, you have a part in the solution. If you have studied what the Bible has to say regarding the problem, what have you done in response to your discovery?

Are you doing whatever God's Word is instructing you to do? No matter how bizarre the command, God wants you to follow it without any complaining. Get ready and obey! Listen, and *"Do whatever he tells you."*

Read: Open your Bible and read Amos 9:13-14.

Reflect: Prayerfully consider the following: What might God's answer to my biggest challenge look like? What do I need him to restore in my life?

Respond: As a result of these truths, what might need to change in my attitude, beliefs, and actions? What steps do I need to take outwardly?

Fill the Jars with Water

"Now there were six stone water jars there for the Jewish rites of purification, each holding twenty or thirty gallons. Jesus said to the servants, 'Fill the jars with water.' And they filled them up to the brim. And he said to them, 'Now draw some out and take it to the master of the feast.' So they took it...the master of the feast called the bridegroom and said to him, 'Everyone serves the good wine first, and when people have drunk freely, then the poor wine. But you have kept the good wine until now.' This, the first of his signs, Jesus did at Cana in Galilee, and manifested his glory. And his disciples believed in him" (John 2:6-9, 11).

What part of your life do you want God to use? Would you say, "I want God to use every part of my life?" Is that truly the passion of your heart? Would you be more inclined to say, "I want God to use as much of my life as he can?" Some might say, "I want God to use my life, but I am still trying to figure out 'What will He use?' and 'How will God use what I have?'"

At the wedding in Cana, the servants found six water jars that were available to be filled with water. Without knowing it, the servants were an active part of Jesus' first public miracle. They were given clear instructions on what to do, and they followed through with their responsibilities.

There are times when we want God to transform a particular area of our lives. This area becomes the major theme of our prayer life. It is often the topic of conversation among close friends. We believe if God takes care of this one thing, everything else will be just fine. In our self-sufficiency we might believe that everything else in our lives is manageable, controllable.

God is not satisfied with having only a part of your life. This would be like finding six water jars and only filling one of them with water. If only one is filled, only one can experience the miraculous. You may give God freedom and access to one area of your life, but that is not all He wants.

God wants to fill and transform every area of your life for His glory. This includes your personal walk with Him, your family, broken relationships, your career, opportunities to serve, sharing your faith, and so much more.

Read: Open your Bible and read Psalm 23:5.

Reflect: Prayerfully consider the following: Have I made all of my life available for God to use? If not, what needs to empty for God to fill?

Respond: As a result of these truths, what might need to change in my attitude, beliefs, and actions? What steps do I need to take outwardly?

Where is Your Passion?

"The Passover of the Jews was at hand, and Jesus went up to Jerusalem. In the temple he found those who were selling oxen and sheep and pigeons, and the money-changers sitting there. And making a whip of cords, he drove them all out of the temple, with the sheep and oxen. And he poured out the coins of the money-changers and overturned their tables. And he told those who sold the pigeons, 'Take these things away; do not make my Father's house a house of trade.' His disciples remembered that it was written, 'Zeal for your house will consume me' " (John 2:13-17).

Do you get bored easily with the way your room is organized? Do you enjoy moving things around every couple of months to give your room a fresh look? Men typically leave things as they are without giving it too much attention. Women are usually the ones who enjoy these changes.

On at least one occasion, Jesus reorganized the layout of the temple. People traveled many miles to make the annual Passover pilgrimage. Savvy business people set up booths to take advantage of the people, charging the people high prices for the animals used to make sacrifices.

Jesus responded quickly. He disrupted their transactions and moved everyone out of the temple courts. It was time to get God's house back in order. Those who set up booths in the temple were robbing the people. This was far from God's purposes for His temple, the place of worship. It was time to get things back in order and restore God's original design.

Do you have a passion to worship God? Do you have a passion to see His church flourish and grow the way He designed it? Consider your role in your local church. You may not be the person organizing each service, but you do have an important responsibility. If you are a member of God's family, you have a responsibility to worship God and serve others.

Jesus was passionate to see God's temple moving in the right direction. It was His personal passion. What are you passionate about in your church? What areas can you begin to serve in? God places you in a local church to serve, and help make the church a better place to worship and grow.

Read: Open your Bible and read Malachi 3:1-3.

Reflect: Prayerfully consider the following: Why do I go to church? Do I go to worship God and grow spiritually or do I have another motive?

Respond: As a result of these truths, what might need to change in my attitude, beliefs, and actions? What steps do I need to take outwardly?

Three Days

*"So the Jews said to him, 'What sign do you show us for doing these things?'
Jesus answered them, 'Destroy this temple, and in three days
I will raise it up.' The Jews then said, 'It has taken forty-six years to build
this temple, and will you raise it up in three days?' But he was speaking
about the temple of his body. When therefore he was raised from the dead,
his disciples remembered that he had said this, and they believed the
Scripture and the word that Jesus had spoken" (John 2:18-22).*

There are times when we simply don't understand something the first time
we hear it. We may not understand the big picture. The implications may
totally escape us, or it may be too complex a subject for us to process.

The Jews did not understand why Jesus was so upset about the conversion
in the temple from house of worship to marketplace. They were still
processing the entire experience. They requested a sign from Jesus. Jesus
spoke to them regarding the resurrection of His body, the temple of God,
after three days of being in the grave. The Jews totally missed the point of
his response. They focused on the physical temple, but Jesus focused on
himself and what things were about to take place. The Jews were confused
by Jesus' response. They were still trying to figure out the puzzle.

It would all make sense to the disciples, but only after Jesus was raised
from the dead. Do you struggle with believing God's Word? Has it been a
tug-of-war experience for you spiritually? Do you agonize over taking
steps of faith in obedience to the scriptures? Be encouraged in your walk
with the Lord. In the right time, He will connect-the-dots for you. Faith is
required for you to know God more intimately and grow spiritually.

There are no shortcuts to spiritual maturity. Even if you don't fully
understand what God wants you to do, or where He wants you to go,
don't lose heart. Obey what you know He wants you to do right now, and
go where He wants you to go today. Let Him take care of the rest. God
promises to be with us and in us throughout this entire adventure. You
may need to wait "three more days" to see how it all fits together.
Remember God's Word, believe God's Word, and obey God's Word.

Read: Open your Bible and read Luke 6:46-49.

Reflect: Prayerfully consider the following: Am I obeying what I
understand about God in His Word? If not, what is holding me back?

Respond: As a result of these truths, what might need to change in my
attitude, beliefs, and actions? What steps do I need to take outwardly?

He Knows What's Inside

"Now when he was in Jerusalem at the Passover Feast, many believed in his name when they saw the signs that he was doing. But Jesus on his part did not entrust himself to them, because he knew all people and needed no one to bear witness about man, for he himself knew what was in man" (John 2:23-25).

Do you remember waiting to open a much-anticipated gift from your family? The wrapping was beautiful, and the bow was almost ready for you to untie. The excitement was due in part to not knowing what you would find. You had absolutely no idea what was inside that beautiful box.

When Jesus began His ministry, people wanted to follow Him. They were amazed by His great teachings. They wanted to see more signs and wonders. There were those who were following Jesus for all the wrong reasons. They loved what they saw on the outside. They enjoyed watching the sick find healing, but their hearts were far from God. Jesus did not place His confidence in those who followed Him with a shallow heart.

Do your circumstances determine your faithfulness to God? When the pressures of life begin to squeeze, does this draw you closer to God, or lead you further away? Is your commitment to God and others unbending? Do you run when trouble arrives at your door? No matter what others see on the outside of your life (the wrapping), God knows what's inside. He knows if your love for Him is real and He knows if it is not.

Jesus' confidence is reserved for those who are truly His followers, God's sons and daughters in the faith. Whether you are a confident person or not, God believes in you. As your Father, He knows you personally. You not only have a new spirit, but you also have a new mission. His confidence is based on the fact that He will finish what He has started in your life. God always finishes what He starts. When people see you they should see what's inside: Jesus. Regardless of the personality of your exterior wrapping, God is the one who lives in you. He is the one changing you from the inside out. Notice Paul's strong confidence: *"And I am sure of this, that he who began a good work in you will bring it to completion at the day of Jesus Christ" (Philippians 1:6).* Let His perfect work continue in your life.

Read: Open your Bible and read Philippians 1:6.

Reflect: Prayerfully consider the following: What is God trying to change in my life right now? What changes am I most thankful for?

Respond: As a result of these truths, what might need to change in my attitude, beliefs, and actions? What steps do I need to take outwardly?

You Must Be Born Again

"Now there was a man of the Pharisees named Nicodemus, a ruler of the Jews. This man came to Jesus by night and said to him, 'Rabbi, we know that you are a teacher come from God, for no one can do these signs that you do unless God is with him.' Jesus answered him, 'Truly, truly, I say to you, unless one is born again he cannot see the kingdom of God' " (John 3:1-3).

It's Friday afternoon, and your teenage son or daughter asks, "Is there anything I can do to help you around the house?" They follow it up with, "Have you lost weight?" or "That shirt looks great on you." After a few minutes they give you a big hug and say, "My friends and I are getting together later for pizza. Can you give me $10.00?" Finally we discover the true motive for their unusual words of kindness and acts of service. In Jesus' day we find what appears to be a similar approach. Nicodemus, a respected religious leader, approached Jesus with words that appear to be flattering affirmation. Jesus cut right through his presentation and arrived at the heart of the matter—Nicodemus needed a spiritual rebirth.

Have you every tried to flatter God with a beautiful selection of large words? Save your voice. God is not impressed at all. God looks at the heart—your heart. Have you ever been born again? If you have never accepted Jesus as Savior and turned from your sin through a prayer of faith, that's your most pressing need. That is God's desire for you right now.

There are two components to being born again. First, believe in the person of Jesus. Believe that He came and died on the cross for your sins. Believe that He was buried, and three days later, raised from the dead. Second, admit to God that you are a sinner. Admit that you have broken His commandments. Ask God to forgive you for all of your sins.

Today is the day of salvation! Take some time right now and get right with God. Jesus said, you must be born again. This is God's plan for your life. Jesus is the only one who can give you direct access to God. Here is His promise: *"If you confess with your mouth that Jesus is Lord and believe in your heart that God raised him from the dead, you will be saved"* (Romans 10:9).

Read: Open your Bible and read John 1:12.

Reflect: Prayerfully consider the following: Have I been born again? If not, what am I waiting for? If I have, who needs to hear my story of hope?

Respond: As a result of these truths, what might need to change in my attitude, beliefs, and actions? What steps do I need to take outwardly?

Please Explain

"Nicodemus said to him, 'How can a man be born when he is old? Can he enter a second time into his mother's womb and be born?' Jesus answered, 'Truly, truly, I say to you, unless one is born of water and the Spirit, he cannot enter the kingdom of God. That which is born of the flesh is flesh, and that which is born of the Spirit is spirit. Do not marvel that I said to you, You must be born again. The wind blows where it wishes, and you hear its sound, but you do not know where it comes from or where it goes. So it is with everyone who is born of the Spirit" (John 3:4-8).

Have you ever asked at a large gathering, "Has anyone here ever seen the wind?" If you have, you will probably get at least one person to raise their hand. The reality is that we cannot see the wind. We can only feel it and see the effect the wind has on trees, street signs, oceans, sand etc.

The work of the Holy Spirit is mysterious. He is someone who we can't fully understand or explain. As with the wind, we can't see the Holy Spirit. We can't say, "Look, I see the Holy Spirit." No, but we can experience His presence within us as He transforms our spirit. We can also see His power in the way He works in the lives of those around us.

The Holy Spirit points us to Jesus. He personally draws people to the Savior. The Holy Spirit teaches us the deep things of God, and leads us into all truth. He is the one who comes alongside to help us as we pray through difficult moments. He is the one who gives us the power to live boldly for Jesus. His work in us is nothing short of a work of art.

You must have two births before you enter God's Kingdom: a physical birth and a spiritual birth. Spiritual transformation is the work the Spirit performs in us. God starts this great work in you and continues this work through the power of the Holy Spirit. This was difficult for Nicodemus to fully understand. Maybe this mystery is difficult for you to understand, too.

Have no fear! Focus on what you know God wants you to do next. Don't worry where the Holy Spirit will lead you to in this next year. Listen to the whisper of His voice. He will make it clear one step of faith at a time.

Read: Open your Bible and read John 14:26. *I Cor. 2: 10-14*

Reflect: Prayerfully consider the following: How does this passage describe the Holy Spirit? What does this mean for my life today?

Respond: As a result of these truths, what might need to change in my attitude, beliefs, and actions? What steps do I need to take outwardly?

Heavenly Things

"Nicodemus said to him, 'How can these things be?' Jesus answered him, 'Are you the teacher of Israel and yet you do not understand these things? Truly, truly, I say to you, we speak of what we know, and bear witness to what we have seen, but you do not receive our testimony. If I have told you earthly things and you do not believe, how can you believe if I tell you heavenly things?' " (John 3:9-12)

Watching magic shows is always entertaining. Whether it involves suspending a woman in thin air, or making an elephant disappear, we love the anticipation. Both children and adults are amazed. They watch carefully and expectantly. Good magicians never reveal their secrets. To do so would be a great insult to those involved in this magical community.

Nicodemus was completely amazed by the words of Jesus. He was in complete disbelief. Jesus' words were making him question the very core of his belief system. It was difficult for him to quickly absorb these simple, but profound, truths. Like a young child at a magic show, Nicodemus was amazed at what was happening. He tried to satisfy his intellectual appetite, but the spiritual reality went far beyond his intellectual capacity.

Jesus understood the spiritual battle Nicodemus faced. We all face this battle. We may initially filter ideas through our intellect, and try to wrap our mind around the implications. As with a food processor, we try to break things down to a simpler form for intellectual consumption. But when spiritual realities are introduced, we are faced with a new paradigm.

Nicodemus was entering new territory. Jesus was challenging him to look beyond his limited capacity. Jesus wanted Nicodemus to understand and accept the spiritual reality of what God really required for Salvation. This was a spiritual reality birthed in Heaven. Do you struggle with accepting the spiritual realities found in the Bible? When you struggle deeply to understand spiritual truths intellectually, do you choose to believe God?

There are spiritual realities that will challenge your thinking and go beyond your reasoning. When you don't fully understand them, choose to trust God and take a step of faith. God may choose to reveal more as you do.

Read: Open your Bible and read Proverbs 3:5-6. Trust in the Lord with all your heart

Reflect: Prayerfully consider the following: What is the promise I receive when I trust God and follow him in every area of my life?

Respond: As a result of these truths, what might need to change in my attitude, beliefs, and actions? What steps do I need to take outwardly?

Eternal Life

"No one has ascended into heaven except he who descended from heaven, the Son of Man. And as Moses lifted up the serpent in the wilderness, so must the Son of Man be lifted up, that whoever believes in him may have eternal life. For God so loved the world, that he gave his only Son, that whoever believes in him should not perish but have eternal life" (John 3:13-16).

Is there such a thing as a fountain of youth? Can we really drink from a source that will help us live longer and defy the laws of aging? Is there a spring of youthfulness somewhere that is yet to be discovered? Some people believe there is such a source. Even if we could stretch our life a little longer or have smoother skin, we cannot escape the reality of death.

Jesus conquered death. He is the source of life—eternal life. Real life on Earth and eternal life from Heaven is found in the person of Jesus. God's plan was to sacrifice Jesus as the punishment for our sins. His death on the cross meant an end to sin's power. God's power for salvation would rest in the finished work of Jesus Christ on the cross at Calvary.

Aren't you glad the perfect work of Jesus is finished? Because Jesus died you can now live. You can live for God without reservation. The story of God's great redemption not only involves your eternal union with God, it involves your daily relationship in Christ Jesus. Eternal life is a present reality. Right now you have eternal life. Right now you are eternally secure. Right now you have the life of Jesus living within you.

So make sure when you talk with those who don't know Christ you mention both the present and the future realities in Christ Jesus. God did not promise to eliminate wrinkles or make people look better in their jeans. He promised us an unlimited source of power. He promised us a Living Hope. He promised us the life that people long for in the depths of their heart. This promise is abundantly fulfilled in the One who died for us.

What does this all mean? As a born again believer you have eternal life living within you. God has made you forever His. God's Spirit longs to freely live through your life to share the hope of eternal life with others.

Read: Take time to study and memorize John 3:16.

Reflect: Prayerfully consider the following: What can I do today to intentionally help people know the true source of eternal life?

Respond: As a result of these truths, what might need to change in my attitude, beliefs, and actions? What steps do I need to take outwardly?

Sent to Save

"For God did not send his Son into the world to condemn the world, but in order that the world might be saved through him. Whoever believes in him is not condemned, but whoever does not believe is condemned already, because he has not believed in the name of the only Son of God" (John 3:17-18).

Being a firefighter is an exciting job. We see their shiny trucks and hear their loud horn as they race to their next stop. We wonder if they are going to rescue someone from a burning house or take care of a hazardous spill. Their dispatch has one focus. Firefighters are sent to save lives.

At times people wonder why Jesus came to this earth. They haven't quite figured out his job description. His purpose was singular. He came to seek and save those who were lost. Jesus was sent to save. His ministry was not one of condemning others. He did point out hypocrisy when it appeared, but He was quick to turn His focus back on the lost.

Without Jesus you stand condemned before a holy and righteous God. There is no earthly remedy for this. Your life in Jesus cancels out your condemnation. Paul wrote, *"There is therefore now no condemnation for those who are in Christ Jesus" (Romans 8:1).* What a great feeling to know that you are no longer condemned to an eternity without God and without Jesus.

There is a difference between godly sorrow, conviction, and guilt. You may feel shame over an unconfessed sin in your life. God's Spirit is convicting you and asking that you repent and turn to God for forgiveness. This is good. God's Spirit shows us our sin. He wants us to live in holiness. But when you have moved passed your repentance, Satan will try to discourage you with guilt and condemnation. Pay attention. In Christ Jesus, there is no longer any condemnation. We are now His eternal sons and daughters. If today, sin is present in your life, confess it to the Lord in prayer.

Don't take this lightly. Prolonged confession leads to more sin. You are no longer condemned, so stop living as a condemned person. Jesus came to set you free from guilt and condemnation. Start living for God with all of your heart, mind, soul, and strength. You have been sent to save others.

Read: Open your Bible and read Romans 8:1-39.

Reflect: Prayerfully consider the following: Am I living as a changed person? Am I sorrowful when I sin? Do I need forgiveness today?

Respond: As a result of these truths, what might need to change in my attitude, beliefs, and actions? What steps do I need to take outwardly?

Exposed

"And this is the judgment: the light has come into the world, and people loved the darkness rather than the light because their works were evil. For everyone who does wicked things hates the light and does not come to the light, lest his works should be exposed. But whoever does what is true comes to the light, so that it may be clearly seen that his works have been carried out in God" (John 3:19-21).

Imagine working at a construction site at night. The power suddenly shuts off, and you can't see what's around you. Working in dark places has many challenges. In the dark, you have a much greater risk for injury. Your chances of getting your work completed in the dark are slim-to-none. When Jesus arrived on the earth, people were very comfortable living in spiritual darkness. They actually loved it. Why? Because the pleasures they enjoyed in spiritual darkness were totally evil. They were not looking to make any personal changes. Their lifestyle opposed God's plan for their lives, but they continued anyways. Are you living in spiritual darkness?

When people remain in spiritual darkness, they have no intention of coming to the light. If you are living to exploit people financially, coming to the light means a sharp reduction in income. If you are misusing authority, coming to the light might mean getting demoted or even fired. If you are comfortable with lying, coming to the light means removing your mask of deception, and making things right with those you have deceived. Those who live in the truth, however, do not need to hide what they do. There is nothing to hide. There is no deception. Those who walk in God's ways want to please God. They live for an eternal purpose. Short-term gains are not part of their agenda. They understand their eternal purpose as a believer. They are committed to making the most of life to glorify God.

What about you? If your actions and your motives were placed in the light of God's truth, what would be exposed? Is there something you enjoy doing in the dark that is contrary to God's Word? Would it bring praise or shame to His name? Would people say that you love the truth or that you love cutting corners, finding loopholes, and creating excuses for your actions? When the light shines on your life, everything is exposed. When totally exposed, what does your life look like from God's point of view?

Read: Open your Bible and read John 3:19-21.

Reflect: Prayerfully consider the following: Is there any work of darkness that I need to stop, confess, and put behind me?

Respond: As a result of these truths, what might need to change in my attitude, beliefs, and actions? What steps do I need to take outwardly?

Given from Above

"Now a discussion arose between some of John's disciples and a Jew over purification. And they came to John and said to him, 'Rabbi, he who was with you across the Jordan, to whom you bore witness—look, he is baptizing, and all are going to him.' John answered, 'A person cannot receive even one thing unless it is given him from heaven' " (John 3:25-27).

Birthday parties and piñatas are a great combination. The children get very close, and open their bags wide to get as much candy as possible. When the strings are pulled, or the piñata is hit with a strong swing of a stick, all of the candy falls out. The children don't waste any time wondering where the candy came from. They know the piñata is the source.

The moment had finally arrived. John's disciples were confused. If John was the prophet, why is everyone going to Jesus and His disciples for baptism? This marked the beginning of Jesus' ministry. John was not troubled for even a minute. He knew who he was and who he was not. John's response was powerful. His understanding of the source of life and the source of all good things was exceptional. John embraced God's sovereignty. He was not trying to win an election or maintain his popularity. John was content because he knew the source of all blessing.

Every good thing in your life comes from God. As James reminds us, *"Every good gift and every perfect gift is from above, coming down from the Father of lights with whom there is no variation or shadow due to change" (James 1:17).* When you get a generous raise, celebrate a birthday, or receive kindness from others, it comes from God. When your health improves, or when you find a good friend, it comes from God. God is the source.

But what happens when others are the recipients of God's blessings? What happens when people advance in their careers or in their personal lives and you seem to get left behind? What happens when these very people have taken advantage of you, or acted in ungodly ways? Well, if every good thing comes from God, you should celebrate their success. If you can't, there may be some unfinished business in your own heart to work through. Celebrate when God blesses others! After all, it is given from above.

Read: Open your Bible and read James 1:17.

Reflect: Prayerfully consider the following: Do I celebrate God's blessings when others receive it? What do I need to adjust in my heart?

Respond: As a result of these truths, what might need to change in my attitude, beliefs, and actions? What steps do I need to take outwardly?

Up and Down

"You yourselves bear me witness, that I said, 'I am not the Christ, but I have been sent before him.' The one who has the bride is the bridegroom. The friend of the bridegroom, who stands and hears him, rejoices greatly at the bridegroom's voice. Therefore this joy of mine is now complete. He must increase, but I must decrease" (John 3:28-30).

Seesaws can be found on many playgrounds. They are great for kids. Two children sit on opposite sides of the toy. One child pushes off from the ground and goes high in the air, while the other child heads downward and remains on the bottom until he or she gives a mighty push down with their legs. When one child goes up, the other must come down. Up and down.

Once again we find the incredible focus of John's purpose unfolding in a simple phrase, *"He must increase, but I must decrease."* John understood his role. He was to move downward on the seesaw in order for Jesus to be elevated among the people. John made it easy for Jesus to have center stage. He wanted Jesus to be "the main attraction" for the people of Israel.

John had to deliberately get himself out of the way for Jesus to be exalted. He was thrilled and content to see Jesus' ministry move forward. He compares himself to a groomsman in a wedding, celebrating the happiness of the bridegroom. John found complete satisfaction in reducing his popularity to point people to the Savior. Receiving recognition is not evil.

People should recognize the good that you do. But do you try too hard to stay on top of the seesaw of life? It is natural to feel pleasure when people praise you for the good that you do, but it should not come at the expense of praise for the work of Jesus in your life. Jesus wants to be exalted through your life. In order for this to happen, you must decrease. You have to get yourself out of the way, even if it hurts.

Your desire for fame or the goals you've established must take a backseat. For Jesus to increase, you must decrease. For Him to go up you, must come down. This involves submitting all that you are to be all who God wants you to be. It means helping others see the Savior through you. It means being content and genuinely grateful with what you have.

Read: Open your Bible and read Galatians 2:20.

Reflect: Prayerfully consider the following: Am I fighting for my own personal fame? What needs to decrease in my life so that Jesus can shine?

Respond: As a result of these truths, what might need to change in my attitude, beliefs, and actions? What steps do I need to take outwardly?

Above All

"He who comes from above is above all. He who is of the earth belongs to the earth and speaks in an earthly way. He who comes from heaven is above all. He bears witness to what he has seen and heard, yet no one receives his testimony."
(John 3:31-32)

"First to market" is a term used by entrepreneurs to describe the first introduction of a new product or service into the marketplace. If managed very well, that head start can prolong the time required for others to successfully introduce a competitive product or service. They become the undisputed market leader because they stand above all other competitors.

Jesus descended from a heavenly kingdom. This kingdom is eternal in nature. It is a kingdom that is above all. Although competition exists for a short time, God's kingdom will prevail. When Jesus came, His perspective was different. He looked at life through the lens of the kingdom. He freely taught everyone who wanted to listen about the realities of God's kingdom.

Although many reject His teachings, the truth about God's kingdom and heavenly realities remains the same. The more you study the Bible, the better you will understand God's eternal Kingdom. The more you know Jesus, the better you know God. The more you trust the Holy Spirit, the more you can join God in His great work of redeeming those who are lost.

Have you found it difficult to witness to others about Jesus, perhaps because of an unexpected rejection by someone you love? This can certainly be difficult, but not impossible to overcome. Remember, when people reject the person of Jesus, they are rejecting God, not you. When they want nothing to do with Jesus, it is a rejection of a spiritual nature.

It has been said that most people want to hear about Jesus. The minority are those who are hostile towards the good news. So if most people are open to talking about Jesus, what are you waiting for? God only created one person just like you. Don't be surprised...it's you! He has uniquely formed your personality, talents, and abilities to connect with others and share your faith. Don't let rejection scare you. Jesus is above all!

Read: Open your Bible and read Isaiah 53:1-12.

Reflect: Prayerfully consider the following: Both Isaiah and Jesus were rejected. What is my biggest fear regarding being rejected by others?

Respond: As a result of these truths, what might need to change in my attitude, beliefs, and actions? What steps do I need to take outwardly?

Without Measure

"Whoever receives his testimony sets his seal to this, that God is true. For he whom God has sent utters the words of God, for he gives the Spirit without measure. The Father loves the Son and has given all things into his hand. Whoever believes in the Son has eternal life; whoever does not obey the Son shall not see life, but the wrath of God remains on him" (John 3:33-36).

An unlimited buffet is not the norm for most restaurants. Most restaurants carefully measure and weigh their portions before serving their customers. This helps them manage costs and provide consistent service. Buffets are totally different. You get to choose from an unlimited amount of food to eat. There are no limitations, measurements, or restrictions.

God anointed Jesus to accomplish His work. Jesus would later quote the prophet Isaiah, *"The Spirit of the Lord God is upon me, because the Lord has anointed me to bring good news to the poor; he has sent me to bind up the brokenhearted, to proclaim liberty to the captives, and the opening of the prison to those who are bound" (Isaiah 61:1).* Jesus was given the Holy Spirit without measure. He was empowered to fully carry out God's work. The words that Jesus spoke were of divine origin. His ministry to the sick, the poor, and the lost were the very works of God. The fullness of God was revealed in the life of Jesus. To experience the person of Jesus was to experience the fullness of God. God's love granted Jesus all things. He did not lack anything. Jesus was fully equipped to accomplish God's mission.

Do you ever feel inadequate when it comes to taking on spiritual responsibilities for others? Do you find yourself thinking, "I need more education and training" or "I need more experience before I can begin?" Does it seem like an insurmountable task to help people grow in their faith? God gave Jesus what was needed to do His work—the Holy Spirit.

Jesus gives you the Holy Spirit without measure to accomplish your mission. The Holy Spirit will lead you and teach you. Any spiritual insecurity we have is usually due to a lack of faith. Believe that God equips and empowers those whom He calls. His Spirit prepares you for what is needed. Don't be afraid or feel inadequate. Keep growing in your knowledge and application of God's Word as His Spirit leads you.

Read: Open your Bible and read Isaiah 42:1.

Reflect: Prayerfully consider the following: Express to God in prayer how grateful you are for placing his Holy Spirit within you.

Respond: As a result of these truths, what might need to change in my attitude, beliefs, and actions? What steps do I need to take outwardly?

A Strategic Detour

"Now when Jesus learned that the Pharisees had heard that Jesus was making and baptizing more disciples than John (although Jesus himself did not baptize, but only his disciples), he left Judea and departed again for Galilee. And he had to pass through Samaria. So he came to a town of Samaria called Sychar, near the field that Jacob had given to his son Joseph" (John 4:1-5).

Road trips can be a great adventure. When given a choice, most of us prefer taking the scenic route to a more direct route. We want to enjoy God's creation rather than speed across boring highways. When Jesus departed for Galilee, He chose the direct route over the scenic coastline. It was much more than a direct route. It was a strategic detour for God's work. Great resentment existed between the Jews and the Samaritans. Some Jews had intermarried with Gentiles of that region, and they were in rebellion against the common Jewish establishment. The "pure" Jews treated them as outcasts, rejecting them, mistreating them, and labeling them as heretics. In short, Jews and Samaritans hated one another with great intensity. The shortest route between Judea and Galilee was Samaria.

Jesus knew that Samaria was spiritually lost, so He made a strategic detour to connect with the Samaritans. There were Jews who had intermarried with the Gentiles of that region. They rebelled against the Jewish establishment of their day. As you can imagine, tension was very high. Jesus made a strategic detour to connect with the Samaritans. God was about to do a powerful work in the heart of this forgotten area. When it comes to finding your place in God's work, where do you look? By nature we tend to want to be involved with activities and ministries that are already flourishing. The thought of seeing many lives changed is exciting.

But what happens to the people who find themselves in dark places? What about those who are rejected and labeled as outcasts by society? Don't these people need a Savior too? God is doing amazing things with families today. Don't think however that He does not want to do a great work in the lives of the forgotten, the abandoned, and the hurting. God is searching for people who are willing to make spiritual detours. Are you willing to take the hard road and reach out to those who are hurting and neglected?

Read: Open your Bible and read I Timothy 2:4.

Reflect: Prayerfully consider the following: Is there a person or a group of people that God is asking me to make a detour and reach out to?

Respond: As a result of these truths, what might need to change in my attitude, beliefs, and actions? What steps do I need to take outwardly?

Give Me a Drink

"Jacob's well was there; so Jesus, wearied as he was from his journey, was sitting beside the well. It was about the sixth hour. A woman from Samaria came to draw water. Jesus said to her, 'Give me a drink.' (For his disciples had gone away into the city to buy food)" (John 4:6-8).

The number one fear in our country is public speaking. Speaking to others can be very intimidating. Many find it tough to simply start a conversation with someone they do not know. Finding common ground takes time. It is easy for some and difficult for others. Jacob's well was a popular spot for thirsty people. A natural spring of water flowed abundantly for all to enjoy. It was common to find people at the well. Jesus knew He would find two things at this location—water and people. At the well, Jesus broke the social and religious rules of His day by speaking with a woman. Both Jesus and the woman were seeking water—the common ground.

This woman was alone. This fact alone spoke volumes. Women generally traveled in groups. What had she done to be left alone? What was it about her lifestyle that created this social vacuum? Whatever her background, Jesus and the woman had a common ground. They were both seeking water. Jesus asked her, *"Give me a drink."* What a shocking request from Jesus: a man, a Jew, and a Rabbi. This was a triple no-no. Jews and Samaritans don't talk to one another. Jewish men, especially a Rabbi, have no business talking to such a woman. Jesus crossed religious, racial, and cultural barriers to connect with this lost soul. He saw an obvious opportunity to establish common ground and He went for it. Jesus initiated direct contact by simply using water as the common denominator.

It may not be as difficult as you think. Your place of work is a common denominator with lost colleagues and employees. It may be the school you attend with your fellow teachers or students. Your neighborhood is another great platform to begin spiritual conversations. Even parks, local sports leagues, and community events can serve as a strong starting point. How can you make better use of each of these platforms to share Christ with others? Who are the people you relate to the most? Start praying for your next spiritual encounter. Ask God to lead and speak through you. If someone says to you, *"Give me a drink,"* give him or her the water of life.

Read: Open your Bible and read I Peter 4:10-11.

Reflect: Prayerfully consider the following: What areas of common ground do I need to make better use of to share Jesus with others?

Respond: As a result of these truths, what might need to change in my attitude, beliefs, and actions? What steps do I need to take outwardly?

Living Water

"The Samaritan woman said to him, 'How is it that you, a Jew, ask for a drink from me, a woman of Samaria?' (For Jews have no dealings with Samaritans.) Jesus answered her, 'If you knew the gift of God, and who it is that is saying to you, 'Give me a drink,' you would have asked him, and he would have given you living water" (John 4:9-10).

We all love to be the recipients of generosity. When people freely give us more than what we expect, it is a positive experience. These are moments we cherish deeply. Hopefully they serve as models for us to follow as we seek to live our lives in an overflow of faith, obedience, and generosity.

It is hard to imagine, but some people believe that God wants nothing to do with them. Overwhelmed by their own sense of guilt, they find that hope seems out of reach; it's not something they pursue or truly believe in. They are unaware of God's compassion, grace, and mercy. The "What?" consistently overrides the "Who?" in their life. They focus almost exclusively on their past actions or their present situation. The thought of God connecting with them on a personal level is totally unimaginable.

Jesus is the gift of God. Jesus is the Living Water. When you receive Jesus as Savior, you begin to discover God's abundant love and generosity. Not only does He cross man-made barriers, He creates new spiritual realities for His children. Jesus gives us eternal life and fills us with His Holy Spirit. The Samaritan had no idea what she was in for. This single encounter would radically change her life and the life of those within her community. Jesus wanted to quench her spiritual thirst. This was more important than her past. It was far more meaningful and lasting than natural water. Jesus offered her Living Water from above. This is what she needed the most.

Jesus looked beyond her physical needs to open up a dialogue about spiritual realities. We need to establish common ground, but not park there forever. We need to help people make the connection between physical needs and spiritual realities. Lead people to Jesus in your conversations. Tell them about the Living Water. Don't be boring. Be creative. Use your surroundings to help others see spiritual realities.

Read: Open your Bible and read 2 Peter 3:9.

Reflect: Prayerfully consider the following: How can I better use my surroundings to help people find Jesus—The Living Water—in their lives?

Respond: As a result of these truths, what might need to change in my attitude, beliefs, and actions? What steps do I need to take outwardly?

Where Do You Get It?

"The woman said to him, 'Sir, you have nothing to draw water with, and the well is deep. Where do you get that living water? Are you greater than our father Jacob? He gave us the well and drank from it himself, as did his sons and his livestock' " (John 4:11-12).

The question, "Where did you get it?" is not a threatening one. We even ask it of total strangers when we see that they have purchased something that we want or need. Most people are willing to point us in the right direction to help us find what we are looking for if we simply ask them.

When the Samaritan woman asked Jesus for the location of living water, she believed it was what she needed to permanently quench her physical thirst. She was only thinking of her physical needs. The woman wanted to find a place to satisfy her thirst. Jesus was leading her to understand that her greatest needed was spiritual transformation, not water.

It didn't matter that Jesus had no vessel to draw water out of the well. He was the source of living water. The woman had some knowledge of Israel's history, but she was missing the most important part—Jesus. You may run into people who know a few stories from the Bible. It may be knowledge gained as a child or a recent effort to learn about God's Word. Don't forget to lead people back to the One who makes all things new.

It is so important that we listen as people share what they know about God. We know that God places a void in the heart of every person. Our job is to help people find the source of living water. Even if they are not looking for Jesus, we need to help them see the importance of finding Him. Let's build a bridge from the physical to the spiritual. This is important!

God will place people in your life for you to lead them to find living water. Some of these people are overwhelmed with meeting their personal needs. Others are wrapped up in the busyness of urban life. Some are so tired that they may fall asleep standing up. But all of these need a Savior. All of these people need us to listen closely to what they are saying and bridge the gap with what they are missing. Help them know how to find Jesus.

Read: Open your Bible and read John 7:37-38.

Reflect: Prayerfully consider the following: What would you say is the biggest change in your life since accepting Jesus? What would others say?

Respond: As a result of these truths, what might need to change in my attitude, beliefs, and actions? What steps do I need to take outwardly?

Thirst Quencher

*"Jesus said to her, 'Everyone who drinks of this water will be
thirsty again, but whoever drinks of the water that I will give him
will never be thirsty again. The water that I will give him will become
in him a spring of water welling up to eternal life" (John 4:13-14).*

You and a group of friends get together for a game of basketball in the middle of the summer. All you really need is a court, a ball, and plenty of water. Water serves to replenish lost fluids. The more you play the more you drink. Water temporarily quenches your thirst unlike any other liquid. Although it works great, it can never eliminate your thirst completely.

Imagine never being thirsty again. Imagine never needing to go to the store and buy a gallon of water. That would be amazing. Jesus was referring to a source of water that would forever satisfy our spiritual thirst. The well was not the source of living water. Jesus was the source. Believing in Jesus would give you unlimited access to the source of living water.

*"On the last day of the feast, the great day, Jesus stood up and cried out, 'If
anyone thirsts, let him come to me and drink. Whoever believes in me, as the
Scripture has said, 'Out of his heart will flow rivers of living water.' Now this he
said about the Spirit, whom those who believed in him were to receive, for as yet
the Spirit had not been given, because Jesus was not yet glorified" (John 7:37-39).*

Few of us would say that our lives have a source of living water. Why is that? Is that not what Jesus promised? Is that not the reality of the Holy Spirit working in us and through us? If we are not living the abundant life Jesus promised, it's not His fault. Maybe we have decided to focus more on our physical needs than on spiritual realities.

You can't simultaneously worry about your physical needs and experience the peace of God's Spirit. You need to make a choice. Do you want your life to be like a spring of living water or a suitcase filled with anxieties? As a believer, you have eternal life right now. You have what everyone needs— a relationship with Jesus. The hope of the world lives in you! Let God take care of your needs. Since you are no longer thirsty, stop worrying.

Read: Open your Bible and read John 4:1-54.

Reflect: Prayerfully consider the following: What do I worry about regularly? Am I allowing God to take care of my needs, worry-free?

Respond: As a result of these truths, what might need to change in my attitude, beliefs, and actions? What steps do I need to take outwardly?

Exposing Our Reality

'The woman said to him, 'Sir, give me this water, so that I will not be thirsty or have to come here to draw water.' Jesus said to her, "Go, call your husband, and come here."' The woman answered him, 'I have no husband.' Jesus said to her, 'You are right in saying, 'I have no husband'; for you have had five husbands, and the one you now have is not your husband. What you have said is true' "
(John 4:15-18).

Hide and Seek is a favorite game among children. You can play it in many different places. Someone counts to fifty and you run to find a good hiding spot. The excitement builds when they can't find you after several minutes. When they do, it's your turn to quickly find and expose those in hiding. The Samaritan woman did not fully understand what she was asking for. She wanted a quick fix to meet her physical need. Her desire to quench her thirst was stronger than her desire to deal with her lifestyle of sin. Jesus got right to the heart of the matter. He wanted her to bring her husband to the well. The woman must have experienced a multitude of emotions as she considered the implications of His penetrating request.

The woman came out of her hiding place. She admitted, *"I have no husband."* Jesus exposed her reality with one powerful question. In spite of her "religious" words, she was living in sin. She may have pretended to be righteous in her initial discussion, but Jesus revealed the true condition of her heart. She had bounced around from one man to another, probably trying to fill her thirst for genuine love and companionship.

When Jesus exposes the true condition of our heart it can be a painful experience. At times we try to flatter God with our long, eloquent prayers. God sees right through us. He knows us better than we know ourselves. He can see the true condition of your heart, even now.

Is there anything in your life that you are trying to hide from God? The thought of hiding something from an omniscient God is rather amusing, but many of us still try. Take some time today and allow God's Spirit to search your heart. Don't let the well of life run dry. Clean it out and let God fill your life with His Spirit. God wants to flow freely through a holy life.

Read: Open your Bible and read I John 1:9-10.

Reflect: Prayerfully consider the following: What do I need to confess that I have kept in hiding? What promise do I find in I John 1:9-10?

Respond: As a result of these truths, what might need to change in my attitude, beliefs, and actions? What steps do I need to take outwardly?

Where's the Place?

"The woman said to him, 'Sir, I perceive that you are a prophet.
Our fathers worshiped on this mountain, but you say that in Jerusalem
is the place where people ought to worship.' Jesus said to her, 'Woman,
believe me, the hour is coming when neither on this mountain nor in
Jerusalem will you worship the Father. You worship what you do not know;
we worship what we know, for salvation is from the Jews' " (John 4:19-22).

Road signs are meant to direct you to a specific location. You don't jump on a road sign that reads, "Texas: 450 miles," and say, "We have arrived." That would be humorous, but strange. People follow all kinds of signs that lead them to the wrong destination. Many people spend fortunes trying to swim in a "holy river," or climb to the top of a "sacred mountain" to worship and find spiritual renewal. They are looking for the right place.

The woman of Samaria understood the religious division between the Jews and the Samaritans. It was a battle between the right place to worship God and the wrong place to worship Him. She was bringing this battle to Jesus to get his opinion. Since Jesus revealed her true condition, the woman considered Jesus a prophet. Her question was probably very sincere.

Jesus explained that a time was coming when the location would no longer be the most important part of worship. You are not more spiritual if you worship God in a big church or in a very small church. It makes no difference if you worship God in Egypt, in China, or in Africa. Worship is not about finding the right place; it's not about "Where?" but "How?" How you worship God is more important than where you worship Him.

It's easy to get involved in religious battles with other believers. We can feel very strongly about certain things that make no difference to our spiritual maturity at all. "What's the best church?" or "Is Saturday night service more or less spiritual than Sunday morning service?" are both questions that lead to nowhere. We are better off remaining silent.

In the eyes of unbelievers, watching two believers argue sends a confusing message about our faith. Don't become a stumbling block for unbelievers. Choose to disagree and drop the subject. Choose to love and move on.

Read: Open your Bible and read Titus 2:9.

Reflect: Prayerfully consider the following: Do I love to argue? What should I do the next time I am challenged to argue publically?

Respond: As a result of these truths, what might need to change in my attitude, beliefs, and actions? What steps do I need to take outwardly?

True Worshipers

"But the hour is coming, and is now here, when the true worshipers will worship the Father in spirit and truth, for the Father is seeking such people to worship him. God is spirit, and those who worship him must worship in spirit and truth" (John 4:23-24).

Doing something the wrong way can be frustrating and costly. When you decide not to read the instructions before assembling a new piece of furniture, trouble awaits you. Things such as balance, stability, and safety are all at risk when the instructions are neglected. It's worth reading through the owner's manual to avoid these mistakes and save valuable time.

Jesus tells the Samaritan woman the kind of worshiper that God is searching for. Jesus simplifies worship. He removes the focus from "Where should I worship" to "How should I worship?" Jesus was essentially saying that today, God is looking for true worshipers. God is searching for people to worship Him in the way He desires—in spirit and truth. He wants people in all places and at all times to worship Him.

People sometimes take pride in worshiping God "in their own way." Some believe worship involves a systematic order of events. Others believe worship requires candles, specific clothing, physical neglect, or repetitious prayers. This is like trying to build new furniture without reading the instructions. One may feel good about it, but in the end, it is not what it should be or what it could be. "I worship God my way" is a sign of spiritual rebellion. True worship is spiritual. It is not a mechanical activity.

The Holy Spirit helps us mature into the image of Christ. He teaches us how to worship. He helps us speak with the Father when we don't know what else to say. The expression of our worship should be spiritual in nature. God's Spirit may lead us to kneel, bow, raise our hands, clap, or even sing. The Holy Spirit teaches us how to worship. He guides us into all truth. God wants you to worship Him in spirit and truth. Worship involves recognizing God for who He is and what He has done. Your worship must be grounded in truth. God has revealed Himself throughout the pages of Scripture. True worship is always grounded in the absolute truth of God's Word. Is the expression of your worship in spirit and truth?

Read: Open your Bible and read Nehemiah 8:6.

Reflect: Prayerfully consider the following: Do I freely express my worship to God in spirit and truth? How can my worship of God grow?

Respond: As a result of these truths, what might need to change in my attitude, beliefs, and actions? What steps do I need to take outwardly?

I Who Speak to You am He

"The woman said to him, 'I know that Messiah is coming (he who is called Christ). When he comes, he will tell us all things.' Jesus said to her, 'I who speak to you am he' " (John 4:25-26).

Piecing together a puzzle can be an adventure. Some puzzles can be completed in a few minutes, but others require hours or even days. It can be tough and even tiring to work through the process. It's always exciting, though, when the time comes to place the last piece. Both Jews and Samaritans were waiting for the promised Messiah. They spent countless hours praying and hoping for their Savior to arrive soon. He was the piece of their spiritual puzzle that was still missing. When the Messiah arrived, it was understood that everything would come together for good. He would be the one who would rule Israel and make all things right.

Jesus finally revealed himself to the Samaritan woman as the promised Messiah. It was a moment filled with great emotion. Jesus was the only one who could transform her sinful life. He was the object of her faith. He was the perfect expression of the God of Israel and the hope of her people. He would be the one to restore all things. And on top of all that, Jesus was the only one who could transform her sinful life. This meeting was more than an answer to prayer; it was a holy experience with God. Jesus is much more than a man or another prophet. Jesus is the eternal Messiah. Not only is he the hope of Israel and Samaria, he is your hope and the hope of the entire world. Jesus was the answer to the greatest puzzle in history. He is also the answer to your greatest challenge.

Jesus came to give you life and a reason for living. He came to remove the weight of your past and give you the power to live a life without regrets. In Christ, you are an overcomer. The purpose for your life is found in the source of life—Jesus Christ. God intentionally meets with you to empower you for His work. He is not trying to hide or make things difficult for you to understand. God wants to help you finish the mission He has purposed for you to do. God enlisted you in His divine plan to make disciples and reproduce His character in the lives of others. Today, He wants to reveal Himself to you in a new way. Today, Jesus has something to say to you.

Read: Open your Bible and read Luke 2:26.

Reflect: Prayerfully consider the following: What is God revealing to me lately about my purpose for living? Am I obeying his leadership?

Respond: As a result of these truths, what might need to change in my attitude, beliefs, and actions? What steps do I need to take outwardly?

Not Ashamed

"Just then his disciples came back. They marveled that he was talking with a woman, but no one said, "What do you seek?" or, "Why are you talking with her?" So the woman left her water jar and went away into town and said to the people, "Come, see a man who told me all that I ever did. Can this be the Christ?" They went out of the town and were coming to him. (John 4:27-30)

Going back to help the community you were raised in is a good idea. Some people go back to their old neighborhoods to work with children, help during a natural disaster, or make a difference in the local economy. Have you heard of someone going back to openly confess his or her sins? Strange, right? It may not be strange at all after an encounter with Jesus.

The Samaritan woman had her world turned upside down in a matter of minutes. Although she lived with a man, she was alone. Recognized as an "easy woman" to those in her community, she was not someone you wanted anyone in your family to associate with. She was trouble. Her bad reputation was known throughout her community. She was a marked girl.

Who knows if the days leading up to her encounter with Jesus were filled with tears and agonizing prayers? Maybe she was ready to change. Maybe she was looking for answers, but too ashamed to talk with anyone. No man in his right mind would give her a moment's thought. No woman would want to come anywhere near her. She was alone, but not forgotten.

God has a way of finding you when you least expect Him to interrupt your life. God reveals your sin to give you freedom from sin's bondage. Without question, the Samaritan woman was spiritually and physically trapped. Jesus provided a way of escape. She no longer had to live in the prison of guilt and shame. She was now free to experience life with God.

Her response was not surprising at all. Since she was condemned publically she wanted everyone to know that she was a changed person. She wanted people to discover for themselves who Jesus was and His power to transform their lives. Do you still get excited about openly sharing God's transforming power with others? What guilt or shame no longer plagues you? Don't keep these things a secret. Make God's work known to all.

Read: Open your Bible and read Matthew 28:18-20

Reflect: Prayerfully consider the following: How can I be more effective in making Jesus known to others? Have I gone back to my community?

Respond: As a result of these truths, what might need to change in my attitude, beliefs, and actions? What steps do I need to take outwardly?

Beyond Hunger

"Meanwhile the disciples were urging him, saying, 'Rabbi, eat.' But he said to them, 'I have food to eat that you do not know about.' So the disciples said to one another, 'Has anyone brought him something to eat?' Jesus said to them, 'My food is to do the will of him who sent me and to accomplish his work.' "
(John 4:31-34)

People can act very strange when they are hungry. Some people complain and get very agitated. Others may grow unusually quiet and lost in thought as they try to concentrate on other things. If we know someone is truly hungry, we feel compelled to take action by offering something to eat. Our generosity compels us to buy him or her a sandwich. We don't like to see people suffer as a result of hunger. It hurts us deeply in our soul. After several hours without food, the disciples were urging Jesus to eat. They cared deeply for Jesus, and did not want to see Him experience hunger. When Jesus refused to eat, they naturally concluded that someone had provided Him with food. But Jesus was focused on a different kind of food.

Jesus said, *"My food is to do the will of him who sent me and to accomplish his work."* Jesus was primarily concerned with fulfilling God's plan from start to finish. Regardless of the extreme physical discomfort or the threat of harsh opposition, Jesus focused on doing and finishing God's will. He was determined to submit Himself without reservations to the will of the Father. Think about your own life and commitment you have to the Lord. Is your commitment to obey God and to finish the mission He has given you the most important thing in your life? Do you find yourself talking more about your favorite restaurant or next meal rather than what is eternal? Your relationship with God is designed to grow. Your love for God and what He desires for you to do should be the priority for your life.

This is not so extreme at all. Many times before we go on vacation we skip our regular breakfast or lunch. Why? Our intense focus on getting everything done before we leave for vacation overrides our hunger. Getting our work done becomes a higher priority. When we think of God's mission for our lives, should we not have a greater motivation? Imagine how many lives could be changed if your focus changed too.

Read: Open your Bible and read Philippians 3:13.

Reflect: Prayerfully consider the following: What do I need to forget in order to reach forward and accomplish God's mission for my life?

Respond: As a result of these truths, what might need to change in my attitude, beliefs, and actions? What steps do I need to take outwardly?

Lift Up Your Eyes and See

"Do you not say, 'There are yet four months, then comes the harvest'? Look, I tell you, lift up your eyes, and see that the fields are white for harvest. Already the one who reaps is receiving wages and gathering fruit for eternal life, so that sower and reaper may rejoice together. For here the saying holds true, 'One sows and another reaps.' I sent you to reap that for which you did not labor. Others have labored, and you have entered into their labor" (John 4:35-38).

Baking is both an art and a science. You can learn a great deal by watching expert chefs in action. They measure and weigh some ingredients very closely while estimating others. They glance at their creations in the oven and at just the right moment, take swift action and pull it out. Why do they take it out at just the right moment? It's simple. They know its ready.

The disciples understood the normal pattern of farming. First you sow seeds. Next, you wait several months. Finally, you gather a crop. What they did not understand was the timetable for a spiritual harvest. Before they arrived, others were already preparing the hearts of the people by sharing God's Word. People were ready to accept Jesus as their Messiah. All they needed was someone to help them understand the Good News.

Jesus wanted the disciples to lift up their eyes and see the spiritual reality. They must have thought that they were only beginning to prepare the harvest. Jesus helped them understand exactly where on the timetable of spiritual harvest they stood. It was time to reap and gather the crops. There are people all around you that are ready to accept Jesus as Savior. They have heard the message of the gospel through radio, cable television, the Internet, friends, neighbors, or family. They don't need a theological course on apologetics. They need someone who loves them enough to show them how they can know Jesus personally. They are ready right now.

As you pray today, lift up your eyes and see whom God has placed in your life. Notice those people who have recently come into your life. Could it be that they are ready to accept Jesus? Is it possible that you are the one God has chosen to lead them to the Savior? Go ahead and gather your crop. Don't wait another few months. Tell them about Jesus today!

Read: Open your Bible and read John 6:44.

Reflect: Prayerfully consider the following: Who has God brought into my life recently? How can I share the gospel with them this week?

Respond: As a result of these truths, what might need to change in my attitude, beliefs, and actions? What steps do I need to take outwardly?

The Power of a Changed Life

"Many Samaritans from that town believed in him because of the woman's testimony, 'He told me all that I ever did.' So when the Samaritans came to him, they asked him to stay with them, and he stayed there two days. And many more believed because of his word. They said to the woman, 'It is no longer because of what you said that we believe, for we have heard for ourselves, and we know that this is indeed the Savior of the world' " (John 4:39-42).

There is something remarkable about transforming communities. When we see an old building that was literally falling apart fully restored to its original design, we stand back in amazement. When a community absorbs the wrath of a hurricane and determines to rebuild, we see transformation one day at a time. These changes are powerful to see and to experience.

Nothing compares, however, with the power of a transformed life. The spiritual transformation in the life of the Samaritan woman was nothing short of extraordinary. It was like nothing she had ever experienced. This powerful transformation overflowed into her community and changed the lives of many. The story of her changed life sparked a desire in others to personally learn more about Jesus. Your story can have the same impact.

Comparing our story with God's story in the lives of others may seem dull. We may not feel that our transformation was as dramatic as it was with others. Maybe we did not have a serious addiction to drugs. Maybe we have not slept with everyone in town, murdered someone in cold blood, or stolen money. This does not mean that our story is any less powerful.

God's story of transformation in your life is more powerful than you realize. Remember, every one of God's children has a testimony, a personal story of transformation. Some people are not moved by dramatic conversions. They don't identify with these individuals. But when they hear about God changing someone like them, the results are powerful.

Write a one-sentence summary of your life before you met Jesus, the events leading up to your conversion and your changed life today as a result of His presence. Get ready! God may send someone to you today.

Read: Open your Bible and read 1 Peter 3:15.

Reflect: Prayerfully consider the following: Am I confident in God's power to work through my testimony? Who needs to hear my story?

Respond: As a result of these truths, what might need to change in my attitude, beliefs, and actions? What steps do I need to take outwardly?

Too Familiar

"After the two days he departed for Galilee. (For Jesus himself had testified that a prophet has no honor in his own hometown.) So when he came to Galilee, the Galileans welcomed him, having seen all that he had done in Jerusalem at the feast. For they too had gone to the feast" (John 4:43-45).

It is easy for brothers and sisters to laugh at one another as adults. They often share unique stories filled with embarrassing moments, great misunderstandings, and unexpected surprises. These stories may be kept out of the public eye, but everyone in the family can look back and laugh.

Jesus was born in Bethlehem, but He was raised in Nazareth of Galilee. Since that is where He spent most of His life, the people of Galilee were familiar with Him. He was the carpenter's son. He worked with Joseph and helped His dad run the family business. Although people knew about Jesus, they did not really know and honor Him for who He really was.

Jesus was more than a carpenter. He was the Son of God. Jesus is the great "I AM." One might think, "How is it possible to live in the presence of God and not recognize Him?" It's possible. Familiarity is dangerous. We can get so used to going to church that we completely miss God's presence around us. We have to be the Church, not simply go to church.

Our faith is often challenged the most right in our own homes and within our spheres of influence. Our own family members can become our greatest challenge to our faith. If you are the only believer in your family, your faith will be constantly tested. If you are the only one who is taking steps to grow spiritually, your faith will be stretched again and again. Don't get discouraged when family or good friends laugh at your desire to grow spiritually. Satan tries to use those who are closest to us to discourage and distract us in our walk with Christ. If those closest to Jesus laughed at His claims, you can be sure that those closest to you will do the same.

Remind those who know you best of God's work in your life. Remind them of your old habits. Show them how God has transformed you for good. Help people see the new you daily, and let your life speak for itself.

Read: Open your Bible and read Philippians 2:22.

Reflect: Prayerfully consider the following: Do I act differently with those who know me best? How can I help them see Jesus in me every day?

Respond: As a result of these truths, what might need to change in my attitude, beliefs, and actions? What steps do I need to take outwardly?

Twenty Miles

"So he came again to Cana in Galilee, where he had made the water wine. And at Capernaum there was an official whose son was ill. When this man heard that Jesus had come from Judea to Galilee, he went to him and asked him to come down and heal his son, for he was at the point of death. So Jesus said to him, 'Unless you see signs and wonders you will not believe' " (John 4:46-48).

Distance is only a problem when you don't have a way or a desire to get to your destination. When you have the means and the will to get there, the number of miles required is no big deal. You simply enjoy the ride. The benefits of arriving at your destination outweigh the challenges of travel.

Jesus was already gaining popularity before his second visit to Cana of Galilee. Like a celebrity on a national tour, many were aware of who Jesus was when He arrived the second time. During this time a government official was experiencing a significant personal struggle. His son was deathly ill. The young man needed healing and he needed it fast. The father was willing to do anything, even travel twenty miles, to find healing for his son.

Up until this point He had turned water into wine and preached to many people, but we don't have any record of Jesus healing anyone. Without question, the people wanted to see another miracle. But why would this man think Jesus could heal his son and make him well? Where did his faith originate? We don't know exactly why this is the case, but the man had enough faith to make this 24-hour journey for his son.

The crowds were gathering to see a bigger show, but the official was not focused on any such thing. He simply wanted his son to be healed. He invited Jesus to travel twenty miles back to Capernaum and heal his son. The request was humble, direct and powerful. This man placed himself at the mercy of our Lord. This is a very good place to be.

How far are you willing to go to be in the presence of Jesus? Are you willing to make significant personal sacrifices to meet with Jesus one-on-one? This official was an unbeliever. He knew about Jesus, but he did not know Jesus. When people understand who Jesus truly is, distance will never be an issue to keep them from connecting with the Savior.

Read: Open your Bible and read Jeremiah 29:13.

Reflect: Prayerfully consider the following: Am I willing to do whatever it takes to meet with Jesus daily? What excuses have I given in the past?

Respond: As a result of these truths, what might need to change in my attitude, beliefs, and actions? What steps do I need to take outwardly?

Believe and Go

"The official said to him, 'Sir, come down before my child dies.' Jesus said to him, 'Go; your son will live.' The man believed the word that Jesus spoke to him and went on his way. As he was going down, his servants met him and told him that his son was recovering. So he asked them the hour when he began to get better, and they said to him, 'Yesterday at the seventh hour the fever left him.' The father knew that was the hour when Jesus had said to him, 'Your son will live.' And he himself believed, and all his household" (John 4:49-53).

It's been said that our actions are what truly prove what we believe. Regardless of what we may claim to value or believe, our worldview reveals itself through what we do, or what we don't do, over a period of time. Behavioral consistency points to a belief system, because it is our core beliefs that compel us into action. When the official from Capernaum faced an uncontrollable crisis, he took action. He humbly approached Jesus and asked Him to take a day's journey and heal his son. The official was desperate and broken, but he had hope. His son was about to die. For this reason, he searched for Jesus, the One who turned water into wine.

Jesus responded to the official's request with a hopeful command, "Go, your son will live." It was a simple command that required a simple faith. That must have been rather strange for this official. He was used to being in authority. He was now submitting himself to the authority of Jesus. He believed and returned home. The official and his entire family believed after his son was healed. Before you go you have to believe.

Think through the last few times when the Holy Spirit was leading you to take action. How did you respond? Did you believe and take action or did you try negotiating your way to inactivity? We are often surprised when God moves our heart to take action. We question the timing and ponder the potential outcome with fear and uncertainty. We get nervous about doing something for the first time. What we need to do is believe and obey. Is this a struggle for you? Do your feet force you to stand still when you hear God's simple instruction from the Bible? Don't let fear or uncertainty grip your heart. God is pleased when we believe and follow Him in faith. Don't wait and miss another miracle. Believe and go!

Read: Open your Bible and read John 4:1-54.

Reflect: Prayerfully consider the following: What keeps me from following all of God's Word? What does my behavior say about my faith?

Respond: As a result of these truths, what might need to change in my attitude, beliefs, and actions? What steps do I need to take outwardly?

A Place Called Hope

"After this there was a feast of the Jews, and Jesus went up to Jerusalem. Now there is in Jerusalem by the Sheep Gate a pool, in Aramaic called Bethesda, which has five roofed colonnades. In these lay a multitude of invalids—blind, lame, and paralyzed" (John 5:1-3).

When you discover a natural spring on vacation, you can count on two things: cold water and a lot of tourists. People love to find these natural wonders and take pictures with their families. The kids love to dive into the ice-cold water and splash family members who dare to get too close.

The pool at Bethesda is believed to have been a natural spring. Some scholars suggest there were high mineral concentrations in the water that could serve to help heal those who were not well. The New King James translation reads, *"An angel went down at a certain time into the pool and stirred up the water."* The healings that took place were either through natural means or possibly through God's miraculous intervention.

It was not your typical recreational pool. Children and their families were not swimming in the pool or having a picnic nearby. It was a place for those who were not well to gather, comfort one another, and wait in hope. This reminds us of those we often find in our church family. They come to church just as they are. Some are very ill. Some have been wounded deeply from past relationships. Others need direction for their lives.

What they all have in common is that God is now the One whom they are searching for. They understand His unlimited power to heal. They believe that He can change their lives. They accept His grace when He asks them to endure. They lean on His wisdom and strength when they find themselves too weak to live. They know deep within their hearts that God is their hope. They comfort one another and encourage one another.

The Church is a place called hope. As with a hospital, people come in hoping to get well. The church is meant to help people relationally, physically, emotionally, financially, and spiritually. It is a place where you can find love, grace, acceptance, and truth in abundance. It's where God's presence flows through His people to touch and impact the lives of others.

Read: Open your Bible and read John 5:1-47.

Reflect: Prayerfully consider the following: How can my past minister, encourage, strengthen, and help heal those who come to my church?

Respond: As a result of these truths, what might need to change in my attitude, beliefs, and actions? What steps do I need to take outwardly?

Do You Want to Be Healed?

"One man was there who had been an invalid for thirty-eight years.
When Jesus saw him lying there and knew that he had already been there
a long time, he said to him, 'Do you want to be healed?' The sick man
answered him, 'Sir, I have no one to put me into the pool when the water
is stirred up, and while I am going another steps down before me.'
Jesus said to him, 'Get up, take up your bed, and walk.' And at once
the man was healed, and he took up his bed and walked" (John 5:5-9).

It's a surprising question. After a few days of high fever, painful stomach
cramps, and a sore throat, your doctor asks, "Do you want to feel better?"
You look at him and say, "But of course I do. That's why I'm here in your
office." He looks at you and replies, "Great! Take this medicine for five
consecutive days, drink plenty of water, and get as much rest as you can."
When Jesus approached the man who was lame, it was a condition he lived
with for the last 38 years. The pool at Bethesda was probably the spot
where he spent most of his time. His disease left him unable to move
freely without the help of another person. The man was discouraged and
communicated a sense of hopelessness to Jesus. It's possible that he felt
trapped and totally defeated by the weaknesses of his own body.

Unlike the official from Capernaum, this man was not able to walk home.
He was completely incapable of overcoming his terrible disease. Yet Jesus
gives him three commands, *"Get up, take up your bed, and walk."* With
those words, the man's life is transformed. He is now able to move freely,
take care of himself, and travel as desired. He is no longer a helpless
prisoner of his own body. He is no longer restricted by disease.

Although we may be physically strong, we can place ourselves in positions
of spiritual bondage. We can get comfortable lying to one another,
practicing sexual immorality, speaking evil of others, or living out other
destructive expressions of our flesh. If not addressed quickly, our sinful
actions turn into ugly habits. These habits, when left alone, lead us into
spiritual bondage and hurt others. We find ourselves in a hopeless
position, trapped by our own willingness to live in this manner.

Read: Open your Bible and read Galatians 5:17.

Reflect: Prayerfully consider the following: Am I doing something
spiritually destructive? What "blind spots" have others pointed out?

Respond: As a result of these truths, what might need to change in my
attitude, beliefs, and actions? What steps do I need to take outwardly?

Above the Law

"Now that day was the Sabbath. So the Jews said to the man who had been healed, 'It is the Sabbath, and it is not lawful for you to take up your bed.' But he answered them, 'The man who healed me, that man said to me, 'Take up your bed, and walk.' They asked him, 'Who is the man who said to you, 'Take up your bed and walk'? Now the man who had been healed did not know who it was, for Jesus had withdrawn, as there was a crowd in the place" (John 5:9-13).

The last decade has been marked by the creation of software, methods, and programs to simplify businesses, organizations, and churches. With all of the information coming through the Internet pipeline at an ever-increasing rate, processing it effectively is a challenge. How and why people make decisions and their reasons is constantly changing. There were certain oral traditions in the time of Jesus that were firmly established within Israel. In addition to the Ten Commandments, Jewish leaders added an additional 39 activities for their people to follow and obey just as they did with the commandments of Scripture. They were given equal weight. The people were expected to follow these commandments closely. Simply put, the leaders turned their opinions and preferences into Law.

When we add to God's Word the result is never good. Traditions have value, but not if they are elevated to the same level of importance as Scripture. Traditions should not remove or add to what God has said. Expressing our culture or using innovative methods to maximize productivity are good, but not if they remove or add to God's Word. God helps simplify our lives. Our tendency is to complicate matters.

God's Word is completely sufficient for all matters of life. You don't need to add additional commandments or traditions to achieve greater spirituality. On the contrary, God wants to remove things from our lives that often serve as distractions from genuine Christianity. In Christ Jesus, you have everything that you need to fulfill God's purposes for your life. This reality is truly liberating. You can be all that God wants you to be without the baggage of complex traditions or 39 additional commandments. Follow every word you find within the Bible. The Holy Spirit will lead you into all truth and clarify what you don't understand. Simple is good.

Read: Open your Bible and read 2 Timothy 3:16-17.

Reflect: Prayerfully consider the following: Do I focus more on following man-made traditions, new rules, and methods, or God's Word?

Respond: As a result of these truths, what might need to change in my attitude, beliefs, and actions? What steps do I need to take outwardly?

Sin No More

"Afterward Jesus found him in the temple and said to him, 'See, you are well! Sin no more, that nothing worse may happen to you.' The man went away and told the Jews that it was Jesus who had healed him. And this was why the Jews were persecuting Jesus, because he was doing these things on the Sabbath"
(John 5:14-16).

Has it happened to you? You make a fast turn and suddenly there are flashing red and blue lights behind you. You neglected to make a full stop before turning. The officer decides to give you a warning instead of a ticket. He tells you, "Next time, make sure you stop. Don't do this again."

The man whom Jesus healed was given a direct command, *"Go and sin no more."* He was made well physically and spiritually by God's power. His life would be forever changed. His life was a living testimony of God's grace and mercy. Since he was well known within the community, the immediate opportunity to spread the good news of Jesus was great.

Despite what some might believe, not all disease is a consequence of sin (John 9:1-3). Not every sickness you experience is connected to a spiritual shortfall. There are times, however, when our spiritual health directly affects our physical health (James 5:13-15). One principle that we can count on is that we always reap what we sow (Galatians 6:7-8). If I sow to my flesh, sin will prosper. If I sow to my spirit, God's plans will prosper.

Think about the day God transformed your life. You accepted Jesus as Savior and confessed your sins to Him. Whether that was yesterday or twenty years ago, what were you doing that God wanted you to stop right away? Are you still doing those things today? If you are, consider the opportunities you are missing to glorify God through your testimony.

If you are well, sin no more. If God has changed your life, sin no more. Why should you sow to your flesh any longer? Why break God's heart? God saved you to use you for His purposes. Don't continue to do what He has commanded you not to do. Stop making excuses for your sin. Stop feeling sorry for yourself. Get up and start living for Jesus Christ!

Read: Open your Bible and read Galatians 6:7-8.

Reflect: Prayerfully consider the following: Am I continuing to flirt with sin in my life? Who can I speak with today to help me stay focused?

Respond: As a result of these truths, what might need to change in my attitude, beliefs, and actions? What steps do I need to take outwardly?

Equal with God

"But Jesus answered them, 'My Father is working until now, and I am working.' This was why the Jews were seeking all the more to kill him, because not only was he breaking the Sabbath, but he was even calling God his own Father, making himself equal with God" (John 5:17-18).

Playing sports as a child has many benefits. A child learns how to work as part of a team, encourage others, and discipline their body. The coach emphasizes the importance of everyone working together. Most children will adapt a collaborative approach as a result of playing on a good team.

God is one, but exists in three distinct persons: Father, Son, and Holy Spirit. Although they have different roles, they are one in essence. Although they are different persons, they are the same God. The Godhead functions as one. The Jews had a difficult time accepting Jesus as part of the triune divinity. They refused to accept that Jesus was equal with God.

Being equal with God was no small claim. Since God was always working and Jesus was God, Jesus continued working. God does not need a day to rest. Jesus was declaring Himself to be above the Sabbath. Jesus was revealing His deity without reservations. It was too much truth for the Jews to handle. The implications of Jesus' statements were overpowering.

There are times when we think that God is on a vacation. We agonize in prayer over a loved one who has walked away from God. We beg God to intervene when our health deteriorates. We plead with God to provide when our employer announces significant reductions in pay. Thankfully, God will never take a vacation. He is always at work, even when we can't see the evidence of His presence. God is actively working in your life, too.

Never think that God has abandoned you. The Father, Son, and Holy Spirit are constantly at work. Even when you don't understand why things are happening or not happening, submit to God and abide in the Lord Jesus. God's Spirit will give you the strength you need to continue forward. In Christ Jesus, you are already on the winning team. The united approach, power, and purpose of the divine Trinity are working with you and for you.

Read: Open your Bible and read Matthew 12:8.

Reflect: Prayerfully consider the following: How does knowing that the Father, Son, and Holy Spirit are always working encourage your faith?

Respond: As a result of these truths, what might need to change in my attitude, beliefs, and actions? What steps do I need to take outwardly?

Identify and Engage

"For this reason the Jews persecuted Jesus, and sought to kill Him, because He had done these things on the Sabbath. But Jesus answered them, 'My Father has been working until now, and I have been working.' Therefore the Jews sought all the more to kill Him, because He not only broke the Sabbath, but also said that God was His Father, making Himself equal with God. Then Jesus answered and said to them, 'Most assuredly, I say to you, the Son can do nothing of Himself, but what He sees the Father do; for whatever He does, the Son also does in like manner. For the Father loves the Son, and shows Him all things that He Himself does; and He will show Him greater works than these, that you may marvel"
(John 5:16-20).

Using the right kind of bait is essential for catching the right fish. Part of fishing well involves identifying what kind of fish you want to catch. This leads to the question, "What do these fish love to eat?" The answer to this question helps you identify and engage these fish more precisely.

God, the vinedresser, is always at work around you. His work of life-transformation is alive and well. This great work takes place with those you come in contact with every day. There are many good activities in life to get involved in. God wants you to be dynamically involved in His work of changing lives. The Christian life is not about staying busy and joining multiple ministries at church. It's about living through the vine and helping others realize this same connection in their lives. Live through the vine!

Identify and engage. God's desire is to magnify His name through your life as you identify His work and get involved. Living through the vine is critical in this process. As you learn to hear God's voice and respond to his ways, your capacity to engage in His work significantly increases.

As you come in contact with others this week, prayerfully consider these questions as you speak with them: "How does the Lord want me to encourage them today? Is there a specific need in their life I can pray for? How can I express just how much God loves them? How can I express just how much I love them? How can I deliver God's love in a meaningful way?" Ask the Lord to help you identify His work and then respond to His lead. Get ready to identify and engage those who need hope and help.

Read: Open your Bible and read I Peter 2:17.

Reflect: Prayerfully consider the following: Am I honoring others by identifying their needs and serving them unconditionally?

Respond: As a result of these truths, what might need to change in my attitude, beliefs, and actions? What steps do I need to take outwardly?

Holy Synchronization

"So Jesus said to them, 'Truly, truly, I say to you, the Son can do nothing of his own accord, but only what he sees the Father doing. For whatever the Father does, that the Son does likewise. For the Father loves the Son and shows him all that he himself is doing. And greater works than these will he show him, so that you may marvel. For as the Father raises the dead and gives them life, so also the Son gives life to whom he will" (John 5:19-21).

Several decades ago, a game named Simon was invented. The game had four sections that would light up in random order. The objective was to duplicate lighted sequences when it was your turn by pressing down on each section of light. As you mastered each sequence, the difficulty and length of each sequence increased. The winner was the one who managed to perfectly duplicate the entire sequence without a mistake.

Jesus followed the lead of the Father in all of His activities. He completely submitted himself to the Father's will. Jesus waited when the Father said to wait, and took action when the Father led Him to take action. Jesus aligned His life with the desires of the Father. He left us a simple model to follow.

Synchronizing your life with God's will is an intentional process. It involves trusting God in every area of your life. It requires you to submit every decision to God's authority. He must be the Master of your life. This is a BIG step for many. You have to believe that God loves you and knows what's best for your life. You have to believe that God rules sovereignly. You have to believe that His ways are the key to winning at life.

God is not trying to hide things from you. He wants to show you what He is doing in the lives of others and how you can be involved. Jesus told His disciples, *"No longer do I call you servants, for the servant does not know what his master is doing; but I have called you friends, for all that I have heard from my Father I have made known to you"* (John 15:15). You are God's friend!

Can you imagine God whispering in your heart and revealing what He wants to accomplish through your life? Can you imagine God doing greater things through your life? Determine to follow God's leading in your life. Allow His perfect plan to be your plan. Listen for His quiet instructions.

Read: Open your Bible and read John 15:15.

Reflect: Prayerfully consider the following: What can you adjust in your schedule each day to spend more time listening to the Father?

Respond: As a result of these truths, what might need to change in my attitude, beliefs, and actions? What steps do I need to take outwardly?

Honor the Son

"The Father judges no one, but has given all judgment to the Son, that all may honor the Son, just as they honor the Father. Whoever does not honor the Son does not honor the Father who sent him. Truly, truly, I say to you, whoever hears my word and believes him who sent me has eternal life. He does not come into judgment, but has passed from death to life" (John 5:22-24).

To lead a group of soldiers through fierce battles is the dream of many young boys. Often these young boys are left speechless when they actually meet a real soldier in person. Without knowing what the word honor even means, they give genuine honor to those who are serving in the military. Those who are worthy of honor should receive it.

In God's Kingdom, the Lamb of God, Jesus, is the One who has been given all honor and all authority. To honor the Son is to honor the Father. To dishonor the Son is to dishonor the Father. For this reason, when you reject Jesus, you reject God. Jesus said, *"I am the way, and the truth, and the life. No one comes to the Father except through me" (John 14:6).* The only way to know God is to know His Son, Jesus Christ.

On the cross, Jesus voluntarily received God's judgment for sin on your behalf. God has given Jesus complete authority to judge His creation. Jesus is the final authority. There is no other. He is the One who gives eternal life. He is the One who provides direct access to the Father to those who accept Him. Jesus is worthy of your highest respect and highest praise. He is worthy of your total honor and worthy of your undivided worship.

If God has given you eternal life through Jesus, honor Him. Worship Him. Serve Him. There is no condemnation in Christ Jesus. You have nothing to fear. You are now God's property. You have passed from death to life. Are you living as one who has been redeemed by the blood of the Lamb? Would others say that your life today shines as a trophy of God's grace?

Don't simply honor the Lord with your words. Honor Him with your life. Let your personal ministry to the Lord and others serve to reflect the new life you have in Jesus. Honoring the Lord is being God's soldier in every mission He provides. Love the Son, honor the Son, and live for the Son.

Read: Open your Bible and read Philippians 2:9-11.

Reflect: Prayerfully consider the following: What part of my life today is not honoring Jesus as Lord? What should I confess and submit to Him?

Respond: As a result of these truths, what might need to change in my attitude, beliefs, and actions? What steps do I need to take outwardly?

The Voice

"Truly, truly, I say to you, an hour is coming, and is now here, when the dead will hear the voice of the Son of God, and those who hear will live. For as the Father has life in himself, so he has granted the Son also to have life in himself. And he has given him authority to execute judgment, because he is the Son of Man. Do not marvel at this, for an hour is coming when all who are in the tombs will hear his voice and come out, those who have done good to the resurrection of life, and those who have done evil to the resurrection of judgment" (John 5:25-29).

Do you find it amazing that you can recognize the voice of your son or daughter in the middle of a crowded room or large event? You may be focused on doing a particular activity or talking with another person. But when you hear their voice you instantly recognize who is calling.

The voice of Jesus attracted great multitudes of people. Without modern technology, Jesus was able to capture the hearts of people through the simplicity of His message. This message of life was the very message of God himself. Jesus, the Son of God, spoke the words of life to those who were spiritually dead. Those who were truly seeking God responded to Jesus' voice. They responded to His personal invitation of eternal life.

Today, Jesus continues His work through His people—the Church. His voice streams through their voice. His love, mercy, and compassion flow through the lives of believers. We are the ones who must continue letting His voice be heard. There are dead people walking all around us. They believe they are living life to the fullest, but they are spiritually empty and therefore spiritually dead. Regardless of their situation, they need Jesus. Consider for a minute those with whom you come in contact every day.

God may be speaking to their hearts right now and trying to get their attention. What if God has specifically planned to use your voice to be His voice for their lives? What if other believers whom they know have silenced their voice and only talk about superficial things? How will these dead friends of yours ever stand a chance to know Jesus? How could they possibly find life in Christ if they never hear His voice through His people? Maybe it's time they hear God's voice of love and hope through you.

Read: Open your Bible and read John 3:16-17.

Reflect: Prayerfully consider the following: Who has God placed around my life recently that is clearly dead? How can I be the voice this week?

Respond: As a result of these truths, what might need to change in my attitude, beliefs, and actions? What steps do I need to take outwardly?

A Greater Testimony

"I can do nothing on my own. As I hear, I judge, and my judgment is just, because I seek not my own will but the will of him who sent me. If I alone bear witness about myself, my testimony is not true. There is another who bears witness about me, and I know that the testimony that he bears about me is true. You sent to John, and he has borne witness to the truth. Not that the testimony that I receive is from man, but I say these things so that you may be saved. He was a burning and shining lamp, and you were willing to rejoice for a while in his light" (John 5:30-35).

Do you remember as a child sharing an amazing story with your friends only to have them respond in total disbelief? Although you gave them many details and showed them several souvenirs from your great adventure, they only laughed at your creative speaking skills. But when your dad suddenly interrupted the conversation and shared a similar story, everything changed. Your friends now believed your entire story.

Testimony from an important and well-respected person can be powerful. It can influence others and change the course of conversations by solidifying the truth in an unexpected way. The testimony of the Father carried an unprecedented influence. Jesus was not sent on His own. The Father was responsible for sending Jesus. The mission of the Father was carried out in the life of the Son. God the Father wrote the script. Jesus fulfilled His part in the power of the Holy Spirit. All of His works flowed from the Father.

"But the testimony that I have is greater than that of John. For the works that the Father has given me to accomplish, the very works that I am doing, bear witness about me that the Father has sent me. And the Father who sent me has himself borne witness about me" (John 5:36-37).

Consider your place of employment for a moment. Does the way you work give evidence that God has sent you? Is it obvious to others by your character and by your attitude that you are on an intentional mission with God? His work in and through your life should be obvious to others. God has your back. When you make what's important to the Father a priority in your life, He will take care of your critics. His influence is greater. Determine to obey God in everything that you learn about His purposes.

Read: Open your Bible and read John 20:21.

Reflect: Prayerfully consider the following: What has the Father sent you to do for His mission? How can you obey God today in this area?

Respond: As a result of these truths, what might need to change in my attitude, beliefs, and actions? What steps do I need to take outwardly?

The Big Clue

"His voice you have never heard, his form you have never seen, and you do not have his word abiding in you, for you do not believe the one whom he has sent. You search the Scriptures because you think that in them you have eternal life; and it is they that bear witness about me, yet you refuse to come to me that you may have life" (John 5:37-40).

A professional detective's occupation can be a frustrating one. There are times when they spend countless hours working on a single case, following each lead closely to exhaust every possibility. When they discover the "big clue" everything changes. All other leads come to a stop. Why? It's simple. The "big clue" is the driving force to help solve the case.

The Jews spent countless hours examining the Scriptures to find eternal life. They meticulously analyzed every paragraph, sentence, word and letter. Their search, however, was meaningless because their hearts were far from God. The leads they followed were superficial. They developed their own conclusions and added lists of additional rules, which resulted in legalism. This was a big mistake. Their case for the Messiah remained open.

These religious leaders had never heard God's voice or seen His face, but they searched diligently to find Him. They searched and they searched, but they missed the "big clue." Can you imagine their frustration? Can you imagine Jesus' frustration with this group? Jesus was and is eternal life. He knew the depths of their stubborn hearts. The "big clue" was present and they totally missed it. Unfortunately, their hearts were filled with unbelief.

Two things jump out at us when we read this text. First, the Jews knew God's Word exceptionally well. However, the Word was not living within them. They knew God's Word intellectually, but not personally. They memorized entire books of the Old Testament and could recite them perfectly from memory. Sadly, it never made it to their hearts.

Second, the Jews did not believe Jesus. Since God's Word was not abiding in their hearts, it was impossible for them to believe the author of life. Believing in Jesus, and allowing His Word to live through your life, is at the very heart of the Christian life. When you accept Jesus everything changes.

Read: Open your Bible and read Luke 6:46-47.

Reflect: Prayerfully consider the following: Does God's Word easily flow from my heart or only from my mind? Do I really believe in Jesus?

Respond: As a result of these truths, what might need to change in my attitude, beliefs, and actions? What steps do I need to take outwardly?

Seek God's Glory

"I do not receive glory from people. But I know that you do not have the love of God within you. I have come in my Father's name, and you do not receive me. If another comes in his own name, you will receive him. How can you believe, when you receive glory from one another and do not seek the glory that comes from the only God? Do not think that I will accuse you to the Father. There is one who accuses you: Moses, on whom you have set your hope. For if you believed Moses, you would believe me; for he wrote of me. But if you do not believe his writings, how will you believe my words?" (John 5:41-47).

There's one at every neighborhood basketball park. These young men play on the team, but they really play for their own egos. They're "ball hogs" that don't pass the ball to their teammates because they hate to share the spotlight. They enjoy being superstars and getting all of the attention more than helping their team win. They play hard only to seek their own glory.

The Jewish leaders in Jesus' day were more concerned with being honored by their peers than receiving the honor that came from God. They wanted to be the religious superstars of their day and take part in what society reserved only for the religious elite. People were very impressed with these men. On the outside they seemed to have it all together.

In public they dressed a certain way and paid attention to every small detail in their man-made laws. They washed their hands continuously, maintained a safe distance from "sinners," and displayed great discipline in public. On the inside it was a different story. God was not impressed with their lack of love and their phony performances. He was certainly not clapping.

Jesus' indictment of their spiritual condition boiled down to three key areas. First, they did not have God's love within them. This is where everything starts. Without God's love dwelling within us, our lives will always head in the wrong direction. Second, they did not receive Jesus as their Messiah and Savior. They rejected the very person they were trying to find because they were too caught up in their own agendas to even recognize Him. Finally, consumed by their own stubborn pride and self-righteousness, they did not seek God's glory. Are you seeking His glory?

Read: Open your Bible and read Proverbs 29:23.

Reflect: Prayerfully consider the following: Would others say that I am prideful, or humble? What has Satan used to enlarge my mind with pride?

Respond: As a result of these truths, what might need to change in my attitude, beliefs, and actions? What steps do I need to take outwardly?

Following Signs

*"After this Jesus went away to the other side of the Sea of Galilee,
which is the Sea of Tiberias. And a large crowd was following him,
because they saw the signs that he was doing on the sick" (John 6:1-2).*

Tourists who travel to New York can purchase what is known as "The City Pass." This coupon book provides discounted tickets to all of the major attractions within the city, making it easy for everyone to see and appreciate the great beauty of New York. Because of its popularity, large crowds can be found traveling from one event to another. With the City Pass in hand, taking in all the Big Apple's museums and skyscraping towers is as easy as following the signs. Following signs comes naturally for us.

Jesus was never impressed with large crowds. He understood that many were following Him because they had a desire to see impressive signs and wonders. They would see Jesus perform miracles, but would totally miss the person of Jesus in the process. Jesus later explained, *"Indeed, in their case the prophecy of Isaiah is fulfilled that says: 'You will indeed hear but never understand, and you will indeed see but never perceive' " (Matthew 13:14).*

Healing the sick struck a cord with the people. You can always find people who are sick. Some get better quickly while others remain in their condition for weeks or even several months. When families struggle through prolonged sickness, it can drain them emotionally, physically and financially. Jesus' healing ministry was the result of His great love and compassion for people. He responded to their faith, however great or small, graciously acting on their behalf to make them well.

What do you do when people pursue you for the wrong reasons? Are you gracious and compassionate? Jesus looked beyond the motives of the crowds. He knew exactly why they were following Him, but He continued to minister to them. He continued to love and He continued to give. Mark writes, *"When he went ashore he saw a great crowd, and he had compassion on them, because they were like sheep without a shepherd. And he began to teach them many things" (Mark 6:34).* Imagine what would happen if you determined in your heart to love and minister to others, regardless of their motives? As people continue following signs, lead them to follow Jesus.

Read: Open your Bible and read Matthew 15:30.

Reflect: Prayerfully consider the following: How can I more effectively love and minister to those who are sick, hurting, alone, and discouraged.

Respond: As a result of these truths, what might need to change in my attitude, beliefs, and actions? What steps do I need to take outwardly?

Not Enough

"Jesus went up on the mountain, and there he sat down with his disciples. Now the Passover, the feast of the Jews, was at hand. Lifting up his eyes, then, and seeing that a large crowd was coming toward him, Jesus said to Philip, 'Where are we to buy bread, so that these people may eat?' He said this to test him, for he himself knew what he would do. Philip answered him, 'Two hundred denarii worth of bread would not be enough for each of them to get a little' " (John 6:3-7).

You stumble across an infomercial for a humanitarian organization working to stop hunger, disease, and oppression. The ad is so direct and so filled with stories of personal suffering that it breaks your heart to watch. The need is great and overwhelming, and you give what you can. But while your contribution can help a few, it is not enough to help everyone.

As Jesus rested with his disciples, a wave of people quickly approached them. The crowd had traveled a long way to find Jesus, and they were hungry. Jesus wanted to meet their needs and teach the disciples an important lesson. It would be a lesson that they would not soon forget.

He decided to test the spiritual maturity of his disciples without warning or advance preparation. The people were approaching and the disciples needed to take action right away. The need was overwhelming. There were thousands of adults and children who decided to follow Jesus. The problem far exceeded the disciples' ability to solve in their own power.

What do you do when you realize that all of your resources are not enough to solve the problems you are facing? Where do you go to find answers? What steps do you normally take? There are times when God will deliberately test your spiritual maturity. He wants to see how you will respond when the need exceeds your personal limitations.

God is the solution. He is not overwhelmed by your circumstances. How you respond speaks volumes about your faith. You can trust Him to lead you. You can trust Him to provide for your needs. Don't focus on what you can't see or what you don't have right now. The next time you are tested just remember, although you may not have enough, God is enough.

Read: Open your Bible and read 2 Corinthians 9:8.

Reflect: Prayerfully consider the following: Am I giving God the first opportunity to lead me through the problems I face each day?

Respond: As a result of these truths, what might need to change in my attitude, beliefs, and actions? What steps do I need to take outwardly?

Divide or Multiply

"One of his disciples, Andrew, Simon Peter's brother, said to him, 'There is a boy here who has five barley loaves and two fish, but what are they for so many?' Jesus said, 'Have the people sit down.' Now there was much grass in the place. So the men sat down, about five thousand in number. Jesus then took the loaves, and when he had given thanks, he distributed them to those who were seated. So also the fish, as much as they wanted" (John 6:8-11).

Watching a teenager work his way through the buffet line at a restaurant is quite entertaining. They pile the food on their plate as high as they can and return again and again to fill their large appetites. Just when you think they have had enough, they make one final visit to the dessert line to satisfy their love for ice cream and cookies. Since the disciples did not anticipate this massive problem, they did not have any food for the people. A search for resources turned up only a boy with five loaves of bread and two fish. It was simply not enough. The disciples considered what the boy had in comparison to the needs of the people. Andrew asked, *"But what are they for so many?"* His question was sincere, but his perspective was wrong.

Andrew focused on their present resources to provide for the people rather than God's unlimited reserves. He was basically saying, "Jesus, no matter how much we divide up what we have, it will not be enough. This won't work. It will fall far short of what's required to meet the need." Have you ever been there? You exhaust all of your resources. You diligently search for a solution, but you find absolutely nothing.

Spiritually speaking, this is a good place to be. Recognizing your limitations can lead you to depend on the Lord to provide. At this point, Jesus took the loaves and the fish. He gave thanks and gave them back to the disciples to distribute to those who were seated. The people ate as much as they wanted to eat that day. This was the start of the picnic buffet festival. Think about your approach to solving big problems. Who or where do you go first? If you are the answer, dividing your resources is your only option. If God is your first choice, however, there's room for a miracle of multiplication. Do you want to feast on God's unlimited buffet, or place a limit on His provision? Do you want to divide or multiply what you have?

Read: Open your Bible and read John 10:10.

Reflect: Prayerfully consider the following: What do I need to adjust in my life to allow God to provide more abundantly for my needs?

Respond: As a result of these truths, what might need to change in my attitude, beliefs, and actions? What steps do I need to take outwardly?

A Place to Replenish

"And when they had eaten their fill, he told his disciples, 'Gather up the leftover fragments, that nothing may be lost.' So they gathered them up and filled twelve baskets with fragments from the five barley loaves left by those who had eaten. When the people saw the sign that he had done, they said, 'This is indeed the Prophet who is to come into the world!' Perceiving then that they were about to come and take him by force to make him king, Jesus withdrew again to the mountain by himself" (John 6:12-15).

Finding places for personal privacy has become more popular in our society. You often hear of people spending a week at a secluded beach. Some prefer a cabin in a remote mountain, or a portable tent near a quiet river. Regardless of personal preferences, their question is often very similar: Where can I go to disconnect from work, find some rest and renew my strength? Jesus was quickly gaining popularity. He was helping people, transforming lives, healing the lame, and feeding the hungry. Jesus was becoming a superstar in the eyes of many. The people saw Him as a prophet and were ready to make Him their King. Despite His growing popularity, Jesus intentionally found a place and carved out time in His schedule to replenish spiritually. It was the top priority in His life.

If Jesus regularly found a place to rest and replenish, don't you think you need to follow His example? If He made the time and the effort to fill His spirit, rest and disconnect from people, don't you think you need to do the same? Serving people is hard work. If you don't control your schedule, it will absolutely control you. Daily renewal is critical to your total health. You are not a machine. Your spiritual life is neither mechanical nor automated. You have to get away every day and connect with the Savior.

Do you have a place where you can go each day to disconnect from people, rest, and allow God to fill your spirit? If not, find a place to listen to the Father, receive His strength, and study His Word. God replenishes your spirit and revives your soul. Find a place right now and let God fill you with His presence. Stop running on empty. Don't procrastinate. Make the time to replenish and listen to what He has to say to you today.

Read: Open your Bible and read Matthew 14:13.

Reflect: Prayerfully consider the following: What place have I determined to meet with God daily for personal replenishing?

Respond: As a result of these truths, what might need to change in my attitude, beliefs, and actions? What steps do I need to take outwardly?

Walking on Water

"When evening came, his disciples went down to the sea, got into a boat, and started across the sea to Capernaum. It was now dark, and Jesus had not yet come to them. The sea became rough because a strong wind was blowing. When they had rowed about three or four miles, they saw Jesus walking on the sea and coming near the boat, and they were frightened. But he said to them, 'It is I; do not be afraid.' Then they were glad to take him into the boat, and immediately the boat was at the land to which they were going" (John 6:16-21).

Unexpected strong winds can quickly change your outdoor deep-sea activities. Fishing in the ocean can change from pleasure to panic. When the seas begin to aggressively rock your boat and toss your supplies into the water, catching fish is the least of your concerns. When the winds are fierce, even the best rowers run out of strength to fight nature's wrath. The weather was not favorable for the disciples once they committed to their voyage. It was dark and the conditions were rough. They rowed three to four miles and battled heavy winds and high waves. Surely they were totally exhausted. Maybe some wondered if they would survive at all.

At that moment they lifted up their eyes and saw Jesus walking on water and approaching their boat. The disciples were really afraid. Can you blame them? It's not every day that you see a ghostly figure walking freely on the water and not being affected by the rough conditions around them! Jesus responded, *"It is I; do not be afraid."* The disciples gladly received Jesus into the boat, and immediately the boat arrived at their destination.

This was a great object lesson. Jesus demonstrated absolute authority over nature. The lesson was dramatic, but it made the point. Have you ever experienced great fear as a result of your surroundings? Have you ever felt severely threatened by the actions of others? Fear can paralyze you and force you to stop rowing. Fear can actually reverse your progress. It can sink you into a deep depression. Fear can cause you to give up on the dreams that God has for you. So how should you respond? Gladly invite Jesus to lead you through your fears. He knows how to direct you through every fear. Let him navigate the course of your life. He can lead you through every challenge you face, even if it means walking on water.

Read: Open your Bible and read 2 Timothy 1:7.

Reflect: Prayerfully consider the following: Am I allowing fear to control and limit God's work through my life? What am I so afraid of?

Respond: As a result of these truths, what might need to change in my attitude, beliefs, and actions? What steps do I need to take outwardly?

The Work of God

"So when the crowd saw that Jesus was not there, nor his disciples,
they themselves got into the boats and went to Capernaum, seeking Jesus.
When they found him on the other side of the sea, they said to him,
'Rabbi, when did you come here?' Jesus answered them, 'Truly, truly,
I say to you, you are seeking me, not because you saw signs, but because
you ate your fill of the loaves. Do not work for the food that perishes,
but for the food that endures to eternal life, which the Son of Man will give to
you. For on him God the Father has set his seal.' Then they said to him,
'What must we do, to be doing the works of God?' Jesus answered them, 'This is
the work of God, that you believe in him whom he has sent' " (John 6:24-29).

It's hard at times to figure out how to finish a task to someone else's satisfaction. They're not always clear about what they want, and it almost takes detective work just to figure out their objectives, expectations, and concerns. This can be frustrating and unproductive. The people were looking for Jesus because He satisfied their physical needs. They were not looking for spiritual confirmation of the Messiah's arrival. Instead, they were pursuing more personal benefits to satisfy their desire for an abundance of food and personal comfort. Yet pursuing things that will ultimately perish is shortsighted, so Jesus challenged their defective motives. In their quest for food, they missed what Jesus was trying to do.

Jesus came to reveal Himself to the people and save them from their sins. Doing the work of God required believing in Jesus as the Messiah. If you believed in Him, you were following God's plan for your life. If you rejected Him as the Messiah, you rejected the work of God altogether. Working for Jesus is working for God. Working for Jesus is working for eternity. Jesus didn't want them to miss that greater purpose.

Think about the driving force of your life. Would people say that your life is governed by wealth, possessions, and power, or by faith in the Lord Jesus? Don't miss this next statement: What you do for God's work will outlast everything else. Rewards for your faith are everlasting. Whatever you do in faith carries over into eternity. Let your faith in God be obvious to others. Do the work of God. His rewards pay eternal dividends.

Read: Open your Bible and read I Corinthians 3:9.

Reflect: Prayerfully consider the following: What does working for God look like in my life? Where do I need to start exercising more faith?

Respond: As a result of these truths, what might need to change in my attitude, beliefs, and actions? What steps do I need to take outwardly?

I AM the Bread of Life

"So they said to him, 'Then what sign do you do, that we may see and believe you? What work do you perform? Our fathers ate the manna in the wilderness; as it is written, 'He gave them bread from heaven to eat.' Jesus then said to them, 'Truly, truly, I say to you, it was not Moses who gave you the bread from heaven, but my Father gives you the true bread from heaven. For the bread of God is he who comes down from heaven and gives life to the world.' They said to him, 'Sir, give us this bread always.' Jesus said to them, 'I am the bread of life; whoever comes to me shall not hunger, and whoever believes in me shall never thirst' " (John 6:30-35).

There is nothing like eating leftovers on the day after Thanksgiving. The slices of turkey are still juicy, and the pumpkin pie so fresh and tasty that it brings a big smile to our faces. But imagine eating a Thanksgiving meal every day for the next calendar year. No one would be smiling. After a while, it might be hard to remain thankful for the same menu day after day.

When God provided sweet bread for Israel to eat each day, they looked at this as the ultimate provision for their people. They wrongly understood Moses as the one who performed the miracle instead of God. Apparently, Jesus' feeding of more than 5,000 people was not impressive enough for the Jews. They wanted to see something greater. Why not feed the entire nation of Israel with mysterious food from the sky? They were unable to see God's provision through the Lord Jesus, the Bread of Life.

Jesus recognized their inability to see and understand spiritual realities. He told them directly, *"For the bread of God is he who comes down from heaven and gives life to the world."* The bread of God is not a loaf of bread, but a living Savior—Jesus. Jesus is the One who satisfies our deepest hunger. In Him we find both eternal life and spiritual satisfaction. He is our Sustainer.

Like the woman at the well, the Jews wanted Jesus to satisfy their immediate physical needs. Once again, Jesus was speaking about satisfying their spiritual hunger and their spiritual thirst. Jesus' "I AM" statements point to His divinity. He was revealing what He could do as a result of who He was. In your prayer life recently, have you focused more on what Jesus can do for you physically, or on what He can do for you spiritually?

Read: Open your Bible and read John 6:48.

Reflect: Prayerfully consider the following: Do I go regularly to Jesus to fill my spirit and satisfy my need for spiritual nourishment?

Respond: As a result of these truths, what might need to change in my attitude, beliefs, and actions? What steps do I need to take outwardly?

Lose Nothing

"But I said to you that you have seen me and yet do not believe. All that the Father gives me will come to me, and whoever comes to me I will never cast out. For I have come down from heaven, not to do my own will but the will of him who sent me. And this is the will of him who sent me, that I should lose nothing of all that he has given me, but raise it up on the last day. For this is the will of my Father, that everyone who looks on the Son and believes in him should have eternal life, and I will raise him up on the last day" (John 6:36-40).

You misplace an important item in your home. It can happen even to the most organized person. You can't remember the exact location, but you know it has not left the property. After searching for days and asking everyone in your home, you can't figure out where it might be. It may be tough to admit, but the reality cannot be denied any longer. It is truly lost.

The religious leaders of Jesus' day were unrelenting in their unbelief towards His claims. In spite of this, God was still regularly leading people to Jesus. Even when it appeared that no one was responding to the gospel, lives were being changed. Jesus told them that He would not lose a single person who was sent to Him from the Father. They were his personal responsibility. The implication was a strong rebuke. If you did not believe in Jesus, you were essentially blocking God's plan to lead you to the Savior.

Jesus came to do His Father's will, not His own will. God's mission was Jesus' singular agenda. God's will has not changed. He wants those who believe in Jesus to have eternal life and be resurrected on the last day. As a reflection of God's perfect sovereignty, He has already selected those who would believe in Jesus. If you believe in Jesus, God has chosen you.

"For those whom he foreknew he also predestined to be conformed to the image of his Son, in order that he might be the firstborn among many brothers. And those whom he predestined he also called, and those whom he called he also justified, and those whom he justified he also glorified" (Romans 8:29-30).

Your life has an eternal purpose. If Jesus is your Savior, celebrate this great privilege. Discover all that God has predestined you to be. Don't pursue things that have no eternal value. You can lose them. Fulfill the mission God has designed for your life. Let your actions display your gratitude.

Read: Open your Bible and read John 10:28-29.

Reflect: Prayerfully consider the following: How can I show God just how much I appreciate being a member of His eternal family?

Respond: As a result of these truths, what might need to change in my attitude, beliefs, and actions? What steps do I need to take outwardly?

The Father Directs

"So the Jews grumbled about him, because he said, 'I am the bread that came down from heaven.' They said, 'Is not this Jesus, the son of Joseph, whose father and mother we know? How does he now say, 'I have come down from heaven'? Jesus answered them, 'Do not grumble among yourselves. No one can come to me unless the Father who sent me draws him. And I will raise him up on the last day. It is written in the Prophets, 'And they will all be taught by God.' Everyone who has heard and learned from the Father comes to me—not that anyone has seen the Father except he who is from God; he has seen the Father"
(John 6:41-46).

Have you seen someone provoke a meaningless argument to avoid facing up to a more painful reality in their life? It can be tough to watch. They deflect direct questions, raise their voice up several notches and dramatize their revised subject of focus. They avoid the truth like a plague by dancing around the facts. You have to be fairly creative to do this effectively, but people do this all of the time when faced with the reality of Jesus' claims.

The religious leaders of Jesus' day did not demand a historical analysis of Jesus' origin. They did not want to consider the possibility of deity in the life of this carpenter from Galilee. This was too uncomfortable for them to evaluate objectively. Since the rulers were the "spiritual authority" of Israel, they wanted to eliminate the very thought that Jesus might be the Messiah before it entered into the minds and hearts of the people.

Jesus wanted them to save their breath. There was something these men were neglecting to consider—God's perfect sovereignty. The Father is the One who directs us to Jesus. Coming to Jesus is never purely the result of winning an intellectual battle or answering all of the critics' objections. The Father serves an active role in the Salvation process. Innovative methods are good, but we must never forget that God is the Initiator and Director.

God's work in your life involves leading you into a deeper relationship with Jesus. This is much more than a one-time activity. It is a daily process. God continuously works to shape you into the image of His Son. He directs your life to perfect your life. Why? He wants you to be like Jesus.

Read: Open your Bible and read Ephesians 1:3-6.

Reflect: Prayerfully consider the following: In what two specific areas do I need to become more like Jesus in my attitude and in my actions?

Respond: As a result of these truths, what might need to change in my attitude, beliefs, and actions? What steps do I need to take outwardly?

I AM the Living Bread

"Truly, truly, I say to you, whoever believes has eternal life. I am the bread of life. Your fathers ate the manna in the wilderness, and they died. This is the bread that comes down from heaven, so that one may eat of it and not die. I am the living bread that came down from heaven. If anyone eats of this bread, he will live forever. And the bread that I will give for the life of the world is my flesh" (John 6:47-51).

Diet companies spend many advertising dollars to convince their audience of the great taste of the foods they manufacture. Even mentioning "diet food" gives some a funny feeling in their stomachs. Regardless of their taste, diet foods can only help people live better on this side of heaven.

Here's the bottom-line statement Jesus delivered to the Jews, "If you eat what your fathers ate you will die as they died. If you eat what I have to offer you will never die. You will live forever with me and with the Father." Jesus offers us eternal life right now. Eternal life is not a place, but a person—Jesus. If you accept Jesus you have eternal life.

What do diet foods, organic foods, and unhealthy foods all have in common? For one, they cannot produce eternal life. Only heavenly food can produce eternal life. Jesus said, *"I am the living bread that came down from heaven."* When we accept Jesus as Savior and Lord, His presence lives within us. We have direct access to the Father right now. We begin living forever right now. The sacrifice of Jesus on the cross made it possible for you to experience eternal life. His death in the flesh produced life in the Spirit for those who follow Him. You are now the recipient of perfect and abundant spiritual nutrition. You not only have what you need to live in this life, but also in the life yet to come. Stop right now and thank Him.

What Jesus has done for you has no comparison. He is your life. He is your Lord. He is your King. From start to finish, Jesus is your all in all. He is the giver of life and the author of your salvation. Jesus came down so that you could come up. He became weak physically so that you would be alive and strong spiritually. The communion He seeks to have with you each day is highly relational and personal. Jesus is your Living Bread.

Read: Open your Bible and read John 6:1-71.

Reflect: Prayerfully consider the following: Am I allowing God to sustain every part of my life? Am I living in light of eternity? How can I tell?

Respond: As a result of these truths, what might need to change in my attitude, beliefs, and actions? What steps do I need to take outwardly?

Eternal Nourishment

"The Jews then disputed among themselves, saying, 'How can this man give us his flesh to eat?' So Jesus said to them, 'Truly, truly, I say to you, unless you eat the flesh of the Son of Man and drink his blood, you have no life in you. Whoever feeds on my flesh and drinks my blood has eternal life, and I will raise him up on the last day. For my flesh is true food, and my blood is true drink. Whoever feeds on my flesh and drinks my blood abides in me, and I in him. As the living Father sent me, and I live because of the Father, so whoever feeds on me, he also will live because of me. This is the bread that came down from heaven, not like the bread the fathers ate, and died. Whoever feeds on this bread will live forever.' Jesus said these things in the synagogue, as he taught at Capernaum" (John 6:52-58).

Different foods affect us in different ways. Those containing high fiber help control our appetites for several hours. Carbohydrates make good fuel, but foods with too much sugar don't satisfy our bodies for very long. All of these foods have one thing in common: they are only temporary solutions to your hunger. Over time, your hunger will eventually return again.

When Jesus used this physical illustration to make a spiritual application, His Jewish audience was angry and offended by the way His words seemed to violate the Law of Moses (Leviticus 17:10-14). They completely missed what Jesus was communicating. The extreme blindness of their hearts would not allow them to make a spiritual application. This was very sad.

As Jesus described the eating of His body and the drinking of His blood, He was illustrating the perfect work that He would finish on the cross. This is a work that must be accepted within our hearts for us to experience eternal life. This is the only way for us to receive forgiveness for all sins. This is the eternal nourishment that we need to live forever. In rejecting Jesus, these Jews also rejected God's exclusive provision for eternal life.

Have you accepted Jesus Christ as Savior? Have you made the perfect work of Jesus on the cross your eternal food and drink? If not, what are you waiting for? If so, are you returning to Him for your daily spiritual nourishment? Jesus is your spiritual fuel for effective Christian living.

Read: Open your Bible and read I Peter 2:1-24.

Reflect: Prayerfully consider the following: Have I accepted the perfect work of Jesus within my heart? Is Jesus my daily source for spiritual fuel?

Respond: As a result of these truths, what might need to change in my attitude, beliefs, and actions? What steps do I need to take outwardly?

Spirit and Life

"When many of his disciples heard it, they said, 'This is a hard saying; who can listen to it?' But Jesus, knowing in himself that his disciples were grumbling about this, said to them, 'Do you take offense at this? Then what if you were to see the Son of Man ascending to where he was before? It is the Spirit who gives life; the flesh is no help at all. The words that I have spoken to you are spirit and life. But there are some of you who do not believe.' (For Jesus knew from the beginning who those were who did not believe, and who it was who would betray him.) And he said, 'This is why I told you that no one can come to me unless it is granted him by the Father' " (John 6:60-65).

Do you remember that subject in high school that was painful for you to work through? Spending late nights with your friends doing homework was no help. They were just as lost as you were. It was frustrating trying to listen to the instructor's every word, when you did not understand what they were saying no matter how hard you tried. You were totally lost.

Jesus understood the frustration provoked by His teaching ministry. It was due primarily to the hard hearts of those who listened. The Spirit of God spoke through the Son of God in powerful ways. Jesus' words penetrated the hearts of the people. His teaching methods were simple, yet profound. But the people were not used to hearing these kinds of sermons. Jesus spoke words of spirit and life. God may be convicting your heart to grow in your relationship with Him. He may be leading you to be more proactive in an area where you have often been reactive or even passive. As God's Spirit speaks to your heart, take decisive action. Don't get offended when He corrects you. Don't grumble when He points something out in your attitude that needs to be changed right away.

God wants to produce life through you. Jesus said, *"It is the Spirit who gives life; the flesh is no help at all."* Even Jesus' disciples were complaining about His teachings. They too struggled to accept and apply His word in their lives. Don't be discouraged and don't be afraid. This struggle between your flesh and God's Spirit is normal. In Christ, you can overcome your personal struggles and live in the power of the Holy Spirit. Following your flesh is never good, but when you follow God's Spirit, you find real life.

Read: Open your Bible and read 2 Corinthians 3:1-6.

Reflect: Prayerfully consider the following: Is my life characterized more by spirit and life flowing through me or by personal struggles and sins?

Respond: As a result of these truths, what might need to change in my attitude, beliefs, and actions? What steps do I need to take outwardly?

The Holy One of God

*"After this many of his disciples turned back and no longer walked with him.
So Jesus said to the Twelve, 'Do you want to go away as well?' Simon Peter
answered him, 'Lord, to whom shall we go? You have the words of eternal life,
and we have believed, and have come to know, that you are the Holy One
of God.' Jesus answered them, 'Did I not choose you, the Twelve?
And yet one of you is a devil.' He spoke of Judas the son of Simon Iscariot,
for he, one of the Twelve, was going to betray him" (John 6:66-71).*

It happens every semester in college. Students who want to major in
medicine sign up for their first chemistry class. They arrive enthusiastically,
but their enthusiasm is short lived. They realize this is only the first of
several chemistry classes, each one being harder than the last. After their
second exam, they drop the class and change their major. They decide it is
much too difficult to continue, so they drop the class, turn away, and leave.

After Jesus' disturbing "flesh-eating sermon," many of the disciples turned
away from following Him. If Jesus had a public relations coach, they would
have urged Him to change the content of His message. Yet Jesus was not
interested in shallow spectators. He was not trying to increase His social
ratings. He was looking for people to continue God's work. He focused
on training men who would be faithful in preaching the gospel to others.

It must have been an uncomfortable feeling for the disciples. Those who
stayed with Jesus watched many of their friends walk away from Him.
Without question, those who stayed may have even questioned their own
faith and commitment. After all, they had more in common with their
fellow disciples than with Jesus. This must have been really tough to watch.

As we would expect, Peter breaks the awkward silence of the disciples and
speaks up first. He responds, *"Lord, to whom shall we go? You have the
words of eternal life, and we have believed, and have come to know, that you are
the Holy One of God."* His assessment of Jesus was right on target. It was a
holy moment. It was a bold proclamation of divine revelation. Peter got it!
Maybe your friends and family have decided to walk away from their faith.
You may find yourself torn on the inside. Don't be discouraged. Although
you might be the only follower of Christ, Jesus is still the *"Holy One of God."*

Read: Open your Bible and read John 6:1-71.

Reflect: Prayerfully consider the following: Am I taking intentional steps
this week to draw closer to Jesus, or to walk away from Jesus?

Respond: As a result of these truths, what might need to change in my
attitude, beliefs, and actions? What steps do I need to take outwardly?

I Testify

"After this Jesus went about in Galilee. He would not go about in Judea, because the Jews were seeking to kill him. Now the Jews' Feast of Booths was at hand. So his brothers said to him, 'Leave here and go to Judea, that your disciples also may see the works you are doing. For no one works in secret if he seeks to be known openly. If you do these things, show yourself to the world.' For not even his brothers believed in him. Jesus said to them, 'My time has not yet come, but your time is always here. The world cannot hate you, but it hates me because I testify about it that its works are evil' " (John 7:1-7).

Have you ever had a string of bad days when nothing seems to go right? It seems that everything you do works backwards. Instead of making progress, you lose ground. Instead of building new relationships, you lose old friends. Instead of saving on an important repair, you find another problem and spend twice the money. Jesus was coming off a tough couple of days. The Jews in Judea were planning to kill Him. This was no secret. The crowds totally rejected Jesus as their Messiah. He was rejected by many of His followers, and even His own family did not believe His claims. They openly mocked His testimony and everything He represented.

Your testimony is one of the most powerful weapons that you possess as a believer. Satan will use all of his tricks to discourage you from sharing God's story in your life with others. Satan will use family, friends, co-workers, neighbors, and even total strangers to intimidate you. He works hard to make you fear others. Satan wants to silence your story. You might not have someone planning to kill you, but you may have someone who is trying to destroy your credibility at work or at school. They begin spreading rumors and lies. Others approach you and begin asking questions. Your faith is put on the spotlight. Will you take a stand for the truth or will you collapse and walk away? Be bold and choose to testify!

Guard your testimony. Do everything with absolute integrity. When you have an opportunity to speak about God's work in your life, say a short prayer and speak boldly for Christ. Your story will always impact the story of another. God will use your witness to change the heart of those around you. Openly share your story within God's story as God opens hearts.

Read: Open your Bible and read Hebrews 11:1-2.

Reflect: Prayerfully consider the following: Do I have a good testimony where I work and where I live? Who can I share my story with today?

Respond: As a result of these truths, what might need to change in my attitude, beliefs, and actions? What steps do I need to take outwardly?

What Do You Say?

"'You go up to the feast. I am not going up to this feast, for my time has not yet fully come.' After saying this, he remained in Galilee. But after his brothers had gone up to the feast, then he also went up, not publicly but in private. The Jews were looking for him at the feast, and saying, 'Where is he?' And there was much muttering about him among the people. While some said, 'He is a good man,' others said, 'No, he is leading the people astray.' Yet for fear of the Jews no one spoke openly of him" (John 7:8-13).

Two attorneys go back and forth in a high profile case. Each of them presents their unique case to the judge to the best of their abilities. The facts have been presented and the witnesses have all shared their stories. The judge takes a deep breath. The quietness in the room is thunderous. Everyone present wonders the same thing: "What will the judge say?"

While the feast of the Jews was in progress, many conversations revolved around Jesus. Those who were familiar with Jesus ruled out any possibility of divinity. Those who searched for Him with impure motives were looking to prove a point or embarrass Him publicly. Others enjoyed talking about this amazing man. They talked about His miracles. They said that He was a great teacher, but they never took any action. Some only believed that Jesus was a "good man." Others insisted that He was a "master deceiver." They concluded that Jesus was leading people in the wrong direction. They concluded that Jesus was not the Son of God.

What do you say about Jesus? When confronted by others, how do you respond to Jesus' claims? If you say that He is only a peacemaker, a good teacher, or a moral leader, you have missed the purpose of His arrival. Jesus is more than all of these things combined. Peter writes, *"But in your hearts honor Christ the Lord as holy, always being prepared to make a defense to anyone who asks you for a reason for the hope that is in you; yet do it with gentleness and respect" (1 Peter 3:15).* Jesus has already defined Himself. Jesus is Lord! He is the *"great God and Savior."* He is your redeemer. Regardless of what others say about Jesus, always be ready to defend your Lord. Let the Word of God speak for itself. Study and know where to help people find the right answer. Prepare yourself and watch God work.

Read: Open your Bible and read 2 Timothy 3:16-17.

Reflect: Prayerfully consider the following: Am I ready to defend Jesus and show others through the Bible how they can know Jesus as Savior?

Respond: As a result of these truths, what might need to change in my attitude, beliefs, and actions? What steps do I need to take outwardly?

Extraordinary Teaching

"About the middle of the feast Jesus went up into the temple and began teaching. The Jews therefore marveled, saying, 'How is it that this man has learning, when he has never studied?' So Jesus answered them, 'My teaching is not mine, but his who sent me. If anyone's will is to do God's will, he will know whether the teaching is from God or whether I am speaking on my own authority. The one who speaks on his own authority seeks his own glory; but the one who seeks the glory of him who sent him is true, and in him there is no falsehood'" (John 7:14-18).

Great teachers are unforgettable. They were the ones who went out of their way to help us better understand a certain subject or skillset. They took their time and viewed their work as an investment rather than a cost. Even if the subject matter was boring, they gave it life. Their enthusiasm for their work was electric. Jesus was a remarkable, one-of-a-kind teacher. The Jews were amazed by His teachings. They were perplexed by His great skills despite His lack of "formal religious education." Jesus explained that His teachings had a divine origin: *"My teaching is not mine, but his who sent me."* His powerful lessons came directly from Almighty God.

Spiritual discernment helps us recognize God's Word. God's Spirit helps us know when people are speaking on God's behalf or not. His Word protects us. If we are not certain, we can always go back to God's Word, because it is always true. Jesus was seeking God's glory in all His teachings. There was no falsehood in Jesus. His words were absolutely true.

If you are in a position of influence or authority, you are a teacher. People are watching your life and learning from your words and your actions. How would people rate your level of truthfulness? Do you speak the truth all of the time? Is your integrity considered extraordinary? Do you "bend the rules" or lie when an opportunity is presented for your personal gain? If you do, you will eventually suffer the consequences of your dishonesty.

Evaluate the message of your life. When you help others, what kind of attitude do you display? Does it inspire others to reach their full potential? Does it help them move beyond their deepest fears? Is it extraordinary?

Read: Open your Bible and read Philippians 2:1-16.

Reflect: Prayerfully consider the following: Does God's truth rule in every part of my life? Am I inspiring others to be their best for God?

Respond: As a result of these truths, what might need to change in my attitude, beliefs, and actions? What steps do I need to take outwardly?

Judge with Right Judgment

"'Has not Moses given you the law? Yet none of you keeps the law. Why do you seek to kill me?' The crowd answered, 'You have a demon! Who is seeking to kill you?' Jesus answered them, 'I did one work, and you all marvel at it. Moses gave you circumcision (not that it is from Moses, but from the fathers), and you circumcise a man on the Sabbath. If on the Sabbath a man receives circumcision, so that the law of Moses may not be broken, are you angry with me because on the Sabbath I made a man's whole body well? Do not judge by appearances, but judge with right judgment'" (John 7:19-24).

When young boys get together to play football in their neighborhood, it is always amusing to see how they view the rules. Some want to spell everything out in the beginning and gain consensus. Others don't really care about the rules. They simply want to start playing. The most interesting ones are those who try to make up the rules as they play.

This last example reminds us of the Jewish leaders in Jesus' day. They did not follow the commandments of Moses as God originally designed. They memorized every commandment. They knew every single word in the Law. Yet sadly, they totally missed the spirit of the Law. They created their own commandments as they went along to supplement what Moses provided, focusing more on the opinions of men rather than God's Word

The Jewish leaders were angry with Jesus because He did not acknowledge their new rules as God's commandments. Instead, He clarified God's original intention for the commandments. He taught them the purpose behind the commandments and the Jews rejected Him as a result of this.

People often say, "Don't judge me. The Bible says, 'don't judge others.'" That statement is not accurate. We make several hundred judgments every day. Jesus told the Jews to *"judge with right judgment."* In other words, don't make up a list of rules and judge others by your personal preferences. This creates big problems and can really hurt people.

God wants you to make right judgments. God's Word is all that you need to rightly judge all matters of life. There is no need to create more rules.

Read: Open your Bible and read Psalm 119:1-176.

Reflect: Prayerfully consider the following: Do I typically place more restrictions on people than what the Bible expects from their lives?

Respond: As a result of these truths, what might need to change in my attitude, beliefs, and actions? What steps do I need to take outwardly?

Speaking Openly

"Some of the people of Jerusalem therefore said, 'Is not this the man whom they seek to kill? And here he is, speaking openly, and they say nothing to him! Can it be that the authorities really know that this is the Christ?' " (John 7:25-26).

Have you ever greeted a detective at your front door to respond to a few confidential questions regarding one of your neighbors? It can be a strange experience indeed. The authorities may share some information with you, but they keep most of what they know to themselves. The other details are not for public consumption. Only those directly involved in the investigation know the details, but they can't speak openly about them.

Jesus made incredible claims about His divine origin. He was not hiding behind a curtain or living in a remote cave somewhere. He spoke in the synagogues, on the streets, and throughout the surrounding villages. Jesus was open about who He was—the Messiah, the Son of God.

The religious leadership of the day was the authority over all matters of life. Jesus now appears on the scene and speaks boldly to the people. He speaks with authority, power and great certainty and addresses the crowds in everyday language. Since the religious leaders were confused and uncertain themselves, their silence sent mixed messages to the people.

The people of Jerusalem were confused. They were waiting for an official position, but they did not receive one. Many wondered, "Could this be the Christ?" No one had ever silenced the religious Jews like Jesus did. They may have wondered if their leaders were holding back important information. Something strange was happening behind the scenes. Surely there was much more to the story than what was being revealed!

The name of Jesus still brings out many emotions and unsettled thoughts. There are some who won't say a word when they hear His name mentioned in a conversation. Others will openly take their questions to people in positions of spiritual authority. But some will not go to church to find their answers. They will ask friends and family who know Jesus. Speaking openly about Jesus may be difficult for you. You don't need to go buy a megaphone, but you do need to grow your faith in this area.

Read: Open your Bible and read Romans 1:16.

Reflect: Prayerfully consider the following: What part of Jesus' life do I know and understand well? Who can I share this with today?

Respond: As a result of these truths, what might need to change in my attitude, beliefs, and actions? What steps do I need to take outwardly?

I Know Him

"'But we know where this man comes from, and when the Christ appears, no one will know where he comes from.' So Jesus proclaimed, as he taught in the temple, 'You know me, and you know where I come from. But I have not come of my own accord. He who sent me is true, and him you do not know. I know him, for I come from him, and he sent me.' So they were seeking to arrest him, but no one laid a hand on him, because his hour had not yet come. Yet many of the people believed in him. They said, 'When the Christ appears, will he do more signs than this man has done?' " (John 7:27-31).

Watching a child's face light up when their parents pick them up from their first day of school is priceless. The child has been introduced to 30 new classmates and a brand new teacher, while at the same time trying to adapt to a new environment. It can be overwhelming. When they see their parents stand at the door at 2:30 PM, they smile and make a beeline for those familiar faces. Just seeing someone they know makes everything better. Jesus loved talking about the Father. He spoke out of His great intimacy and familiarity with the Father. He told the critics, *"I know him, for I come from him, and he sent me."* Knowing the Father was not a great mystery for Jesus. It was His daily reality. He personally knew the Father.

Jewish leaders in Jesus' day knew about God, but they did not know Him intimately. They had no lack of intellectual knowledge, but the connection to their hearts was non-existent. They lacked the spiritual intimacy exhibited in every word and action of our Lord. Their solution was simple, arrest Jesus and remove Him from the spotlight. After all, something had to be done before things really got crazy. The common people were not religious scholars, scribes, or rising political figures, but they began believing in Jesus. They were convinced that the Messiah was among them.

Would those who know you best say that you know the Father intimately? Can they see the qualities of Jesus in the way that you speak and in the things that you do? Make it your goal today to spend time knowing more about your Savior. Did you notice what happened when Jesus' work became obvious to those around Him? The people believed. When God's work in your life is obvious, more people will believe and follow Jesus.

Read: Open your Bible and read John 4:39-42.

Reflect: Prayerfully consider the following: Am I seeking to know God more intimately? Do I believe that God can use me to change lives?

Respond: As a result of these truths, what might need to change in my attitude, beliefs, and actions? What steps do I need to take outwardly?

Unsolved Mysteries

"The Pharisees heard the crowd muttering these things about him, and the chief priests and Pharisees sent officers to arrest him. Jesus then said, 'I will be with you a little longer, and then I am going to him who sent me. You will seek me and you will not find me. Where I am you cannot come.' The Jews said to one another, 'Where does this man intend to go that we will not find him? Does he intend to go to the Dispersion among the Greeks and teach the Greeks? What does he mean by saying, 'You will seek me and you will not find me,' and, 'Where I am you cannot come'?" (John 7:32-36).

Unsolved mysteries have evolved into popular shows on cable television. Old crime files are reopened to see if new clues can be found. Detailed reenactments are performed to help stimulate the memory of potential witnesses. New conversations begin. Families of the victims regain a measure of hope. Some of these cases are solved. Others remain open. The Pharisees had a real dilemma. Jesus was gaining enormous popularity with the people. The Pharisees were fighting with one another and being challenged by the very people who had once adored them. Each of their attempts to arrest Jesus failed miserably. They remained divided as a group, and felt threatened regarding Jesus' claims and His upcoming plans.

Despite their opposition, Jesus continued His ministry. He gave the Pharisees a riddle to solve, an unexpected mystery to unfold. He told these leaders that He was leaving to a place where they had no access. Although they would search for Jesus, their efforts would be useless. Jesus was returning to the Father. He was getting ready to go home. The Jews asked two questions, "Where does He intend to go? What does He mean?" Right now, Jesus is at the right hand of the Father. His original plan was to finish His mission and return to the Father's presence. Jesus' first coming was temporary, but His Kingdom is forever.

As a believer in Christ, you reign with Jesus right now. Your spiritual mystery has been solved. You are seated at the right hand of the Father. Jesus' presence is not an unsolved mystery for you. His presence lives within you. You know where He is and you know where you are going. You have the Living Hope of God. You have His presence forever.

Read: Open your Bible and read Acts 2:28.

Reflect: Prayerfully consider the following: When I think of God's awesome presence, what three things bring a smile to my face?

Respond: As a result of these truths, what might need to change in my attitude, beliefs, and actions? What steps do I need to take outwardly?

Rivers of Living Water

"On the last day of the feast, the great day, Jesus stood up and cried out, 'If anyone thirsts, let him come to me and drink. Whoever believes in me, as the Scripture has said, 'Out of his heart will flow rivers of living water.' Now this he said about the Spirit, whom those who believed in him were to receive, for as yet the Spirit had not been given, because Jesus was not yet glorified" (John 7:37-39).

Many years ago a company called Nestea ran a commercial to help people visualize what they would feel like after drinking their iced tea. A person who was sweating and very thirsty grabbed a glass of iced tea and drank. Immediately they began falling backwards into a large pool filled with water. There's nothing like an irresistible invitation to quench your growing thirst.

Jesus did not run a commercial. He did something much more powerful. Jesus leveraged the powerful symbolism of God's Word and the events of that day to make a profound spiritual application. The prophet Isaiah wrote, *"With joy you will draw water from the wells of salvation"* (Isaiah 12:3). Jesus presented Himself as the Source of Life. Believing in Jesus meant tapping into a well that provided complete spiritual satisfaction, eternal life.

When the priests poured out their containers of water before the people, it pointed to the living waters yet to come. Jesus stepped in as a fulfillment to this powerful illustration. Jesus is eternal life. He is the source. He told the woman at the well, *"If you knew the gift of God, and who it is that is saying to you, 'Give me a drink,' you would have asked him, and he would have given you living water." The woman said to him, "Sir, you have nothing to draw water with, and the well is deep. Where do you get that living water?"* (John 4:10-11)

Jesus' invitation is clear. If you are thirsty, come to Jesus and drink. But get ready. When you drink from the source of all life, your life will change. The Holy Spirit will begin transforming you into the image of Jesus. You will experience an inner spiritual cleansing. Your spirit will be permanently reinvigorated. You can start living in the power of the Holy Spirit.

What's flowing from your heart today? Have you allowed a difficulty or some tradition to block God's Spirit from flowing through your life? You already have what you need to live the Christian life and bear much fruit.

Read: Open your Bible and read 2 Corinthians 3:5.

Reflect: Prayerfully consider the following: Is Jesus the source of my life? Do I live as if He is my sufficiency, or is my focus on something else?

Respond: As a result of these truths, what might need to change in my attitude, beliefs, and actions? What steps do I need to take outwardly?

Born and Raised

"When they heard these words, some of the people said, 'This really is the Prophet.' Others said, 'This is the Christ.' But some said, 'Is the Christ to come from Galilee? Has not the Scripture said that the Christ comes from the offspring of David, and comes from Bethlehem, the village where David was?' So there was a division among the people over him. Some of them wanted to arrest him, but no one laid hands on him" (John 7:40-44).

Where were you born? Surely the location comes to your mind quickly. Is it the same city or region where you grew up? These days, it seems like most of us are born in one place and raised in another. Although they represent different phases of our history, we often identify equally with both locations. Jesus was born in Bethlehem of Judea, but raised in Galilee. Galilee was in the northern part of Israel and Bethlehem in the south. Although a resident of Galilee, Jesus had been born in David's hometown, Bethlehem. His adulthood was shaped in Galilee. Jesus' accusers practiced poor investigative skills. His birthplace was well documented.

The prophet Micah declared, *"But you, O Bethlehem Ephrathah, who are too little to be among the clans of Judah, from you shall come forth for me one who is to be ruler in Israel, whose coming forth is from of old, from ancient days"* (Micah 5:2). Bethlehem was a special place for Israel. King David was born in this small town. The Messiah would also find His birthplace here as well. To accept Jesus as the Messiah meant recognizing Him as heir to the throne of King David. For those who took the time to research His rich history, the discovery was truly amazing. *Psalm 89:3-4* reads, *"You have said, 'I have made a covenant with my chosen one; I have sworn to David my servant: I will establish your offspring forever, and build your throne for all generations.' Selah."*

What's your history like? You may not have been born in Bethlehem, but your place of birth is important. It is important because God was involved in the process. You may not understand its significance now, but never underestimate God's perfect plans. The place where you were raised has equal importance. It shaped your thinking in some ways and your personality in others. How can your experience as a young person be used to encourage others? You might be very surprised after you get started.

Read: Open your Bible and read Isaiah 9:6.

Reflect: Prayerfully consider the following: What words are used in this passage to describe our Lord Jesus? What are the implications for my life?

Respond: As a result of these truths, what might need to change in my attitude, beliefs, and actions? What steps do I need to take outwardly?

Search and See

"The officers then came to the chief priests and Pharisees, who said to them, 'Why did you not bring him?' The officers answered, 'No one ever spoke like this man!' The Pharisees answered them, 'Have you also been deceived? Have any of the authorities or the Pharisees believed in him? But this crowd that does not know the law is accursed.' Nicodemus, who had gone to him before, and who was one of them, said to them, 'Does our law judge a man without first giving him a hearing and learning what he does?' They replied, 'Are you from Galilee too? Search and see that no prophet arises from Galilee' " (John 7:45-52).

It is always a good idea to investigate matters before jumping to fast conclusions. We have all made the mistake of taking sides prematurely, or making assumptions about others unfairly. We question the apparent discrepancies without thoroughly understanding the context. In the end, relationships are damaged and we learn a very painful lesson in the process.

The chief priests and the Pharisees were such a group. Fearing the end of their own doctrine, influence, and traditions, they quickly condemned Jesus. They ignorantly scorned His actions and mocked His words. Since their hearts were cold, their ears were deaf and their eyes were blind. They were furious that the officers who arrested Jesus seemed swayed by His teachings. The officers were totally amazed and believed in Jesus' words.

Nicodemus, a respected religious leader asked, *"Does our law judge a man without first giving him a hearing and learning what he does?"* In other words, "Hey guys, you are violating your principles to satisfy your preferences. How can we condemn a man without a fair trial?" These leaders were not pleased with Nicodemus' concern for the law. They focused on hearsay instead. Ironically, the Pharisees and the chief priests urged Nicodemus to *"search and see"* if a Prophet was supposed to come from Galilee or not. Obviously, Isaiah 9:1 was not part of their reasoning. Jesus would find His place of birth in Bethlehem, but discover His mission in Galilee.

These leaders needed to *"search and see"* for themselves. Since they did not do their homework, it was easy to arrive at the wrong conclusion. Do you arrive at fast conclusions about others without doing your homework? Please don't do that. Make good judgments. Search and see for yourself.

Read: Open your Bible and read Matthew 7:2.

Reflect: Prayerfully consider the following: Am I judging others fairly? Do I react too quickly and condemn? How can I better *"search and see"*?

Respond: As a result of these truths, what might need to change in my attitude, beliefs, and actions? What steps do I need to take outwardly?

So What Do You Say?

"They went each to his own house, but Jesus went to the Mount of Olives. Early in the morning he came again to the temple. All the people came to him, and he sat down and taught them. The scribes and the Pharisees brought a woman who had been caught in adultery, and placing her in the midst they said to him, 'Teacher, this woman has been caught in the act of adultery. Now in the Law Moses commanded us to stone such women. So what do you say?' This they said to test him, that they might have some charge to bring against him"
(John 7:53-8:1-6).

Interruptions all too often arrive at the wrong place and at the wrong time. They have the ability to distract, reduce productivity and interfere with helpful rhythms. How you handle distractions is very important. People sometimes take special notice when sudden interruptions invade our lives. For better or for worse, our attitude and our actions may be long remembered. Jesus got up early one morning and went to teach at the temple. While He was speaking to the people, the scribes and the Pharisees marched in with a woman who had been caught in the act of adultery. Can you imagine the embarrassment and shame she must have felt as they placed her right in the middle of the harsh crowd? The religious leaders were not concerned at all about this woman's dignity.

The religious leaders had a hidden agenda. They were determined to trap Jesus and make Him say something contrary to either God's Law or to Rome's. Doing this would destroy Jesus' ministry and give them significant justification to accuse Him of being either a false prophet or a traitor.

The scribes and the Pharisees began their questioning with an equation: Adultery + God's Law = Death. To deny that she was worthy of death meant that Jesus was contradicting God's Law. Calling for her death meant that He was provoking rebellion against the Roman Empire. How could Jesus possibly avoid their trap? You can hear the sarcasm in their voices as they call Jesus *"teacher"* and then ask, *"So what do you say?"* This was a very public test for Jesus. There were only two options—pass or fail. Put yourself in Jesus' place. How would you respond? What would you say?

Read: Open your Bible and read James 1:3.

Reflect: Prayerfully consider the following: Am I allowing interruptions to grow my faith, or do I complain and get upset when they quickly surface?

Respond: As a result of these truths, what might need to change in my attitude, beliefs, and actions? What steps do I need to take outwardly?

Has No One Condemned You?

"Jesus bent down and wrote with his finger on the ground. And as they continued to ask him, he stood up and said to them, 'Let him who is without sin among you be the first to throw a stone at her.' And once more he bent down and wrote on the ground. But when they heard it, they went away one by one, beginning with the older ones, and Jesus was left alone with the woman standing before him. Jesus stood up and said to her, 'Woman, where are they? Has no one condemned you?' She said, 'No one, Lord.' And Jesus said, 'Neither do I condemn you; go, and from now on sin no more' " (John 8:6-11).

Many years ago a company called Crayola introduced a new product called Crayola Sidewalk Crayons. It was a brilliant invention. Children who loved to express their creative abilities were now able to make colorful drawings on the sidewalk of their homes without leaving any permanent marks. Since the product was made out of chalk, it washed away easily with water.

When Jesus was pressed to answer the question regarding the woman caught in adultery, He began writing on the ground. We don't know exactly what Jesus wrote down. He may have written some or all of the Ten Commandments. Maybe He wrote down a few recent sins committed by the woman's accusers. Although Jesus did not have Crayola's Sidewalk Crayons, His message to these leaders was both colorful and powerful.

Jesus got right to the heart of the matter when He said, *"Let him who is without sin among you be the first to throw a stone at her."* Jesus did not have to defend His reputation for demonstrating grace, mercy, and compassion. He needed to point out an obvious fact. All of us are sinners *(Romans 3:23)*. There is no one righteous *(Romans 3:10)*. We all fall short of God's perfect standard. To pretend that you are without sin is ridiculous.

Jesus extends incredible grace and mercy to this woman. He got rid of all of her accusers. He gave her a second chance at life. Jesus removed all condemnation from her life. He wanted her to know that she was free to stop sinning. She was now free to start living a holy life. In Christ, you too are free to stop sinning. You can live a holy life. Don't worry if others still condemn you. God's perspective is what really matters. Sin no more.

Read: Open your Bible and read Mark 2:13-17.

Reflect: Prayerfully consider the following: Is my life holy before God? Am I being used by God to change sinners or are they changing me?

Respond: As a result of these truths, what might need to change in my attitude, beliefs, and actions? What steps do I need to take outwardly?

I Am the Light of the World

"Again Jesus spoke to them, saying, 'I am the light of the world. Whoever follows me will not walk in darkness, but will have the light of life.' So the Pharisees said to him, 'You are bearing witness about yourself; your testimony is not true.' Jesus answered, 'Even if I do bear witness about myself, my testimony is true, for I know where I came from and where I am going, but you do not know where I come from or where I am going" (John 8:12-14).

Good lighting has many benefits. Studies find that adequate lighting helps improve employee performance at work. Good lighting helps people maintain a positive attitude. It helps keep people safe by allowing them to avoid hidden dangers and drive around unexpected debris on the highways. A traditional lighting ceremony was part of the celebration of the Feast of Tabernacles. People danced and praised the Lord with music and lighted torches under large lamps. Light was a symbolic part of the celebration. It served to remind the people of God's presence and how He used light to lead His people at night and provide safety through a pillar of fire.

"And the Lord went before them by day in a pillar of cloud to lead them along the way, and by night in a pillar of fire to give them light, that they might travel by day and by night. The pillar of cloud by day and the pillar of fire by night did not depart from before the people" (Exodus 13:21-22).

Light and salvation are connected with God's salvation. The Messiah, Jesus Christ, is our salvation. The psalmist wrote, *"The Lord is my light and my salvation; whom shall I fear? The Lord is the stronghold of my life; of whom shall I be afraid?"* (Psalm 27:1) Jesus used the symbolism of the lights in the Feast of Tabernacles to position Himself as the *"Light of the World."* He revealed Himself in this metaphor as the Salvation for every man, woman, and child.

One day, the light of Jesus will serve as the light of heaven. *"And the city has no need of sun or moon to shine on it, for the glory of God gives it light, and its lamp is the Lamb. By its light will the nations walk, and the kings of the earth will bring their glory into it"* (Revelation 21:23-24). There is no need to live in fear, darkness or uncertainty. Jesus is ready to lead your life and show you the way to go. He is ready to protect you and help you overcome all darkness.

Read: Open your Bible and read John 12:35.

Reflect: Prayerfully consider the following: Is fear, uncertainty or darkness winning the battle over my mind? How can God change this?

Respond: As a result of these truths, what might need to change in my attitude, beliefs, and actions? What steps do I need to take outwardly?

Double Testimony

"'You judge according to the flesh; I judge no one. Yet even if I do judge, my judgment is true, for it is not I alone who judge, but I and the Father who sent me. In your Law it is written that the testimony of two people is true. I am the one who bears witness about myself, and the Father who sent me bears witness about me.' They said to him therefore, 'Where is your Father?' Jesus answered, 'You know neither me nor my Father. If you knew me, you would know my Father also.' These words he spoke in the treasury, as he taught in the temple; but no one arrested him, because his hour had not yet come" (John 8:15-20).

In a court of law, having two expert witnesses on your side can make a big difference in an important case. They have the ability to build the jury's confidence by their explanation and clarification of important matters as they make their final decision. These witnesses provide a unique credibility to the case. Having two expert witnesses can often help close the case. People typically make judgments based upon their education, experience, preferences, and other factors. God's judgments originate from a divine perspective. His judgments are true. They are not biased. God is perfectly just in all of His decisions because He is righteous and true. Both the Father and the Son give indisputable testimony to the validity of Jesus as Messiah. They uniquely serve as divine witnesses and heavenly judges.

Jesus' critics once again lacked true spiritual understanding. They asked Jesus, *"Where is your Father?"* They had no idea who Jesus was referring to. The critics did not know the Father nor did they know the Son. With this in mind, it is easy to understand why they rejected the witness of both Father and Son. It was impossible for these belligerent men to know the Father due to their rebellion towards the Son. Jesus made this point clear.

When people consider the truthfulness of your statements, does it point back to a holy character? Do your words infuse confidence in others and help alleviate confusion and tension? Can people count on every word you say as the truth? If people don't believe your words, they won't believe your Savior either. If the way you live reflects a lack of integrity, your witness for Jesus will surely suffer. God will back up your life's story when it reflects His character because a double testimony can change lives.

Read: Open your Bible and read Acts 22:15.

Reflect: Prayerfully consider the following: Do I live my life in total truthfulness? Where is my integrity being challenged the most recently?

Respond: As a result of these truths, what might need to change in my attitude, beliefs, and actions? What steps do I need to take outwardly?

Unless You Believe

"So he said to them again, 'I am going away, and you will seek me, and you will die in your sin. Where I am going, you cannot come.' So the Jews said, 'Will he kill himself, since he says, 'Where I am going, you cannot come'?' He said to them, 'You are from below; I am from above. You are of this world; I am not of this world. I told you that you would die in your sins, for unless you believe that I am he you will die in your sins' " (John 8:21-24).

It may be hard for a young person to understand, but if they want to drive a car legally, they have to get a license. It may seem trivial, but there is no other option. If they don't study and practice they won't pass the test. And if they don't pass the test, they cannot drive. There is no other option. Young people and adults are not always fans of limited options, but they don't always have a selection of choices. The religious leaders were scratching their heads as Jesus spoke. Since they did not believe in Jesus as their Messiah, they could not accept Him as their Savior and King.

Jesus is eternal. He came from heaven. Jesus' origin was divine and not earthly. His purposes were eternal in nature and not temporary. Jesus told the Jews that unless they believed they would all die in their sins. Jesus was the only access to the Father. There was no other. He was the only Redeemer for Israel and for the entire world. The Apostle Peter makes this point very clear, *"And there is salvation in no one else, for there is no other name under heaven given among men by which we must be saved"* (Acts 4:12).

Do you know people who are looking for God in all the wrong places? Unlike the scribes and the Pharisees in Jesus' day, these people may be very sincere. They may have all of the right motives, and they may even invest a significant portion of their resources on pilgrimages and other "spiritual" pursuits. But if Jesus is not the One they are seeking to know, they will never be able to connect with the Father. They remain spiritually lost and without hope. There are certain things that will not happen unless you believe. Finding freedom from your sins and eternal life is one of them. Growing spiritually is another. You have to believe in God's power to save those friends and family members who are spiritually lost. God wants to reach those people through you. Love them and pray for them every day.

Read: Open your Bible and read Matthew 19:16.

Reflect: Prayerfully consider the following: How can I more effectively help my lost friends and family understand their true spiritual condition?

Respond: As a result of these truths, what might need to change in my attitude, beliefs, and actions? What steps do I need to take outwardly?

Lessons From The Father

"So they said to him, 'Who are you?' Jesus said to them, 'Just what I have been telling you from the beginning. I have much to say about you and much to judge, but he who sent me is true, and I declare to the world what I have heard from him.' They did not understand that he had been speaking to them about the Father. So Jesus said to them, 'When you have lifted up the Son of Man, then you will know that I am he, and that I do nothing on my own authority, but speak just as the Father taught me. And he who sent me is with me. He has not left me alone, for I always do the things that are pleasing to him.' As he was saying these things, many believed in him" (John 8:25-30).

A father plays a critical role in the life of his family. He serves as his family's primary provider and protector, and his influence impacts multiple generations. The lessons we learn from our fathers deeply influence how we think, how we invest our time and how we respond to problems.

Jesus submitted Himself to the will of the Father in every situation. He lived completely dependent on God's Word to accomplish His mission as the Messiah. Jesus did not make up things as He went along. His first activity was to pray and listen to the Father's heart. As a result of this communion, Jesus carried out the mission given to Him by the Father. He was not impulsive. He lived on mission with God moment by moment.

The time spent with the Father was foundational to the ministry of Jesus. Everything flowed from that daily relationship with the Father. Jesus later asked His disciples, *"Do you not believe that I am in the Father and the Father is in me? The words that I say to you I do not speak on my own authority, but the Father who dwells in me does his works"* (John 14:10). This relationship was continuous, thriving, and active. Jesus modeled how we should live.

Do you depend fully on God to lead your daily plans, conversations and activities? Spiritually speaking, are you an active listener? There are so many lessons the Father wants to teach you. He knows what is best for His glory and for your life. He pursues you to use you. The Spirit of God takes the Word of God and adjusts your life to do the work of God. Listen attentively to the Father and follow His lead. His lessons are eternal.

Read: Open your Bible and read Ephesians 6:18.

Reflect: Prayerfully consider the following: How can I adjust my schedule today to increase the time I spend listening to the Father?

Respond: As a result of these truths, what might need to change in my attitude, beliefs, and actions? What steps do I need to take outwardly?

The Truth Will Set You Free

"So Jesus said to the Jews who had believed him, 'If you abide in my word, you are truly my disciples, and you will know the truth, and the truth will set you free.' They answered him, 'We are offspring of Abraham and have never been enslaved to anyone. How is it that you say, 'You will become free'?' Jesus answered them, 'Truly, truly, I say to you, everyone who practices sin is a slave to sin. The slave does not remain in the house forever; the son remains forever. So if the Son sets you free, you will be free indeed' " (John 8:31-36).

Walk through any prison hallway and you will find a common denominator. Every prisoner lacks the freedom to live as they choose. They are forced to follow a strict schedule. Time spent speaking with family is limited. The prisoners can't take a vacation and come back. The crimes they have committed keep them locked up in a cell until the time served is completed. The Jews assumed that they were spiritually free as a result of being descendants of Abraham. They did not believe they were enslaved to anyone or anything. They were mistaken. No matter what family you come from, sin is not lacking. It is part of the experience. The Jews had grown very comfortable with practicing sin and living through the limited power of their own flesh. They were living in spiritual bondage.

Jesus' conclusion was shocking. Although they were not slaves of any particular nation, they were slaves to their own flesh. Practicing sin proves its mastery over your life. No matter what you say, your practice points to your master. Jesus wanted these Jews to understand that sin has been their master. He was giving them an opportunity to find true freedom.

Jesus is the truth. He is the one who gives you true freedom. Studying God's Word regularly will lead you to obey God's Word fully. Finding freedom is about knowing Jesus, knowing the Bible, and applying the truth in every part of your life. Living in the truth will set you free from your sin. God has so much for you to know and experience, but you have to remain in His Word. When Jesus transformed your spirit, it was only the start of your freedom. As you determine to follow God's Word in whatever He shows you, experiencing more and more freedom will become your reality. If you know the Son and remain in His Word, the truth will set you free.

Read: Open your Bible and read Galatians 5:1.

Reflect: Prayerfully consider the following: What benefits do I receive when I exchange the weight of my sins for the freedom I have in Jesus?

Respond: As a result of these truths, what might need to change in my attitude, beliefs, and actions? What steps do I need to take outwardly?

No Space No Place

"'I know that you are offspring of Abraham; yet you seek to kill me because my word finds no place in you. I speak of what I have seen with my Father, and you do what you have heard from your father.' They answered him, 'Abraham is our father.' Jesus said to them, 'If you were Abraham's children, you would be doing the works Abraham did, but now you seek to kill me, a man who has told you the truth that I heard from God. This is not what Abraham did. You are doing the works your father did.' They said to him, 'We were not born of sexual immorality. We have one Father—even God'" (John 8:37-41).

Have you ever found a great piece of furniture that would look great in your home? It's a perfect match in style and comfort. There is only one problem. There is no place in your home to put it. Your layout is much too tight. You can't squeeze in one more piece of furniture. The Jewish leaders had no place for Jesus' teachings. Their hearts were crowded with pride, unbelief, and endless man-made commandments to supplement God's Word. There was no room for Jesus or His teachings. They were stubborn and filled with darkness. No wonder they could not believe.

Jesus recognized their ancestral connection to Abraham, but He wanted them to understand the difference between physical descendants and spiritual descendants. Abraham lived by faith. Although he was not perfect, his life was marked by faith and obedience to God's Word. Jesus could not say the same for the Jews in His day. Since they practiced evil, they could not be Abraham's children. Their works simply did not match.

This was a convicting conclusion indeed. If these Jews were not Abraham's true descendants, they were in big trouble. If their works reflected the deeds of the flesh rather than the power of the Holy Spirit, something was terribly wrong. We can understand why they dismissed Jesus' words so bitterly. It pointed to their true spiritual condition—darkness. Your words, attitudes, and actions over time point to your true spiritual condition. Do you crowd out God's Word from penetrating your heart? Is there room for the Holy Spirit to make some changes? Regardless of what you say or think, your words, attitudes, and actions reveal the real you. You cannot continually behave in a manner that is inconsistent with who you really are.

Read: Open your Bible and read Luke 6:46.

Reflect: Prayerfully consider the following: What do my words, attitudes, and actions this last week say about God's place in my heart?

Respond: As a result of these truths, what might need to change in my attitude, beliefs, and actions? What steps do I need to take outwardly?

Not of God

"Jesus said to them, 'If God were your Father, you would love me, for I came from God and I am here. I came not of my own accord, but he sent me. Why do you not understand what I say? It is because you cannot bear to hear my word. You are of your father the devil, and your will is to do your father's desires. He was a murderer from the beginning, and does not stand in the truth, because there is no truth in him. When he lies, he speaks out of his own character, for he is a liar and the father of lies. But because I tell the truth, you do not believe me. Which one of you convicts me of sin? If I tell the truth, why do you not believe me? Whoever is of God hears the words of God. The reason why you do not hear them is that you are not of God' " (John 8:42-47).

Have you ever taken a class in college that left you dizzy after each session? The subject matter is extremely difficult to understand. You are faced with a choice: Should I drop the class or get help? You decide to hire a tutor. The tutor helps you understand the subject and they make it enjoyable to learn. You listen carefully to every word and apply it quickly.

There were many reasons the Jews questioning Jesus could not comprehend His words. For starters, they blocked out the work of the Holy Spirit in their lives. The Holy Spirit is the divine tutor. He teaches us the deep things of God. He points us to Jesus. These Jews could not stand to hear the subject of Jesus. It made them sick to the core. To them Jesus was more than repulsive, He was blasphemous. They hated Him deeply.

Jesus unapologetically told them who they truly descended from—the devil. Why would Jesus say such a thing? Isn't that harsh? Not really. Religious though they were, they were mirroring the works of the devil. Their motives aligned with evil rather than good. The evil within was coming out. They were liars and did not live in the truth. They were even planning to murder Jesus. They could not hear God because they were not of God.

Are you of God? You might ask, "How can I know?" Meditate on Jesus' words, *"Whoever is of God hears the words of God."* Are you hearing God and responding to His commands? This is so important to your daily walk with God. Today, read His Word, believe His Word, and do His works.

Read: Open your Bible and read I John 4:7-11.

Reflect: Prayerfully consider the following: Am I obeying God's Word? How can I express my love for God and others more clearly?

Respond: As a result of these truths, what might need to change in my attitude, beliefs, and actions? What steps do I need to take outwardly?

Honor

"The Jews answered him, 'Are we not right in saying that you are a Samaritan and have a demon?' Jesus answered, 'I do not have a demon, but I honor my Father, and you dishonor me. Yet I do not seek my own glory; there is One who seeks it, and he is the judge' " (John 8:48-50).

When a judge puts on his black robe, he is doing far more than simply changing clothes. When he takes his place on the bench, the judge's robe represents his unique position, responsibility, and authority in a court of law. No longer are they just like everybody else. They have a unique function. Their position commands special respect and great honor.

After being accused of communicating messages of demonic origin, Jesus replies that to the contrary, honoring the Father is His chief priority. His whole purpose in teaching, healing, and rescuing people was to connect people to the Father. He placed the supreme desires of the Father above everything else. Honoring the Father was His singular purpose.

What the religious leaders did not understand was that when you dishonor the Son, you dishonor the Father. Conversely, when you honor the Son, you honor the Father. It is a direct relationship. The Apostle John previously wrote, *"The Father judges no one, but has given all judgment to the Son, that all may honor the Son, just as they honor the Father. Whoever does not honor the Son does not honor the Father who sent him"* (John 5:22-23).

Think about your life for a moment. Are you trying to honor God by serving Christ and His church? Are you more concerned with getting recognition from others than helping people see God's glory in all matters? You cannot simultaneously seek your own personal recognition and God's. It cannot happen. It won't happen. Give honor to the Lord Jesus and give honor to God. He will honor you when you honor His Son (John 12:23).

Jesus is worthy of your honor. There is no greater authority and there is no greater power. When you place the greatest value of life on the creator of life, living for His glory can become your reality. Honor the Lord in your daily submission to His Word and to His will for your life.

Read: Open your Bible and read I Timothy 1:17.

Reflect: Prayerfully consider the following: Am I honoring Jesus with the decisions I'm making this week? What do they say about what I value?

Respond: As a result of these truths, what might need to change in my attitude, beliefs, and actions? What steps do I need to take outwardly?

I Know Him

"'Truly, truly, I say to you, if anyone keeps my word, he will never see death.'
The Jews said to him, 'Now we know that you have a demon! Abraham died,
as did the prophets, yet you say, 'If anyone keeps my word, he will never taste
death.' Are you greater than our father Abraham, who died? And the prophets
died! Who do you make yourself out to be?' Jesus answered, 'If I glorify myself,
my glory is nothing. It is my Father who glorifies me, of whom you say, 'He is our
God.' But you have not known him. I know him. If I were to say that I do not
know him, I would be a liar like you, but I do know him and I keep his word' "
(John 8:51-55).

It does not happen every day, but it is exciting when it does. You see a friend being interviewed by a news reporter on the evening news. You know how he will respond to the questions before they even speak. Inside you begin cheering for them to do well. Why? You know him personally. He is your friend. It's almost as if you were the one being interviewed.

The eternal intimacy between the Father and the Son goes far beyond anything words could describe. It was more than the religious leaders of Jesus' time could handle or comprehend. How could Jesus possibly know Abraham or the prophets? How could He heal people? Was Jesus trying to deceive the people? Was His teaching of demonic origin?

Jesus was making the point that He is eternal. His relationship with the Father has always been and always will be. His words bring life. They overcome the reality of sin and death. Jesus pointed people to the Father and the Father pointed people to Jesus. God the Father glorifies the Son.

Can you say with all of your heart, "I know God intimately and I seek to know Him more each day?" This is central to the Christian life. Growing in your love and knowledge of God is where spiritual closeness begins. Learning to worship and pray on a regular basis draws you closer to the Savior. Our closeness to our Lord fuels our worship and our prayers.

Can you say with all of your heart, "I keep His Word?" Love and knowledge of God should lead us to complete obedience in every area of our lives. The more you know God the more you will obey His Word.

Read: Open your Bible and read Exodus 19:5.

Reflect: Prayerfully consider the following: Which of these three do I need to work on the most: love, knowledge, or obedience to God's Word?

Respond: As a result of these truths, what might need to change in my attitude, beliefs, and actions? What steps do I need to take outwardly?

Looking Forward

*"'Your father Abraham rejoiced that he would see my day. He saw it
and was glad.' So the Jews said to him, 'You are not yet fifty years old,
and have you seen Abraham?' Jesus said to them, 'Truly, truly, I say to you,
before Abraham was, I am.' So they picked up stones to throw at him,
but Jesus hid himself and went out of the temple" (John 8:56-59).*

After several months of waiting and planning, vacation finally arrives. You determine to leave work at the office for at least one week while you enjoy spending time with your family. You have been looking forward and dreaming about this week for a long time, and you carefully make the most of every moment. Looking forward now paints a big smile on your face.

Back in the book of Genesis, Abraham was also dreaming. He was trying to understand how God would unfold His promise to future generations. *"Now the Lord said to Abram, 'Go from your country and your kindred and your father's house to the land that I will show you. And I will make of you a great nation, and I will bless you and make your name great, so that you will be a blessing. I will bless those who bless you, and him who dishonors you I will curse, and in you all the families of the earth shall be blessed' "* (Genesis 12:1-3).

Abraham lived with great expectancy. He was looking forward to the fulfillment of a divine promise. Abraham welcomed these promises by faith. He knew that God would eventually use his physical seed to accomplish His divine plans. *"These all died in faith, not having received the things promised, but having seen them and greeted them from afar, and having acknowledged that they were strangers and exiles on the earth"* (Hebrews 11:13). Unlike Abraham, the Jews who picked up rocks to kill Jesus failed to look forward and see God's plan unfold right before their eyes. Their response to Jesus was to seek to end His life rather than objectively investigate His claims. They couldn't see that Jesus was the Messiah, God's Son.

Are you waiting expectantly for God to fulfill a promise in your life? Are you praying for a spiritual breakthrough? Don't allow your past or your present situation to discourage you from persevering in prayer. God is alive! He is doing His work even when you can't detect His activity. In times of waiting be cheerful. God always delivers on His promises.

Read: Open your Bible and read Genesis 12:1-3.

Reflect: Prayerfully consider the following: Is my family blessing others as God intended? How can I lead my family to make an eternal impact?

Respond: As a result of these truths, what might need to change in my attitude, beliefs, and actions? What steps do I need to take outwardly?

Not "Who?" but "What for?"

*"As he passed by, he saw a man blind from birth. And his disciples asked him,
'Rabbi, who sinned, this man or his parents, that he was born blind?'
Jesus answered, 'It was not that this man sinned, or his parents, but that
the works of God might be displayed in him. We must work the works
of him who sent me while it is day; night is coming, when no one can work.
As long as I am in the world, I am the light of the world' " (John 9:1-5).*

Machines inevitably break, weather patterns change, and crowds behave in ways beyond anyone's control. Yet when things go terribly wrong, the first question on everyone's mind is "Who is responsible?" It is not always fair. It is not always predictable. It is not even always right. But someone always ends up taking the blame when things go terribly wrong.

When Jesus' disciples saw a man who was blind, they immediately connected his condition with sin. Sin can lead to suffering, sickness and even death *(1 Corinthians 11:30)*. But this situation was different. Sin was not the reason for this man's blindness. It was not anyone's fault. God strategically chose to use this man in a way that would magnify His name. This man was destined to become a living example of God's great power.

Extended personal suffering can lead to a greater manifestation of God's unlimited power. The Apostle Paul understood this principle when he wrote, *"So to keep me from becoming conceited because of the surpassing greatness of the revelations, a thorn was given me in the flesh, a messenger of Satan to harass me, to keep me from becoming conceited" (2 Corinthians 12:7).*

We don't know exactly what physical struggle Paul continuously battled. He begged God to remove it on at least three occasions. We know it kept Paul humble. The results of his life and his ministry were unparalleled. God was glorified in a mighty way through his pain and personal suffering. Similarly, Jesus was helping His disciples develop the right spiritual perspective. God wants to reveal Himself through our struggles, hurts and limitations. Think through your most challenging physical and personal limitations. Could it be that God has allowed this reality in your life to display His unlimited power? Do you regularly get upset over this condition? Are you allowing God to use this as a tool for His glory?

Read: Open your Bible and read Job 1:1-22; 2:1-13.

Reflect: Prayerfully consider the following: Do I allow my personal struggles and limitations to negatively affect my witness for God?

Respond: As a result of these truths, what might need to change in my attitude, beliefs, and actions? What steps do I need to take outwardly?

What's Your Part?

*"Having said these things, he spit on the ground and made mud with the saliva.
Then he anointed the man's eyes with the mud and said to him,
'Go, wash in the pool of Siloam' (which means Sent).
So he went and washed and came back seeing" (John 9:6-7).*

Great teachers are marked by their simplicity rather than their complexity. They don't try to make things too technical or spend time highlighting irrelevant details. Great teachers simplify difficult concepts by breaking them down into smaller pieces and using only the most basic terminology.

In Jesus' day, mud was sometimes placed on the eyes to heal infections, but never to restore sight. Jesus used a combination of natural resources, divine power, and His own saliva to give sight to the man born blind. After placing the mud on his eyes, Jesus gave the blind man a simple two-step instruction: *"Go, wash in the pool of Siloam."* Jesus' instructions were clear and simple. It was now time for the blind man, the student, to exercise faith and personally apply the lesson. As God speaks, do I listen and follow?

Sometimes in seeking to place all our burdens on God, we forget our role in the process. God has chosen to do His work through His people. God has a part, and so do you. Don't forget your part. Don't just say, "I'm leaving this in the Lord's hands." That may sound spiritual, but what's your part? As you pray through a great difficulty, God may want you to take a new step of faith beyond what you are currently willing to consider.

The question remains, "What's your part?" If you are praying for God to return your child to the faith, what role do you play in this prayer? If tension at work has multiplied, what steps of peace is God leading you to begin? If your spouse is troubled by broken family relationships, how can you bring healing to their soul? You may not need to go down to the pool and wash your eyes, but you still need to discover what role you need to play. The blind man had a choice. He could have laughed at Jesus' divine prescription or even removed the mud from his face. Instead, he chose to follow God's Word. He determined to do exactly as Jesus instructed. The man obeyed, and immediately received his sight. What about you? Are you willing to obey God, regardless of the instruction?

Read: Open your Bible and read 2 Corinthians 5:7.

Reflect: Prayerfully consider the following: Do I live by faith or by sight? What part is God asking me to do before I experience my next miracle?

Respond: As a result of these truths, what might need to change in my attitude, beliefs, and actions? What steps do I need to take outwardly?

I Am the Man

"The neighbors and those who had seen him before as a beggar were saying, 'Is this not the man who used to sit and beg?' Some said, 'It is he.' Others said, 'No, but he is like him.' He kept saying, 'I am the man.' So they said to him, 'Then how were your eyes opened?' He answered, 'The man called Jesus made mud and anointed my eyes and said to me, 'Go to Siloam and wash.' So I went and washed and received my sight.' They said to him, 'Where is he?' He said, 'I do not know' " (John 9:8-12).

When those who are overweight lose 100-250 pounds, the results are transformational. It is not uncommon for friends and family who have not seen them for a few months to fail to recognize them as they walk down the street. It may take a second look or the sound of their voice for the reality of their transformation to sink in. The man who was born blind experienced an even greater transformation. It was a divine miracle. The one who had been limited to begging on the streets was now a changed man with a new purpose for living. He doesn't fully understand who Jesus is right away, but God often reveals Himself to us one step at a time.

Even with a limited knowledge of the Savior, this man's witness was already starting to shake up his world. Neighbors, friends, family and casual acquaintances were all astonished by the radical change in his life. They had more questions than answers. At one point they even questioned if this was the same man. He insisted, *"I am he."* What a powerful story indeed.

Your spiritual transformation is a powerful witness. God's work in your life is designed to be shared with others. The way God changed your thinking and removed you from sin is important for others to know. Maybe your story is not as dramatic as the man who was born blind. Make no mistake about it; every God Story is a powerful story.

Practice sharing your story in the mirror if this will help you gain greater confidence. Always remember that God will place the words on your mouth as needed. There's no need to fear or panic. God can use every weakness you have for His purposes. Keep it simple and take confidence in the fact that God's work of transformation always impacts those around us.

Read: Open your Bible and read Romans 1:16.

Reflect: Prayerfully consider the following: What does the man who was born blind teach me about sharing my faith and sharing my story?

Respond: As a result of these truths, what might need to change in my attitude, beliefs, and actions? What steps do I need to take outwardly?

Indecision

"They brought to the Pharisees the man who had formerly been blind. Now it was a Sabbath day when Jesus made the mud and opened his eyes. So the Pharisees again asked him how he had received his sight. And he said to them, 'He put mud on my eyes, and I washed, and I see.' Some of the Pharisees said, 'This man is not from God, for he does not keep the Sabbath.' But others said, 'How can a man who is a sinner do such signs?' And there was a division among them. So they said again to the blind man, 'What do you say about him, since he has opened your eyes?' He said, 'He is a prophet' " (John 9:13-17).

The persistent waiter brings out the dessert tray for you and your family. These life-like creations help provide a tempting visual, but your stomach is quite full. Surprisingly, there is space for dessert. You absolutely love chocolate. Ice cream cools your soul. But the cheesecake looks like something out of a celebrity baking show. You find it so hard to decide.

The Pharisees had a hard time finalizing their official position regarding Jesus. They were divided in their opinions, and their debate was anything but civil. Strong emotions took over quickly. At least two contradictory conclusions surfaced: first, He is not from God because He does not keep the Sabbath; second, He must be from God because sinners are not miracle workers. The man who was blind concluded, *"He is a prophet."*

This debate must have been entertaining to those looking on. Never had anyone shaken up the religious establishment like Jesus did. It was truly a moment to remember. What they wrestled with had significant implications for their religion and for their lifestyle. If Jesus was the promised Messiah, they had to abandon their traditions and submit to Jesus as their Lord and King. He would have the final authority on what traditions were acceptable and those that would be discontinued.

Recognizing Jesus as Messiah would represent more than a little shake up. As Messiah, Jesus would dethrone these religious leaders and radically change the leadership structure in Jerusalem and in Israel. The Pharisees were not ready for such a "hostile takeover." They had no intention of giving up control. How about you? Are you willing to give up control of your life for Jesus to reign freely? Decide today to please your Lord.

Read: Open your Bible and read Galatians 2:20.

Reflect: Prayerfully consider the following: Why is it hard for me to live for Christ daily and die to my personal desires for fame, status and wealth?

Respond: As a result of these truths, what might need to change in my attitude, beliefs, and actions? What steps do I need to take outwardly?

Relentless Unbelief

"The Jews did not believe that he had been blind and had received his sight, until they called the parents of the man who had received his sight and asked them, 'Is this your son, who you say was born blind? How then does he now see?' His parents answered, 'We know that this is our son and that he was born blind. But how he now sees we do not know, nor do we know who opened his eyes. Ask him; he is of age. He will speak for himself.' (His parents said these things because they feared the Jews, for the Jews had already agreed that if anyone should confess Jesus to be Christ, he was to be put out of the synagogue.) Therefore his parents said, 'He is of age; ask him' " (John 9:18-23).

Is it easier for someone to convince you of great news or terrible news? Chances are you more readily believe one than the other. Regardless of your preference, your temperament and your past leave you with a distinct tendency that may be extremely difficult to overcome quickly.

The Pharisees were known for being unbending and meticulous when it came to following the Law. This naturally spilled over into their unfair prosecution of Jesus. Regardless of the evidence, they refused to believe in Jesus as their Messiah. Likewise, they refused to believe in the obvious miracle of the man who was born blind. They were unrelenting in their unbelief. You can hear their prosecutorial tone as they question the parents of this transformed man. Their approach reminds us of the emptiness and desperation that arises when false religion is confronted with the truth. What is most disheartening is the response of the man's parents. They were more concerned with maintaining their social status within the Jewish community than giving God the glory for this miracle.

How do you respond when you are afraid? Do you take charge, talk nervously, remain frozen, or start shaking? Don't allow the influence of others to derail your faith. If God has done a miracle in your life, call it what it is—a divine intervention. Miracles are not common, but they are memorable. If God has performed a miracle in your family or within your place of work, don't ignore it. Celebrate the miracle and give God the glory. Stand up and proclaim what God has done. If you don't, others may remain in unbelief. If you do, you may be the voice that helps them believe.

Read: Open your Bible and read Colossians 1:28.

Reflect: Prayerfully consider the following: Am I a consistent proclaimer of Jesus' miracles? Which ones do I need to verbalize more?

Respond: As a result of these truths, what might need to change in my attitude, beliefs, and actions? What steps do I need to take outwardly?

One Thing I Do Know

*"So for the second time they called the man who had been blind
and said to him, 'Give glory to God. We know that this man is a sinner.'
He answered, 'Whether he is a sinner I do not know. One thing
I do know, that though I was blind, now I see' " (John 9:24-25).*

Having first-hand knowledge about a particular subject can produce unusual confidence. When your intellect and your experience arrive at the same destination, it can be a powerful moment. When you prepare to take an exam, the knowledge gained through the pain of your preparation and practice is priceless. Regardless of what others say, you know your stuff.

The religious leaders continued to pour out their wrath on the testimony of Jesus. They even went so far as to call him a sinner without any evidence to back up their claim. It was a desperate measure to persuade the people in their favor. The problem was that the miracle that stood before them could not be explained without God as part of the equation. The man who was healed was not buying their drama, and they knew it.

They tried one more tactic to close their case. They asked the man to come clean and confess the truth much like Joshua demanded of Achan (Joshua 7:19). He accepted their offer and responded confidently. He was unaware of Jesus' past or His capacity to sin. He was however fully convinced of His power, and he knew how radically Jesus had changed his life. His personal testimony and changed life were beyond debate.

If someone were trying to build a case against Jesus using the changes He has made in your life, would they find sufficient evidence to persuade others to believe in Jesus? God's work through your life serves as a powerful testimony for the Lord Jesus. It's what the world needs to see.

Consider the single most significant change that God has made in your life. Can you summarize in one sentence the difference in your life before and after this change? What is the one thing you do know about God's transforming work that no one can challenge? This is not something that you should keep to yourself. Everyone needs to hear. Everyone needs to see. Everyone needs to know and experience God's transforming power.

Read: Open your Bible and read 2 Timothy 1:7.

Reflect: Prayerfully consider the following: Am I remaining silent when critics attack Jesus? What is God's greatest miracle and change in my life?

Respond: As a result of these truths, what might need to change in my attitude, beliefs, and actions? What steps do I need to take outwardly?

Bewildered

"They said to him, 'What did he do to you? How did he open your eyes?'
He answered them, 'I have told you already, and you would not listen.
Why do you want to hear it again? Do you also want to become his disciples?'
And they reviled him, saying, 'You are his disciple, but we are disciples
of Moses. We know that God has spoken to Moses, but as for this man,
we do not know where he comes from' " (John 9:26-29).

Have you ever witnessed adults getting visibly irritated as a result of waiting in a long line at a store? They pace back and forth, openly complaining about the manager and disturbing other customers. They may eventually vent their anger by attacking the cashier with sarcasm to make their point. Similarly, the Pharisees had tried every trick in the book to persuade the man who was born blind to publically deny Jesus. They failed miserably, and now they were out of ammunition. They finally resort to attacking the man directly in an effort to shut him up. Personal attacks are usually desperate tactical measures; this strategy would also fail miserably.

The man could have repeated his story another 100 times, but the Pharisees were unwilling to receive the truth about the Lord Jesus. Repeating the story would not make a difference. They did not want to research His origins, and had no desire to submit to His Lordship as their promised Messiah. Their unbelief was beyond repair. It had turned into heartless rebellion. Their unbelief was truly incomprehensible. There are people who will never understand the good news of Jesus Christ. They refuse to believe in His name. They process everything through their natural abilities and remain in darkness. Paul reminds us, *"The person without the Spirit does not accept the things that come from the Spirit of God but considers them foolishness, and cannot understand them because they are discerned only through the Spirit" (1 Corinthians 2:14, NIV).*

The work of spiritual transformation is spiritual in nature. The battle takes place in a spiritual domain. This is where you need to fight. Helping your family and friends know Jesus is a spiritual activity. They may ridicule your faith, attack your beliefs, or reject you altogether. Don't get discouraged. Keep praying for their spiritual blindness to be removed. Only Jesus can help them see the truth. Pray for them every day, and lead them to Jesus.

Read: Open your Bible and read Luke 9:22.

Reflect: Prayerfully consider the following: How can I pray differently and more effectively today for those who are spiritually blind?

Respond: As a result of these truths, what might need to change in my attitude, beliefs, and actions? What steps do I need to take outwardly?

An Amazing Thing

"The man answered, 'Why, this is an amazing thing! You do not know where he comes from, and yet he opened my eyes. We know that God does not listen to sinners, but if anyone is a worshiper of God and does his will, God listens to him. Never since the world began has it been heard that anyone opened the eyes of a man born blind. If this man were not from God, he could do nothing.' They answered him, 'You were born in utter sin, and would you teach us?' And they cast him out" (John 9:30-34).

Watching a child stand in amazement is very exciting. When they see an airplane, an elephant, or a cruise ship for the first time, their reaction is priceless. They may point to the object without speaking a single word. The experience overwhelms their capacity to explain what they see or feel.

The man who was born blind was amazed at the Pharisees' unwillingness to believe in Jesus. Healing a man who was born blind is a big deal and it was a first for their people. Since God was responsible for the miraculous, Jesus' origin was obviously divine. These religious experts surely had more answers than what they were willing to share. They were hiding the truth.

What this man was unable to figure out was why the Pharisees hated Jesus so much. Jesus was restoring sight to the blind. He was releasing people from a world of darkness and hopelessness. Why would you hate the person behind this activity? God was obviously answering His prayers. He summarized his argument in one sentence, *"If this man were not from God, he could do nothing."* That was the truth and nothing but the truth.

Needless-to-say, the Pharisees rejected the man's epic conclusion. How they had responded earlier paved the way for their final verdict. Since they were the final authority, this man did not stand a chance in their presence. His voice was considered inferior in matters of judgment, and his teaching was brutally ridiculed. These Pharisees were a hopeless case.

You may not be a theologian. You may not be a professor at your local seminary. You may not be a pastor, either. You can, however, teach others about Jesus. God's Word is all that you need. The Bible is sufficient to handle every argument and give evidence to the Savior's amazing power.

Read: Open your Bible and read Matthew 10:22.

Reflect: Prayerfully consider the following: Am I handling spiritual opposition in a way that honors God? How can I better prepare for this?

Respond: As a result of these truths, what might need to change in my attitude, beliefs, and actions? What steps do I need to take outwardly?

Spiritual Sight

"Jesus heard that they had cast him out, and having found him he said, 'Do you believe in the Son of Man?' He answered, 'And who is he, sir, that I may believe in him?' Jesus said to him, 'You have seen him, and it is he who is speaking to you.' He said, 'Lord, I believe,' and he worshiped him. Jesus said, 'For judgment I came into this world, that those who do not see may see, and those who see may become blind.' Some of the Pharisees near him heard these things, and said to him, 'Are we also blind?' Jesus said to them, 'If you were blind, you would have no guilt; but now that you say, 'We see,' your guilt remains' " (John 9:35-41).

When your eyes require corrective lenses, it is usually a slow process of discovery. You begin experiencing slight headaches as a result of straining your eyes throughout the day. You can see large objects, but you struggle to see the details. It's not until you have an eye exam that your problem becomes evident. Lenses corresponding to your prescription suddenly bring a fuzzy world into sharp focus; they help you see everything better. Jesus came to seek and save the lost. He restored sight to the blind, healed the sick, and raised the dead. But Jesus did something greater: He became the living prescription for our salvation when He died on the cross for our sins. More than restoring people physically, He changed them spiritually.

The greater miracle in this story is the spiritual sight given to this man in his final encounter with Jesus. The blind man's understanding of who Jesus was is seen in three phases as Jesus revealed Himself one step at a time. He first described Jesus as *"a man."* God became man in the flesh to identify with His creation. Secondly, the man described Jesus as *"a prophet"* after receiving his sight. Experiencing this one-of-a-kind healing was nothing short of divine intervention. This man knew that Jesus was from God.

Thirdly, the man recognized Jesus as *"the Son of Man."* This took things to a whole new level. Jesus is now recognized as deity. He is now recognized as God in the flesh. For this reason, the man places His faith in Jesus and begins to worship Him. This is the place where our faith begins. It is also the position where our faith should remain. Your attitude can change very rapidly when being in the presence of God is your constant focus. He uses worship to adjust your vision. God wants to give you the right perspective.

Read: Open your Bible and read Matthew 10:32.

Reflect: Prayerfully consider the following: Am I acknowledging Jesus in my public life? Is He trying to correct my vision in a particular area?

Respond: As a result of these truths, what might need to change in my attitude, beliefs, and actions? What steps do I need to take outwardly?

The Shepherd of the Sheep

" 'Truly, truly, I say to you, he who does not enter the sheepfold by the door but climbs in by another way, that man is a thief and a robber. But he who enters by the door is the shepherd of the sheep. To him the gatekeeper opens. The sheep hear his voice, and he calls his own sheep by name and leads them out. When he has brought out all his own, he goes before them, and the sheep follow him, for they know his voice. A stranger they will not follow, but they will flee from him, for they do not know the voice of strangers.' This figure of speech Jesus used with them, but they did not understand what he was saying to them"
(John 10:1-6).

Museums are wonderful places to expand your imagination. If you love world history or enjoy different styles of contemporary art, museums will delight your soul. Artifacts on display provide rich illustrations from the past. Paintings, sculptures, furniture, weapons, tools, and other discoveries open up new windows of historical reality as you see their role in history.

Jesus used a similarly powerful illustration to help us better understand how foolish it is to try to enter God's family outside of God's plan. God has provided exclusive access to His Kingdom through the Shepherd of the sheep—Jesus. It is through Jesus that we have access to the Father.

Jesus uses the familiar image of a door to make His point. God is the gatekeeper. He does not open the door to those who have no business coming in to be with the flock. Jesus alone is the Door. Only those who know Him and follow His voice can walk through this door. He is the One who pursues you. He is the One who initiates a personal relationship with you. As His child and heir, Jesus knows your name personally.

Jesus identifies Himself as the Shepherd of the sheep. Everyone present knew the responsibilities of a shepherd. The shepherd knows his sheep intimately. He calls them individually by name. The sheep only respond to His voice. They will not respond to other shepherds. The shepherd leads the sheep to find rest. He feeds his sheep and protects them from danger.

Follow the voice of your Shepherd. You know His voice. If other voices try to distract you away from His purposes for your life, do not listen.

Read: Open your Bible and read Hebrews 3:7.

Reflect: Prayerfully consider the following: Am I actively listening for God's voice to lead me? What would I say are my biggest distractions?

Respond: As a result of these truths, what might need to change in my attitude, beliefs, and actions? What steps do I need to take outwardly?

I AM the Door of the Sheep

"So Jesus again said to them, 'Truly, truly, I say to you, I am the door of the sheep. All who came before me are thieves and robbers, but the sheep did not listen to them. I am the door. If anyone enters by me, he will be saved and will go in and out and find pasture' " (John 10:7-9).

Large sporting events require a tremendous amount of organization. A sophisticated ticketing system helps direct fans to their seats, each ticket providing access to specific areas. Only those with special access can make their way onto the playing field. Your ticket determines your access.

The Jews must have thought, "Is Jesus the Shepherd or is He the Door?" They were confused enough already. It is not one or the other, but both. Jesus is the Shepherd and Jesus is the Door. He faithfully leads people to the Father while simultaneously serving as our mediator and our redeemer. Jesus is our salvation. He is the One who provides us with spiritual rest.

"For through him we both have access in one Spirit to the Father. So then you are no longer strangers and aliens, but you are fellow citizens with the saints and members of the household of God, built on the foundation of the apostles and prophets, Christ Jesus himself being the cornerstone, in whom the whole structure, being joined together, grows into a holy temple in the Lord" (Ephesians 2:18-21).

Shepherds in the New Testament times would lead their sheep into an enclosed area at night to rest. These enclosed areas did not have a door. The shepherd would lie down and serve as the living door. He would then be able to protect the sheep from any sudden danger. The shepherd was responsible for the health of the sheep, and, if necessary, would sacrifice his life for the sheep. Jesus is our Savior, and He is our sacrifice.

The spiritual rest you need is found in Jesus. There is no reason for you to stay up at night worrying about tomorrow. Jesus not only provides eternal rest, but He also protects you from danger. If He is your Savior, He will work everything out for God's fame, His glory. You therefore no longer need to worry. You can rest in His faithfulness. You can trust Him to be a faithful Shepherd and lead you on the right path. As Savior, Jesus is the One who gives you access to the Father. He is the Door of the Sheep.

Read: Open your Bible and read John 14:6.

Reflect: Prayerfully consider the following: Am I trusting Jesus to lead my life and draw me closer to the Father? Am I finding rest in my Savior?

Respond: As a result of these truths, what might need to change in my attitude, beliefs, and actions? What steps do I need to take outwardly?

I AM the Good Shepherd

"The thief comes only to steal and kill and destroy. I came that they may have life and have it abundantly. I am the good shepherd. The good shepherd lays down his life for the sheep" (John 10:10-11).

If you have ever been robbed, you know how horrible it feels. Something that belonged to you was forever removed from your possession. Other items of great personal value may even have been dropped and destroyed in the process. Anger, frustration, and sadness are just the beginning of the emotions that arise from being surprised, caught off guard, and taken advantage of by a thief. Satan is such a thief. He is not your friend. His mission is to steal, kill and destroy, and he does not care who gets hurt in the process. If he can't destroy you, he will try everything in the book to discourage you in your faith. Never forget this reality.

In Christ Jesus, you have a unique life-advantage. You are a chosen family member of the Eternal King. God is for you, not against you. He has blessed your life for the sake of His Kingdom and His glory. You are spiritually rich in Christ. All resources are available for you to advance the King's agenda. You already have all that you need to live for your King. Don't wait. Begin serving God and watch Him provide what is needed.

Jesus is the Good Shepherd. He did not come to remove life, but to give life to all who believed in His name. Abundance begins with Jesus. But your abundant life did not arrive without a high cost. The Good Shepherd paid the penalty of your sins to make this life possible. The writer of Hebrews tells us, *"He [Jesus] entered once for all into the holy places, not by means of the blood of goats and calves but by means of his own blood, thus securing an eternal redemption" (Hebrews 9:12).* Jesus secured your eternity and abundant life with His precious blood on the cross at Calvary.

Do those around you know the Good Shepherd? Think about those friends, family members, and co-workers who seem to spend their lives walking in endless circles. Make an extra effort this week to tell them about Jesus. Eternal life and abundant living is only found in Him. If Jesus paid a high cost, we should make sacrifices to reach others with the truth.

Read: Open your Bible and read Isaiah 40:11.

Reflect: Prayerfully consider the following: What does the care of the Good Shepherd say about God's love for me and others?

Respond: As a result of these truths, what might need to change in my attitude, beliefs, and actions? What steps do I need to take outwardly?

Shepherd Your Flock

"He who is a hired hand and not a shepherd, who does not own the sheep, sees the wolf coming and leaves the sheep and flees, and the wolf snatches them and scatters them. He flees because he is a hired hand and cares nothing for the sheep. I am the good shepherd. I know my own and my own know me, just as the Father knows me and I know the Father; and I lay down my life for the sheep" (John 10:12-15).

There is a significant difference between owning a home and renting a home. Owners make investments and take care of their property. They are often proactive when it comes to maintenance and repairs. Renters have a different mindset. They do not invest in the home and they are not responsible for big repairs. When something breaks, they contact the owner. The contrast between a hired hand and a shepherd is equally clear. The hired hand protects and feeds himself before the sheep. Israel's leaders were rebuked by God for acting as hired hands over the people in Ezekiel 34:2-6. They neglected God's sheep and sinned in the process. The priests were not feeding the people with the Word of God, and the people of God were scattered. This neglect was detrimental to the people.

Jesus is the Owner of the sheep. We belong to Him. He never abandons us. He never neglects us. As the Owner of the sheep, Jesus cares for you. He calls you by name to enter His fold. Jesus knows your name and He knows your voice. He seals you with the Holy Spirit and promises to provide for all of your needs. Jesus protects you through the storms of life. His care for you is profound and very personal. Do you truly believe this?

The Apostle Peter reminds godly leaders to *"Shepherd the flock of God that is among you, exercising oversight, not under compulsion, but willingly, as God would have you; not for shameful gain, but eagerly" (1 Peter 5:2).* Could it be that God wants you to care for others in the same way that He cares for you? This may involve using your home or apartment as a place where small group ministry can begin. For others it may mean coordinating bags of groceries to help a family in need. Some may simply care for others by sending cards of comfort. Since these actions depend largely on the gifts, resources and abilities that God has given us, we each have a responsibility to serve and care for others. Are you intentionally shepherding someone?

Read: Open your Bible and read John 21:16.

Reflect: Prayerfully consider the following: Am I regularly serving others with my gifts? What do my actions say about my love for God and others?

Respond: As a result of these truths, what might need to change in my attitude, beliefs, and actions? What steps do I need to take outwardly?

No Distinction

"'And I have other sheep that are not of this fold. I must bring them also, and they will listen to my voice. So there will be one flock, one shepherd. For this reason the Father loves me, because I lay down my life that I may take it up again. No one takes it from me, but I lay it down of my own accord. I have authority to lay it down, and I have authority to take it up again. This charge I have received from my Father.' There was again a division among the Jews because of these words. Many of them said, 'He has a demon, and is insane; why listen to him?' Others said, 'These are not the words of one who is oppressed by a demon. Can a demon open the eyes of the blind?'"
(John 10:16-21).

In families with more than one child, sibling rivalry inevitably surfaces at one time or another. Children compare birthday gifts, activities, and other items that lead to competitive conflicts. Sharing skills are neglected and the "it's mine" attitude dominates their thinking. Parents have to step in and explain, "You need to treat one another with love. We love both of you the same." Jesus came to bring together people from all ethnic groups to form one church, one body, one family, and one flock. His first priority was naturally to reach the Jews, the immediate heirs of God's promises to Abraham. Second, Jesus commanded His disciples to go into the entire world and preach the gospel to people from every nation. Jesus would break down all spiritual, ethnic, social, gender, and cultural barriers.

"For in Christ Jesus you are all sons of God, through faith. For as many of you as were baptized into Christ have put on Christ. There is neither Jew nor Greek, there is neither slave nor free, there is no male and female, for you are all one in Christ Jesus. And if you are Christ's, then you are Abraham's offspring, heirs according to promise" (Galatians 3:26-29).

The promise to Abraham is a promise that extends to every believer. Faith in Christ makes you an heir of the promises of God! As part of God's spiritual family, there is no need for sibling rivalry. You can worship freely with brothers and sisters in Christ from any community, city, or nation. Whatever divided us from other ethnic groups is no longer relevant. The greater the diversity of God's people, the greater God's glory when we are all beautifully united as one body in Jesus Christ. There is no distinction.

Read: Open your Bible and read Romans 8:14-16.

Reflect: Prayerfully consider the following: Does my attitude and my actions reflect a "No Distinction Policy" with other believers?

Respond: As a result of these truths, what might need to change in my attitude, beliefs, and actions? What steps do I need to take outwardly?

The Father's Hand

"At that time the Feast of Dedication took place at Jerusalem. It was winter, and Jesus was walking in the temple, in the colonnade of Solomon. So the Jews gathered around him and said to him, 'How long will you keep us in suspense? If you are the Christ, tell us plainly.' Jesus answered them, 'I told you, and you do not believe. The works that I do in my Father's name bear witness about me, but you do not believe because you are not among my sheep. My sheep hear my voice, and I know them, and they follow me. I give them eternal life, and they will never perish, and no one will snatch them out of my hand. My Father, who has given them to me, is greater than all, and no one is able to snatch them out of the Father's hand. I and the Father are one' " (John 10:22-30).

No one appreciates a party crasher. They arrive with no tickets or formal invitations and eat food meant for invited guests. They have a tendency to disrupt planned activities, interrupt the flow of communication, and make a mess. These crashers only serve their own personal interests. During the Feast of Dedication, Jesus was confronted by a few party crashers. Although these men were invited to the feast, they came to interrogate the Messiah rather than celebrate the occasion. They repeated their questioning in total unbelief. Regardless of how Jesus responded, they stubbornly clung to their unbelief and refused to accept that Jesus was the Messiah. They could not believe because Jesus was not their Shepherd.

Jesus knows His sheep and His sheep recognize His voice. For this reason, Jesus' sheep follow His leadership. Those who don't obey Him do not recognize or follow His voice. Jesus gives you eternal life. He guarantees your salvation. Your identity in Christ is forever secure. God has placed you in the care of the Good Shepherd; this is the work of Almighty God.

Jesus extends this point one step further. Not only is your eternal security in the perfect care of the Shepherd, it is securely gripped by the Father's hand. Nothing that exists can separate you from the Father's love. The constant care of the Shepherd and the eternal grip of the Father are impenetrable. Nothing that you have done or will do can remove you from God's family. And no person, whether dead or alive, visible or invisible, can remove you from God's power. You are cared for and secure.

Read: Open your Bible and read I John 2:25.

Reflect: Prayerfully consider the following: Have I been uneasy about my eternal security? What is the promise that I should hold on to?

Respond: As a result of these truths, what might need to change in my attitude, beliefs, and actions? What steps do I need to take outwardly?

Throwing Rocks

"The Jews picked up stones again to stone him. Jesus answered them, 'I have shown you many good works from the Father; for which of them are you going to stone me?' The Jews answered him, 'It is not for a good work that we are going to stone you but for blasphemy, because you, being a man, make yourself God' "
(John 10:31-33).

Skipping rocks across a quiet lake is something that many young children enjoy doing. Dads review the proper technique for their kids to follow. If friends are present, their competitive nature drives them to outperform one another. Unless someone else is in the water, the game is harmless.

The Jews were ready to throw rocks at Jesus for a different purpose. They were not playing any lakeside games. They were infuriated by Jesus' claims to be God, and they planned to put an immediate end to His life. This was not a new claim. On at least two prior occasions, Jesus described His equality with God. In John 5:18, Jesus said that He was equal with God in power by calling God His Father. In John 8:59, Jesus said that He was eternal as He described His existence before Abraham and Moses.

The word blasphemy carries the idea of words that are spoken to injure. In the case of Jesus, it meant that the Jews viewed Jesus' claims as an insult to the God of Israel. For this reason, they wanted to put Him to death themselves. This action clearly violated Roman law, but their intense anger clouded their thinking. Jesus was making Himself out to be God and the Jews could not handle it. For this reason, verbal rock throwing followed.

Do you throw verbal rocks to purposely injure others? Have you criticized others unfairly because they have different dreams and goals than you do? As a believer, walking in the Spirit means practicing self-control in every area of your life. If the Spirit of God does not control you, your flesh will dominate your life. Live in the Spirit and refuse to throw rocks at others:

"But the fruit of the Spirit is love, joy, peace, patience, kindness, goodness, faithfulness, gentleness, self-control; against such things there is no law. And those who belong to Christ Jesus have crucified the flesh with its passions and desires" (Galatians 5:22-24).

Read: Open your Bible and read Proverbs 25:28.

Reflect: Prayerfully consider the following: Am I guilty of throwing verbal rocks at others? What is the danger of not practicing self-control?

Respond: As a result of these truths, what might need to change in my attitude, beliefs, and actions? What steps do I need to take outwardly?

Believe the Works

*"Jesus answered them, 'Is it not written in your Law, 'I said, you are gods'?
If he called them gods to whom the word of God came—and Scripture cannot
be broken—do you say of him whom the Father consecrated and sent into the
world, 'You are blaspheming,' because I said, 'I am the Son of God'? If I am
not doing the works of my Father, then do not believe me; but if I do them,
even though you do not believe me, believe the works, that you may know and
understand that the Father is in me and I am in the Father' " (John 10:34-38).*

How much evidence is enough? That may depend not only on the quality
of the evidence, but also the opinion of the judge. The judge may
determine that the evidence is valid or invalid. Fair and balanced judgments
can lead to good rulings. Unfair and biased judgments will often lead to
poor decisions. In the Old Testament (Psalm 82:6), judges were compared
to gods as a result of their power and sovereignty. Although they were not
God, they did represent Him in the way they led the courtroom.

Unjust judges misused that authority by perverting God's Word and
neglecting to apply its teachings to their methods of justice. As a result,
these judges arrived at the wrong conclusions and made poor decisions.
Since God's Word used the word "god" to refer to these unjust judges,
surely it can be used to refer to the Son of God. It was a good argument.

In similar fashion, the Jews were arriving at their conclusions through evil
methods. They were unjust in their evaluation of Jesus and His claims.
Why? Two words describe their condition, total unbelief. The word
"believe" is used at least 99 times in the book of John. It was John's theme
and central message to his readers. The works of Jesus proved His deity.

Those who evaluated His claims justly arrived at the right conclusion:
*"Again they sought to arrest him, but he escaped from their hands. He went
away again across the Jordan to the place where John had been baptizing
at first, and there he remained. And many came to him. And they said,
'John did no sign, but everything that John said about this man was true.'
And many believed in him there"* (John 10:39-42). In your evaluation of Jesus
and His claims, have you been completely honest? Have you given Him a
fair and thorough evaluation? Do you believe in His mighty works?

Read: Open your Bible and read Proverbs 31:9.

Reflect: Prayerfully consider the following: Do I believe that Jesus is the
Son of God? What evidence can I share with others to help them believe?

Respond: As a result of these truths, what might need to change in my
attitude, beliefs, and actions? What steps do I need to take outwardly?

48 Hours

"Now a certain man was ill, Lazarus of Bethany, the village of Mary and her sister Martha. It was Mary who anointed the Lord with ointment and wiped his feet with her hair, whose brother Lazarus was ill. So the sisters sent to him, saying, 'Lord, he whom you love is ill.' But when Jesus heard it he said, 'This illness does not lead to death. It is for the glory of God, so that the Son of God may be glorified through it.' Now Jesus loved Martha and her sister and Lazarus. So, when he heard that Lazarus was ill, he stayed two days longer in the place where he was" (John 11:1-6).

When a good friend is very sick, you do all that you can to contact them and pay them a visit. You might deliver beautiful flowers to brighten up their room, or buy a container of hot chicken soup to keep them warm. More than gifts or even words, though, it is your presence that matters most. Without saying many words, your presence speaks volumes. It communicates genuine love, true friendship, goodness, and personal care.

Jesus was a good friend to Mary, Martha, and Lazarus. He knew their family personally and loved each one of them deeply. But now, the man He loved deeply was not doing well. Instinctively, when the sisters discovered that their brother Lazarus was not well, they called for Jesus. One would think that Jesus' first response would be to make immediate plans to go visit His friend Lazarus as soon as possible. Surely He would heal him, right?

Jesus' response was puzzling at best. He purposely delayed His arrival, waiting two more days before leaving. Martha and Mary did not anticipate the extra wait. They expected Jesus to come right away. They were counting on His presence. They may have questioned Jesus' motives or even been angry about His decision. But He had a purpose in mind that was more amazing than they ever could have possibly imagined.

Why does God take so long in answering some of our prayers? Three words: He Loves You! "He loves me?" Yes! He loves you deeply. God is fully aware of your circumstances. You may be asking Him to make His presence known in the life of your children or in a difficult relationship. Even if God delays longer than you expect, His love for you is real and unshakable. Don't get upset at God when He delays. Trust His wisdom.

Read: Open your Bible and read Job 10:12.

Reflect: Prayerfully consider the following: Do I allow God's love to preserve me completely while I wait for Him to respond to my prayers?

Respond: As a result of these truths, what might need to change in my attitude, beliefs, and actions? What steps do I need to take outwardly?

What is He Thinking?

"Then after this he said to the disciples, 'Let us go to Judea again.'
The disciples said to him, 'Rabbi, the Jews were just now seeking to stone you,
and are you going there again?' Jesus answered, 'Are there not twelve hours
in the day? If anyone walks in the day, he does not stumble, because he
sees the light of this world. But if anyone walks in the night, he stumbles,
because the light is not in him' " (John 11:7-10).

Stunt people get paid very well to do the unthinkable: jumping out of tall buildings, battling multiple villains, hanging from soaring helicopters, and walking through intense fires, are just some of their spectacles. "What are these guys thinking?" They embrace these dangers to add intensity and realism to action scenes and protect the stars of the film from any harm.

When Jesus announced His new mission, His disciples thought, "What is He thinking? He's crazy to go back to Judea again! They are trying to kill Him." The disciples must have been scratching their heads in disbelief. Was this a joke? Apparently, Jesus was not joking. How do you face such great danger with this kind of confidence and unbending resolve? How can you face such opposition with absolute certainty? King David wrote: *"Even though I walk through the valley of the shadow of death, I will fear no evil, for you are with me; your rod and your staff, they comfort me"* (Psalm 23:4).

King David understood what it felt like to walk through danger. David's life was filled with life-threatening opposition from King Saul, one of David's own sons, and countless other enemies. Yet he remained fearless because he knew that God's presence was with him. David was a godly man. He stayed faithful to God's Word, and pursued Him with all of his heart. As we submit our lives to God, we can have this same confidence today.

The time for you to serve God is right now. The daylight represents the believer who obeys God and does His work. You won't fall into a large hole in the daylight if you can see what is before you. When you do God's work, God is responsible for protecting you from danger. When you live your life outside of God's Word, you are walking in the darkness. You can get hurt because of your lack of visibility; there are dangers beyond your capacity to see. If you choose to disobey God, "What are you thinking?"

Read: Open your Bible and read 1 John 2:10.

Reflect: Prayerfully consider the following: Would those who know me best say that my actions reflect someone who is walking in the daylight?

Respond: As a result of these truths, what might need to change in my attitude, beliefs, and actions? What steps do I need to take outwardly?

Let Us Go

"After saying these things, he said to them, 'Our friend Lazarus has fallen asleep, but I go to awaken him.' The disciples said to him, 'Lord, if he has fallen asleep, he will recover.' Now Jesus had spoken of his death, but they thought that he meant taking rest in sleep. Then Jesus told them plainly, 'Lazarus has died, and for your sake I am glad that I was not there, so that you may believe. But let us go to him.' So Thomas, called the Twin, said to his fellow disciples, 'Let us also go, that we may die with him' " (John 11:11-16).

Sunday morning before church is the most difficult time for children to get up. After sleeping in on Saturday morning, they go from one activity to the next. It is not uncommon for them to go to bed a little later than usual on Saturday evening. It takes time for their adrenaline to wear off. But, tickling their feet and removing their blankets can wake them up quickly!

The disciples were trying to avoid returning to Judea. If Lazarus was "*sleeping*" they assumed he would get better. But Jesus was telling His disciples that Lazarus was already dead. The New Testament uses the word "*sleep*" to refer to the death of the believer's body. Our soul does not sleep. There is no such thing as "Soul Sleep." Don't miss this: we immediately enter Christ's presence upon our death (2 Corinthians 5:8).

How could Jesus be glad that He was not there? Didn't Jesus love Lazarus, Martha, and Mary? The disciples must have discussed such things during their journey. They were growing in their understanding of Jesus, but they had much to learn. Jesus would use the death of Lazarus as a powerful tool to teach and encourage His disciples. But He left them in suspense until He was ready to act in a way that they would never forget.

Can you relate to the disciples? You think God is making things clearer when suddenly He throws you a curveball. You try to understand how everything works together, but you are left with unresolved tension within your heart. You find yourself forced to tackle your dilemma directly. Instead of leading you around danger, He walks you right into the heart of it. If you can hear the voice of Jesus shouting, "*Let us go!*" do not fear. Don't try to figure everything out. Follow His lead and watch Him work.

Read: Open your Bible and read John 14:5.

Reflect: Prayerfully consider the following: Do my questions about God's plans for my life prevent me from following His Word?

Respond: As a result of these truths, what might need to change in my attitude, beliefs, and actions? What steps do I need to take outwardly?

Grieving

"Now when Jesus came, he found that Lazarus had already been in the tomb four days. Bethany was near Jerusalem, about two miles off, and many of the Jews had come to Martha and Mary to console them concerning their brother. So when Martha heard that Jesus was coming, she went and met him, but Mary remained seated in the house" (John 11:17-20).

People respond differently to the death of a loved one. Some prefer to talk through the pain with family and friends while others prefer to get away to a quiet place and spend time alone. They separate themselves from the crowds to allow for private reflection. And whatever the preference, grieving is always a process that takes time. It is more than an event.

By the time Jesus arrived, Martha and Mary had been grieving for several days. Their brother Lazarus was dead. A large group of people were already present to minister to the family. After being four days in the tomb, all hope was lost for Lazarus. Jesus was clearly too late to save him. Consider these next two points: God is always on time. He is never late.

Martha and Mary were both awaiting His arrival. They may have wrestled personally with His extended delay. As each day passed, the reality of death sank further into their soul. They must have thought, "What will our life be like without Lazarus? Who will replace his love and care for our family? How will we make it without him?" During their time of grief, these questions must have added additional tears and heartache. Martha immediately left to meet with Jesus as He was entering their town. She was ready to connect with her friend. Mary remained seated in the house. Maybe she was too tired to travel. Perhaps she preferred to stay close to her consolers. Maybe she decided to pray until Jesus arrived at the home.

When you find yourself struggling to find hope, where do you go for answers? Do you expect Jesus to show up when life hurts you the most? If you are grieving over the death of a loved one or a friend, it may still hurt when you think about how much they meant to you. You may find yourself reflecting on the memories of their presence. If so, it can be good to cry and share your grief with others. But don't forget to share your pain with God as well. He understands, and He cares. Let God grieve with you.

Read: Open your Bible and read 2 Corinthians 1:3.

Reflect: Prayerfully consider the following: Am I sharing with God those moments that hurt me the most? Do I let Him grieve with me?

Respond: As a result of these truths, what might need to change in my attitude, beliefs, and actions? What steps do I need to take outwardly?

I AM the Resurrection and the Life

"Martha said to Jesus, 'Lord, if you had been here, my brother would not have died. But even now I know that whatever you ask from God, God will give you.' Jesus said to her, 'Your brother will rise again.' Martha said to him, 'I know that he will rise again in the resurrection on the last day.' Jesus said to her, 'I am the resurrection and the life. Whoever believes in me, though he die, yet shall he live, and everyone who lives and believes in me shall never die. Do you believe this?' She said to him, 'Yes, Lord; I believe that you are the Christ, the Son of God, who is coming into the world' " (John 11:21-27).

As a culture, we are fascinated with the future. Movies do their best to show us how we may one day dress and function in society. Car shows provide a sneak peek as to what cars will look like in twenty years. Top innovative companies share a small portfolio of what new gadgets we can expect. Martha's future was deeply troubled by Jesus' absence. If there was any hope for Lazarus while he was sick, Martha believed it rested on Jesus. She believed in the power of His presence. She believed that God would heal her brother. Martha was a living witness of Jesus' power.

As she shared her sorrow with Jesus, Martha arrived at a powerful conclusion: *"But even now I know that whatever you ask from God, God will give you."* Her growing faith believed that Jesus was able to raise her brother from the dead. Jesus is the resurrection and the life. Today, He can raise the dead. Today, He can change lives. Today, He is the hope and the encouragement that we need to find real life. God's power for your life right now is not limited by the events of your past. His power is not limited by distance or time or circumstances. God will not be taken by surprise by what the future brings. He is fully capable to rule in the present to accomplish His perfect will. Remember, God created the future.

Jesus promises eternal life to all who believe in Him. That means that although our body may eventually perish, our spirit will live forever. You may already believe in Jesus' power to give eternal life, but do you believe in His power to change your circumstances today? Do you believe He can radically turn things around? Today, He can give life to what was once without life and without hope. Today, He is ready to change your life.

Read: Open your Bible and read Matthew 16:16.

Reflect: Prayerfully consider the following: What have you been praying for God to resurrect in your life? Believe that Jesus has the power to do it.

Respond: As a result of these truths, what might need to change in my attitude, beliefs, and actions? What steps do I need to take outwardly?

He's Calling for You

"When she had said this, she went and called her sister Mary, saying in private, 'The Teacher is here and is calling for you.' And when she heard it, she rose quickly and went to him. Now Jesus had not yet come into the village, but was still in the place where Martha had met him. When the Jews who were with her in the house, consoling her, saw Mary rise quickly and go out, they followed her, supposing that she was going to the tomb to weep there" (John 11:28-31).

Junk mail is an everyday reality wherever mailboxes are found. We scan our mail to see if there's anything important mixed in with the stack of flyers, special offers, political advertising, and ads for new restaurants. When we receive a personal invitation it is very powerful. It gets our attention. There is something about it that makes us take action.

When Jesus first approached Bethany, Mary remained seated in her home. But now Martha was coming to deliver a private invitation to Mary. Jesus wanted to see her. He was personally calling for Mary and wanted to spend time talking with His friend. This personal invitation sent Mary scurrying out the door to find Jesus. It was time for Mary to take action. The question, "Where is God when I need Him?" was being answered. Martha was basically saying, "Immanuel, God is with us. God is here! Everything will work out. Jesus wants to be a part of our lives. God has not forgotten us. He wants to be personally involved because He cares."

Does it scare you to know that God wants to be actively involved in every part of your life? He wants to get up and dance when you achieve personal milestones, give your family special memories, and celebrate another birthday. God wants to draw near when tragedy strikes those whom you love. He is present to give you courage when fear grips your heart. He is ready to provide strength and comfort when you are at your weakest.

God has invited you to become a part of His spiritual family. His invitation is direct and personal. God wants you to know that there is a specific purpose for you to fulfill. When you accept His invitation, you accept His mission and His provision for your adventure. The Master is calling for you. If you hear His voice, it's time to get up and take action.

Read: Open your Bible and read John 13:13.

Reflect: Prayerfully consider the following: Am I responding to Jesus' call for my life? Am I allowing Him to give me courage and strength?

Respond: As a result of these truths, what might need to change in my attitude, beliefs, and actions? What steps do I need to take outwardly?

137

Deeply Moved

"Now when Mary came to where Jesus was and saw him, she fell at his feet, saying to him, 'Lord, if you had been here, my brother would not have died.' When Jesus saw her weeping, and the Jews who had come with her also weeping, he was deeply moved in his spirit and greatly troubled. And he said, 'Where have you laid him?' They said to him, 'Lord, come and see.' Jesus wept. So the Jews said, 'See how he loved him!' But some of them said, 'Could not he who opened the eyes of the blind man also have kept this man from dying?' "
(John 11:32-37).

There are songs that have the ability to shake our soul. These songs are masterfully produced and delivered with great skill and passion. There are events that move us at our very core. They awaken deep emotions and connect with what we believe and highly value. These emotional tsunamis arrive without warning and overwhelm us with their tremendous intensity.

It is hard to see people suffer. It is even more difficult when the ones who are suffering are your friends. When they hurt, you hurt. Such was the case with Jesus and Mary. Mary immediately fell at the feet of Jesus and started weeping. It must have been soul shattering for Jesus to hear everyone around Him weeping. It must have broken His heart to see His friend Mary deeply troubled in her soul and shedding her tears on His feet.

Doubtless Mary and Martha had often prayed and told one other, "If only the Lord were here!" "If only you had been here, Lord!" When Mary repeated those words to Jesus, He was deeply moved by the sorrow of His friends. Reflecting on their sadness and on the consequences of sin (death), Jesus wept. He too shared their feelings of grief and personal loss.

The crowd was weeping loudly as if all hope was lost. But in a matter of moments they would discover that all hope was not lost! We are not to weep and sorrow as pagans who have no hope. The scriptures reveal the reality of the resurrection. Jesus is the Living Hope. Jesus is the Resurrection and the Life, and for this reason alone, we can grieve with tears of gladness. The resurrection is guaranteed for all who believe. Connect with those who are suffering. Let them cry on your shoulder. Point them to Jesus. Share with them the hope that He makes available.

Read: Open your Bible and read Philippians 3:10.

Reflect: Prayerfully consider the following: How can the Lord use my personal suffering to encourage and comfort others this week?

Respond: As a result of these truths, what might need to change in my attitude, beliefs, and actions? What steps do I need to take outwardly?

Take Away the Stone

"Then Jesus, deeply moved again, came to the tomb. It was a cave, and a stone lay against it. Jesus said, 'Take away the stone.' Martha, the sister of the dead man, said to him, 'Lord, by this time there will be an odor, for he has been dead four days.' Jesus said to her, 'Did I not tell you that if you believed you would see the glory of God?' So they took away the stone" (John 11:38-41).

Moving out of your home is an adventure. It's wonderful when friends arrive to help carry appliances and large items of furniture that are too big for you to handle by yourself. But there are certain things that no one else can do but you: organizing important papers, working through random items to sort, and gathering precious belongings to carefully pack. As much as your friends might wish to help, those tasks are yours alone.

When Jesus arrived at the cave where Lazarus was buried, He found a large stone covering the opening. Jesus gave a simple, but surprising command: *"Take away the stone."* Martha interrupted right away. Maybe Jesus was not aware of how long Lazarus was in the tomb. Maybe He did not realize that Lazarus' body was already starting to decompose and smell. Jesus was all too aware of those things. But He also knew something Martha didn't.

Jesus reminded Martha of His promise: she would see God's glory if she believed in Jesus. This is still true today. There are areas of our lives with the smell of death and decay all around them. We think it is much too late for a miracle to take place. We abandon hope and resign ourselves to the situation. We refuse to remove the large stone. We refuse to make any changes. If we are honest, we don't want Jesus to see what's inside.

The stone represents the difference between hope and hopelessness, it separated life and death. One side reflected the past, while the other represented the present and the future. Is there something in your life today that you keep hidden behind a large stone? Is it something from your past that troubles you? Is there a loss you are presently grieving? Is there something else troubling you that is too painful to discuss openly? If there are large stones in your life, only you can choose to remove them. You have to let God inside to start His perfect work of restoration. Don't live in this pain any longer. Obey Jesus' voice as He says, *"Take away the stone!"*

Read: Open your Bible and read James 5:16.

Reflect: Prayerfully consider the following: What large stones have I kept away from God? Who can I trust to bear this burden with me?

Respond: As a result of these truths, what might need to change in my attitude, beliefs, and actions? What steps do I need to take outwardly?

Come Out

"And Jesus lifted up his eyes and said, 'Father, I thank you that you have heard me. I knew that you always hear me, but I said this on account of the people standing around, that they may believe that you sent me.' When he had said these things, he cried out with a loud voice, 'Lazarus, come out.' The man who had died came out, his hands and feet bound with linen strips, and his face wrapped with a cloth. Jesus said to them, 'Unbind him, and let him go' "
(John 11:41-44).

After many months of waiting, the show is ready to begin. The audience is sitting on the edge of their seats. The ambiance is electrifying. You can hear the anticipation throughout the audience; the expectations are high. Suddenly, the lights are dimmed, and silence fills the room. The lead actor comes out to center stage, and the applause begins to thunder.

Before He took one step towards Bethany, Jesus knew how the show would begin and end. He needed to demonstrate His deity in a different way to encourage and strengthen His disciples in their still growing faith. Jesus was ready to reveal Himself as God through one of the most powerful miracles ever recorded—the resurrection.

Jesus gave thanks to the Father and called out Lazarus with a loud voice. The result was astonishing. The man Lazarus came out. The one who was dead and buried was now alive, walking and speaking. The one whose memory brought great sorrow and pain was now delivering immeasurable joy and hope. This miracle was so much more than the people expected. It was far greater than anything they had ever experienced or imagined.

In the same way that Jesus called Lazarus out of the tomb, He calls you to *"come out"* of the tomb. Jesus gave life to Lazarus while he was dead. When you accepted Christ as Savior, Jesus gave you life while you were spiritually dead. Jesus gave you His Spirit. Live in the power of the Spirit!

Think about these last few weeks: have you been running back to the tomb? Are you going back to your "old ways" of thinking and living? Listen closely, its time to *"come out"* for good. Leave the life you once lived buried in the tomb. This is where it belongs. *"Come out"* and find life!

Read: Open your Bible and read Philippians 1:21.

Reflect: Prayerfully consider the following: Am I running back to the tomb of my past? What is keeping me there? What am I so afraid of?

Respond: As a result of these truths, what might need to change in my attitude, beliefs, and actions? What steps do I need to take outwardly?

Choices

"Many of the Jews therefore, who had come with Mary and had seen what he did, believed in him, but some of them went to the Pharisees and told them what Jesus had done. So the chief priests and the Pharisees gathered the council and said, 'What are we to do? For this man performs many signs. If we let him go on like this, everyone will believe in him, and the Romans will come and take away both our place and our nation' " (John 11:45-48).

The waiter extends the menu over your right shoulder and smiles. He knows your taste will be delighted with any entrée. The biggest challenge you have is choosing what to order. They all look so good. You can't select multiple entrees. You cannot afford multiple choices. Only one.

The resurrection of Lazarus was the peak of Jesus' ministry. It would be a story found on the lips of many within the reach of Jewish society. How can a man who is dead come back to life? This question would no longer be a mystery. Even small children would understand this great story.

The religious leaders panicked. If they were passive in their dealings with Jesus, everything would now change. If Jesus had the power to raise the dead, imagine what else He could do? They could not deny His power. There were too many witnesses who observed first-hand the signs and wonders He performed. These miracles could not be kept a secret.

You have to make some important choices about your faith: will your faith be real or will it be a show; will you choose to let your life serve as an instrument for God's glory; will you allow the evidence of God's power to flow through every part of your day; will you deliberately elevate Jesus beyond yourself so that people worship God rather than you? God wants to use your life in an amazing way, but He is the One who wants the glory.

You also have the choice to live your life in such a way that others applaud your skills, accomplishments, and talents without you pointing them back to the Savior. This is when you try to minimize the person of Jesus by removing His voice from your daily routine. You realize that the more He shines, the less you shine. These choices have everlasting consequences for you and others. You can't love what this life has to offer and follow Jesus.

Read: Open your Bible and read Psalm 71:8.

Reflect: Prayerfully consider the following: Are my lips filled with giving God glory? Which of the choices above is a reality in my life today?

Respond: As a result of these truths, what might need to change in my attitude, beliefs, and actions? What steps do I need to take outwardly?

One for All

"But one of them, Caiaphas, who was high priest that year, said to them, 'You know nothing at all. Nor do you understand that it is better for you that one man should die for the people, not that the whole nation should perish.' He did not say this of his own accord, but being high priest that year he prophesied that Jesus would die for the nation, and not for the nation only, but also to gather into one the children of God who are scattered abroad. So from that day on they made plans to put him to death" (John 11:49-53).

Superheroes captivate the depths of our imagination. We read about them in comic books and watch their adventures evolve at the movie theatre. An ofter repeated theme is the willingness of each individual superhero to sacrifice their own lives in order to to save the lives of many people. This is more than a theme; it is the key job description of a superhero.

Jesus is more than a superhero. He is God in the flesh. Jesus is the full expression of the Father. When you see Jesus, you see the Father. John reminds us, *"And the Word became flesh and dwelt among us, and we have seen his glory, glory as of the only Son from the Father, full of grace and truth"* (John 1:14). Jesus gave up the glory of heaven to save all of humanity. He humbled Himself and lived among us as a mere man. We were able to hear His voice and shake His hand. God became man to save us from our sins.

Unknowingly, Caiaphas, the High Priest, would predict Jesus' purpose for dying—to save the people. Jesus' death on the cross would replace the penalty for our sins. Paul writes, *"For our sake he made him to be sin who knew no sin, so that in him we might become the righteousness of God"* (2 Corinthians 5:21). Believing in Jesus' perfect work on the cross and the resurrection would justify all people and bring them together in Christ.

Caiaphas and the religious leaders tried stopping Jesus' revolution from taking over Jerusalem and causing their nation's downfall. What happened instead was nothing short of a spiritual revolution. Peter writes, *"He himself bore our sins in his body on the tree, that we might die to sin and live to righteousness. By his wounds you have been healed"* (1 Peter 2:24). Now you have a new purpose for living. Live as a superhero by loving God and serving others. Die to sin every day and do what is right in every decision.

Read: Open your Bible and read 2 Corinthians 10:5.

Reflect: Prayerfully consider the following: Am I proactively loving God and serving others? What decisions test my character the most?

Respond: As a result of these truths, what might need to change in my attitude, beliefs, and actions? What steps do I need to take outwardly?

Purify Yourself

"Jesus therefore no longer walked openly among the Jews, but went from there to the region near the wilderness, to a town called Ephraim, and there he stayed with the disciples. Now the Passover of the Jews was at hand, and many went up from the country to Jerusalem before the Passover to purify themselves. They were looking for Jesus and saying to one another as they stood in the temple, 'What do you think? That he will not come to the feast at all?' Now the chief priests and the Pharisees had given orders that if anyone knew where he was, he should let them know, so that they might arrest him" (John 11:54-57).

Taking time to reflect on major national events is very important. Some of these events remind us of our strengths as a nation while others remind us of our unspoken vulnerabilities. They serve as key historical lessons and serve to remind us of our personal responsibility to make a difference.

The Passover is a major national event for Israel. All Jews participate in this great celebration. This feast serves to remind the Jews of God's mighty deliverance of their people from the Egyptians. It is a celebration that represents freedom from national bondage. It is a time for teaching, for remembering, and for purification on a personal and national level.

Jesus and His disciples separated themselves from the crowds to spend time together before the Passover. It was a time of reflection, teaching, and prayer. The Jews were waiting for Jesus to arrive to have him arrested and unlawfully condemned to death. How can such evil take place during a time of personal and national holiness? This serves as an ugly reminder of our capacity to sin when we live according to our flesh. Stay pure!

It is customary for Jews to purify themselves before the Passover. The preparation is not an event, but a process. It involves a variety of rituals, prayers, washings, and offerings. The process carries rich symbolism and serves to help the people remember the true meaning behind the Passover.

What do you do to help you remember the meaning of Christ's sacrificial death on the cross? Make sure where you go matches with what you do. Yes, going to church is great. But, don't forget to read your Bible and spend an extended time in private prayer. Don't forget to purify yourself!

Read: Open your Bible and read Isaiah 53:4.

Reflect: Prayerfully consider the following: How does it make you feel to know that Jesus was mistreated, afflicted, and killed for your sins?

Respond: As a result of these truths, what might need to change in my attitude, beliefs, and actions? What steps do I need to take outwardly?

Precious Scents

"Six days before the Passover, Jesus therefore came to Bethany, where Lazarus was, whom Jesus had raised from the dead. So they gave a dinner for him there. Martha served, and Lazarus was one of those reclining with him at table. Mary therefore took a pound of expensive ointment made from pure nard, and anointed the feet of Jesus and wiped his feet with her hair. The house was filled with the fragrance of the perfume" (John 12:1-3).

Preparing a special dinner for a dear friend is a real honor. You bring out the best china, prepare a delicious meal, and create a warm environment for them to enjoy. It goes far beyond what you normally do for an evening; your guest is well worth the time and the investment of your resources.

Jesus was given a special dinner when He returned to Bethany with His disciples. This certainly brought a smile to Jesus' face. It must have been good for the disciples to laugh and talk with their friends. They shared many experiences together. They may have talked about their recent retreat with Jesus and how it refreshed their spirits. It was a great night.

Mary did something unexpected that changed the mood of the party. Mark tells us that Mary broke a bottle of fragrant oil and poured it on Jesus' head as He sat down. Next, Mary rubbed the oil on Jesus' feet and wiped His feet with her hair. It was customary to rub the head of your guest with oil, but not their feet. Mary was going beyond the call of duty, but why?

To say that Mary was performing an act of service is an understatement. Mary was performing an act of worship. She was illustrating her love and commitment to her Lord and Savior. The bottle she used represented an entire year's worth of wages for a laborer. Her commitment was real. Mary paid a high price to worship her Lord and demonstrate her devotion.

Can the same be said about you? Do you hold back when you worship God? God wants you to express your love for Him without reservations. Are you worshiping God in spirit and in truth? God is not looking for a show, He is searching for broken hearts. There was a personal cost and a generous offering connected with her worship. Mary was declaring that Jesus is well worth your sacrifice. Nothing is too great to give to Jesus.

Read: Open your Bible and read Romans 12:1-2.

Reflect: Prayerfully consider the following: Am I regularly making personal sacrifices to demonstrate my love and worship to the Lord?

Respond: As a result of these truths, what might need to change in my attitude, beliefs, and actions? What steps do I need to take outwardly?

Prepare

"But Judas Iscariot, one of his disciples (he who was about to betray him), said, 'Why was this ointment not sold for three hundred denarii and given to the poor?' He said this, not because he cared about the poor, but because he was a thief, and having charge of the moneybag he used to help himself to what was put into it. Jesus said, 'Leave her alone, so that she may keep it for the day of my burial. For the poor you always have with you, but you do not always have me' " (John 12:4-8).

We see these crooked characters on the evening news: they present themselves as defenders of the weak and voices for the poor. In reality, they are nothing more than creative thieves with a new sales pitch. These individuals don't care about the poor and they deceive the weak. They are driven by pride and unyielding greed. Stay far away from them at all costs.

Not all of Jesus' disciples were pursuing Him for the right reasons. Judas Iscariot was pursuing Jesus for personal gain. Without anyone knowing, Judas was helping himself to a steady revenue stream. He was exploiting the poor to make himself rich. And when his financial plan was threatened, Judas could not remain silent. He quoted the value of Mary's sacrifice without hesitation and demanded an answer to resolve his tension.

If there was silence in the room when Mary wiped Jesus' feet with her hair, there was an extended silence when Judas asked his abrupt question. Jesus broke the tension with a tough reality—he was going to die very soon. The cross was approaching. Mary was essentially preparing Jesus for burial. The poor would always be with them, but Jesus would not. She was making the most of the opportunity to worship and serve her Savior.

Your greatest opportunities for spiritual maturity will often be found in the way you prepare for important events rather than in the event itself. The process of preparation will shape your character. The events simply highlight the preparation. The day for Jesus' death was not something anyone wanted to use as a conversation starter. They knew that the time was near. It was time for their commitment to grow even more, and Mary grew first. Her act of extraordinary loyalty and worship served to accentuate the importance of personal preparation for what was ahead.

Read: Open your Bible and read Ephesians 2:10.

Reflect: Prayerfully consider the following: Growing spiritually means planning to grow. Am I following a spiritual growth plan to grow my faith?

Respond: As a result of these truths, what might need to change in my attitude, beliefs, and actions? What steps do I need to take outwardly?

Dead Man Walking

"When the large crowd of the Jews learned that Jesus was there, they came, not only on account of him but also to see Lazarus, whom he had raised from the dead. So the chief priests made plans to put Lazarus to death as well, because on account of him many of the Jews were going away and believing in Jesus"
(John 12:9-11).

When you take your family to see a popular parade, you can count on large crowds and plenty of excitement. Since the parade comes through the main artery of the city, people stand on the sidewalk for a better view. When the sponsor float appears, everyone wants to get closer and take pictures. It's a gorgeous work of art, and a beautiful creation to behold.

Word got out regarding Jesus' visit to Bethany. Jesus and Lazarus were creating great anticipation among the people. The crowds were forming into something more than any parade could match. They came out to see life transformation rather than moving floats. This beauty was even more precious to behold. It was much more than amazing. It was glorious.

The power of a transformed life draws a crowd. It forces people to look at their own lives and ask, "Can God change me too? Is God able to transform my circumstances? Can God bring hope to my hopelessness?" Because of the incredible transformation in the life of Lazarus, many believed in Jesus. Lazarus was a living example of God's unlimited power.

Not only did the religious leaders want to kill Jesus, they added Lazarus to their list of death. The witness of Lazarus was a huge threat to their political and national stability. Lazarus' life shouted the obvious—Jesus is the Messiah! Even if they killed Jesus, Lazarus would have an enormous impact of the continuation of this new faith. He had to be silenced!

This is exactly what the enemy tries to accomplish in your life today. He does everything within His power to stop your witness for Jesus. He makes plans to discourage you, uses other people to ridicule your faith, and intentionally leads you into hidden traps. Why? He understands how your story can transform others. He wants to stop this at any cost. Refuse to give in. Let people hear and see the change. Let them see the dead walk.

Read: Open your Bible and read 1 Corinthians 2:9.

Reflect: Prayerfully consider the following: Have I imagined recently what God might do through my testimony? Have I given Him a chance?

Respond: As a result of these truths, what might need to change in my attitude, beliefs, and actions? What steps do I need to take outwardly?

The King of Israel

"The next day the large crowd that had come to the feast heard that Jesus was coming to Jerusalem. So they took branches of palm trees and went out to meet him, crying out, 'Hosanna! Blessed is he who comes in the name of the Lord, even the King of Israel!' And Jesus found a young donkey and sat on it, just as it is written, 'Fear not, daughter of Zion; behold, your king is coming, sitting on a donkey's colt!' " (John 12:12-15).

Teaching children how to give honor to others can be challenging and entertaining. Looking at people in the eyes when you speak, preferring others before yourself, and respecting others does not come naturally to children. Frankly, it doesn't come naturally to many adults, either. Honoring those to whom honor is due is an important life skill to learn.

Word continued to spread regarding Jesus' trip to Jerusalem. Many had gathered to see and give honor to the man who raised the dead. What happened next was a fulfillment of prophecy: *"Blessed is he who comes in the name of the Lord! We bless you from the house of the Lord" (Psalm 118:26).* Jesus was bringing together what the Jews had prayed and hoped for all this time—their Messiah and Salvation. Rest and peace for Israel was present.

"Rejoice greatly, O daughter of Zion! Shout aloud, O daughter of Jerusalem! Behold, your king is coming to you; righteous and having salvation is he, humble and mounted on a donkey, on a colt, the foal of a donkey" (Zechariah 9:9).

Daughter of Zion represents the Jews. *Hosanna* means, "give salvation now" and "save now, we pray you." The people recognized Jesus as the Messiah, the Son of God and the King of Israel. At the very center of their praise was a song of salvation and hope. The Messiah was understood to bring salvation along with His presence. The people were ready to be released from Roman rule. They were ready for their King to rule and lead Israel.

What the people neglected to understand was that the Messiah would first come to destroy the works of darkness. Jesus fulfilled His prophecy by bringing salvation, rest, and peace through His death on the cross. This is where true freedom is found. Jesus is the one who can release us from our spiritual oppression. He has conquered death. He is the King of Israel.

Read: Open your Bible and read Psalm 113-118.

Reflect: Prayerfully consider the following: How often do I celebrate what Jesus has conquered in my life? Am I a praise-filled believer?

Respond: As a result of these truths, what might need to change in my attitude, beliefs, and actions? What steps do I need to take outwardly?

Winning and Losing

"His disciples did not understand these things at first, but when Jesus was glorified, then they remembered that these things had been written about him and had been done to him. The crowd that had been with him when he called Lazarus out of the tomb and raised him from the dead continued to bear witness. The reason why the crowd went to meet him was that they heard he had done this sign. So the Pharisees said to one another, 'You see that you are gaining nothing. Look, the world has gone after him' " (John 12:16-19).

Competition can help elevate an athlete to the next level. It forces them to work with their team rather than perform as a soloist. It creates a positive interdependency. Weaknesses are worked through collectively, and strengths are leveraged for the benefit of the team. Everyone celebrates the big wins and encourages one another during those difficult losses.

At this time in history, Jesus and His disciples were winning the hearts of the people. There was plenty of excitement in the air and hope for all to receive. The momentum was multiplying, and the Pharisees were finding themselves losing their share of respect and popularity. Jesus was evolving into a national celebrity. The Pharisees were in big trouble. Jesus' ministry was an unstoppable force. It transcended ethnic and cultural barriers.

While the Pharisees were trying to figure out what to do, the disciples were trying to figure out what was going on. Maybe Jesus did not share the details of these unfolding events during their recent retreat. Surely He neglected to share this during dinner with His friends. This was not a deal breaker for this team. The disciples continued to follow and serve Jesus. They trusted Jesus even when they could not totally understand His ways.

Does this sound all too familiar? Do you find yourself today trying to figure out what God is doing around you? You have been praying for God to change lives and change your circumstances. Your circumstances have become more complex, but more lives are being changed in the process. You suffer personal loss, but produce spiritual fruit. It seems that the more you lose personally the more you gain spiritually. Have you ever wondered if this strategy is part of God's plan for your life? Ask, "Am I winning *and* losing? Is this what God desires in order for His spiritual team to win big?"

Read: Open your Bible and read Philippians 3:7-8.

Reflect: Prayerfully consider the following: Am I willing to make sacrifices and experience personal loss in order for lives to be changed?

Respond: As a result of these truths, what might need to change in my attitude, beliefs, and actions? What steps do I need to take outwardly?

Spiritual Dividends

"Now among those who went up to worship at the feast were some Greeks. So these came to Philip, who was from Bethsaida in Galilee, and asked him, 'Sir, we wish to see Jesus.' Philip went and told Andrew; Andrew and Philip went and told Jesus. And Jesus answered them, 'The hour has come for the Son of Man to be glorified. Truly, truly, I say to you, unless a grain of wheat falls into the earth and dies, it remains alone; but if it dies, it bears much fruit. Whoever loves his life loses it, and whoever hates his life in this world will keep it for eternal life. If anyone serves me, he must follow me; and where I am, there will my servant be also. If anyone serves me, the Father will honor him' " (John 12:20-26).

"What was the return on your investment?" is a popular question among investors. They love to share stories of how their small investments produced big returns. Your investments drive your results. The greater the investment, the greater the potential for high returns or heavy losses. Where and when you make your investments is also important. Jesus points out to His disciples that seeds only produce fruit when they die. There was only one-way for Jesus to save sinners: He had to die. He had to shed His blood to pay for your sins, losing His life for you to gain eternal life. His personal loss was your eternal gain. His death produced life.

This reflects an unusual equation of spiritual life: losing equals finding. When you lose your life you actually find true life. In other words, when you pursue God's purposes over your own, you find your true purpose for living. Deliberately submitting every area of your life to the Lord Jesus brings freedom, purpose, and eternal rewards. As you follow Jesus, make it a priority to love His people and serve His church. God honors those who serve His Son. Imagine what God could do through your life if you lived in light of eternity. Imagine the spiritual dividends that would remain in your spiritual bank account. Are you ready to start investing in eternity?

Your spiritual investments must be intentional. Establish spiritual priorities and plan your life around them; not doing so allows non-spiritual priorities to control your schedule. Spiritual living is what lasts forever. The alternative is to settle for living in order to gain what this world has to offer. Talk about a low expectation for living! God has so much more planned for your life to produce. Live to produce spiritual dividends.

Read: Open your Bible and read Philippians 2:5-8.

Reflect: Prayerfully consider the following: Am I trying to lose my life for God each day or am I living to experience the pleasures of this world?

Respond: As a result of these truths, what might need to change in my attitude, beliefs, and actions? What steps do I need to take outwardly?

Soul Trouble

"Now is my soul troubled. And what shall I say? 'Father, save me from this hour'? But for this purpose I have come to this hour. Father, glorify your name.' Then a voice came from heaven: 'I have glorified it, and I will glorify it again.' The crowd that stood there and heard it said that it had thundered. Others said, 'An angel has spoken to him.' Jesus answered, 'This voice has come for your sake, not mine. Now is the judgment of this world; now will the ruler of this world be cast out. And I, when I am lifted up from the earth, will draw all people to myself.' He said this to show by what kind of death he was going to die" (John 12:27-33).

Passing a kidney stone can be unbelievably agonizing. In severe cases, the pain can trigger uncontrollable shaking and even keep patients from walking or getting dressed without help. Unpredictable waves of horrible pain continue for as long as it takes for the stone to pass. The experience is physically and emotionally exhausting. It troubles both body and soul.

As Jesus considered the reality of His suffering, the pain was difficult to process. His violent death was one week away, and He was already feeling the distress of that terrible hour. Yet any dread He may have felt for His coming violent death was outweighed by His singular purpose. He was determined to glorify God's name at all costs. Are you determined also?

The power, penalty, and presence of death had to be defeated. The fight was inevitable. Jesus would finish His work. Paul later wrote, *"When the perishable puts on the imperishable, and the mortal puts on immortality, then shall come to pass the saying that is written: 'Death is swallowed up in victory. O death, where is your victory? O death, where is your sting?' The sting of death is sin, and the power of sin is the law. But thanks be to God, who gives us the victory through our Lord Jesus Christ"* (1 Corinthians 15:54-47).

There are events and situations that may be very difficult for you to walk through alone. Moving far outside your preferences and comfort zones may cause your stomach to churn and create major stress. Yet you can be sure of one thing: God will be with you. God will give you the strength, the wisdom and the character to overcome the troubles of life. In every challenge, seek to glorify His name. Soul trouble is good trouble. It helps you to depend more on God and wait for His strength.

Read: Open your Bible and read Psalm 37:7.

Reflect: Prayerfully consider the following: What can I courageously do to honor God and make His name known through my current challenges?

Respond: As a result of these truths, what might need to change in my attitude, beliefs, and actions? What steps do I need to take outwardly?

You Have the Light

"So the crowd answered him, 'We have heard from the Law that the Christ remains forever. How can you say that the Son of Man must be lifted up? Who is this Son of Man?' So Jesus said to them, 'The light is among you for a little while longer. Walk while you have the light, lest darkness overtake you. The one who walks in the darkness does not know where he is going. While you have the light, believe in the light, that you may become sons of light' " (John 12:34-36).

Camping trips and flashlights have at least one thing in common: Neither lasts forever. When the sun is gone and the light from the moon is nowhere to be found, flashlights become your friend. But, they have a limit as to how long they can be used. It's an uncomfortable thing when a camping trip outlasts the batteries in your flashlight. When you have light to see by, you make the most of it. When you don't have it, you can't see.

Jesus is the Light of the World. As this light was preparing to leave the earth, unbelief still permeated His critics. When you are used to living your life in darkness, outside of God's will, the light seems irrelevant! Jesus' challenge to them was direct, *"Walk while you have the light."* He was returning to His major theme: He is the Messiah, the Son of God, and the Light of the World. But His time on the earth would soon come to an end.

You can only reject the light for so long. There comes a time when God no longer pursues those who want to continue their life of sin, leaving them alone in the darkness they have chosen. After a while, this darkness will completely overwhelm you. It will knock you out and control your life. It will drive your thinking, control your words and lead your actions. If you choose to live in darkness, you will have no purposeful direction.

The challenge before us today is to wholeheartedly believe in Jesus, the Light of Life. Jesus wants you to believe in Him right now. He wants you to trust Him to lead your life in the right direction. If you have rejected Jesus, know this: His light will not always be available. The opportunity for you to know God through placing your faith in Jesus Christ has a time limit. Now is your time to believe in Jesus. Now is the time to accept Him. The Bible says, *"And without faith it is impossible to please him, for whoever would draw near to God must believe that he exists and that he rewards those who seek him"* (Hebrews 11:6). You have the light. Believe in the light.

Read: Open your Bible and read 1 John 1:9-10.

Reflect: Prayerfully consider the following: Is God stirring my heart today to believe in Jesus as my Savior? Am I ready to follow the light?

Respond: As a result of these truths, what might need to change in my attitude, beliefs, and actions? What steps do I need to take outwardly?

Beyond Unbelief

"When Jesus had said these things, he departed and hid himself from them. Though he had done so many signs before them, they still did not believe in him, so that the word spoken by the prophet Isaiah might be fulfilled: 'Lord, who has believed what he heard from us, and to whom has the arm of the Lord been revealed?' Therefore they could not believe. For again Isaiah said, 'He has blinded their eyes and hardened their heart, lest they see with their eyes, and understand with their heart, and turn, and I would heal them.' Isaiah said these things because he saw his glory and spoke of him" (John 12:36-41).

Though designed to be a friendly game among friends, one of the players was determined to win. When things did not work out to his advantage, harsh words and shouting rapidly followed. He became increasingly more physical. No one was smiling. Eventually a fight broke out between two friends. Those who watched asked, "How did things get this point?"

When you read through the gospels and repeatedly see rejection, hatred, and violence towards Jesus, there are questions that come to mind. At times these responses are difficult to understand. What happens when you repeatedly reject God? What happens when you say "no" to God over and over again? Does God sit back and do nothing? No. He allows you to reap what you sow. Ultimately God steps in and hardens your heart.

The Jews who rejected Jesus had moved beyond unbelief to unreasoning hatred. Their spiritual darkness was beyond rescuing. God predicted their opposition to the Son of God, and He permitted them to deteriorate in progressive unbelief. There is a personal responsibility for every individual to believe in Jesus for salvation, or to reject Him. Jesus told His critics, *"I told you that you would die in your sins, for unless you believe that I am he you will die in your sins" (John 8:24).* It was time for Jesus' critics to respond.

God always has a part in our spiritual response, and so do we. It is critically important for you to keep your heart in check with God. People walk away from God one step at a time. Whenever you decide to reject God's Word, you risk sliding down a slippery slope of no return. That "small lie" may not seem like a big deal, but it is. It might serve as the first of many unwise choices that pull your heart away from God. In everything, obey God quickly and believe in His Word. Don't go beyond unbelief.

Read: Open your Bible and read Revelation 3:8.

Reflect: Prayerfully consider the following: Since God knows my heart, how should that motivate me to believe in Him more and obey His Word?

Respond: As a result of these truths, what might need to change in my attitude, beliefs, and actions? What steps do I need to take outwardly?

Undercover Faith

"Nevertheless, many even of the authorities believed in him, but for fear of the Pharisees they did not confess it, so that they would not be put out of the synagogue; for they loved the glory that comes from man more than the glory that comes from God" (John 12:42-43).

Undercover secret agents live in a different world. This world is sneaky and mysterious. They don't publically announce their true identity, because that could cost them their lives. These agents operate in the shadows and use code names to remain anonymous. They have important missions, but only a few people know their real identities and their real assignments.

One of the challenges for those accepting Christ was the public declaration of their new faith. Confessing Jesus publically as Messiah and Son of God was no small matter. The implications would be felt at every part of Jewish life and practice. It meant loving the Law, but choosing grace. It meant submitting your life to the Lord Jesus and following His ways. It meant losing friends and family members who would reject your new faith.

There were many social consequences as well. Your position as a council member in the synagogue would be terminated. You could even be kicked out of the synagogue altogether, and labeled as a heretic. So although many of these authorities believed, their faith was weak. They believed in Jesus, but the cost of giving up the acceptance of their peers and the people was too much for them to leave behind. Is the personal cost for you too much?

There is always a personal cost when you follow Jesus. You have to decide if you will love Jesus more than you love acceptance by others. John reminds us, *"And now, little children, abide in him, so that when he appears we may have confidence and not shrink from him in shame at his coming" (1 John 2:28).* Does your position at work keep you from talking about Jesus openly? Does it involve practices that are contrary to God's Word?

If you live in fear of people rejecting you because of your faith in Jesus, your faith is weak. Knowing the King of Kings should bring you great joy and confidence. You are an ambassador for Jesus Christ. You need to please Him. Live for an audience of One. God is the One who places you in positions of influence and authority. Don't let your faith go undercover.

Read: Open your Bible and read John 2:23-25.

Reflect: Prayerfully consider the following: How can I show God today that I love Him much more than the praises of the people around me?

Respond: As a result of these truths, what might need to change in my attitude, beliefs, and actions? What steps do I need to take outwardly?

153

Perfect Representation

"And Jesus cried out and said, 'Whoever believes in me, believes not in me but in him who sent me. And whoever sees me sees him who sent me. I have come into the world as light, so that whoever believes in me may not remain in darkness' " (John 12:44-46).

A young artist was gifted beyond her years. She decided to make her own painting to honor the work of the great Picasso. The results were beautiful to behold. With her skills and resources, she was able to create a picture that represented her artistic hero. It was indeed a work of art.

God was a mystery to the Jewish people, but Jesus was the perfect representation of the Father. Since Jesus was with God from eternity past, He could reveal the Father's nature perfectly, and visibly express His character. John reminds us, *"No one has ever seen God; the only God, who is at the Father's side, he has made him known" (John 1:18).* Jesus came to make the Father known in a way that people could understand and believe.

"He is the radiance of the glory of God and the exact imprint of his nature, and he upholds the universe by the word of his power. After making purification for sins, he sat down at the right hand of the Majesty on high" (Hebrews 1:3).

When you see Jesus, you see the Father who sent Him. Paul writes, *"He is the image of the invisible God, the firstborn of all creation" (Colossians 1:15).* What we see here is nothing less than the fullness of God the Father revealed in and through the life of God the Son. It is a picture of holiness.

"As obedient children, do not be conformed to the passions of your former ignorance, but as he who called you is holy, you also be holy in all your conduct, since it is written, 'You shall be holy, for I am holy' " (I Peter 1:14-16).

God wants you to live in holiness. In Christ, you have been separated from darkness to light, from sinful to holy. As a Christian, you should no longer live in darkness. You don't need to hang out there any longer. You are now the light of this world, and you have a new mission. God's plan for your life is discovered and carried out in the light. In Christ, you are God's representative on earth. Let His character flow through your life.

Read: Open your Bible and read 2 Corinthians 7:1.

Reflect: Prayerfully consider the following: Is there any darkness in my life that I need to remove today for Christ's character to flow through?

Respond: As a result of these truths, what might need to change in my attitude, beliefs, and actions? What steps do I need to take outwardly?

Life or Judgment

*"If anyone hears my words and does not keep them, I do not judge him;
for I did not come to judge the world but to save the world. The one who
rejects me and does not receive my words has a judge; the word that
I have spoken will judge him on the last day"* (John 12:47-48).

When policemen knocked at their door, their first thoughts were negative:
"Did we break the law? Did our son get in trouble?" After a smile, the
policemen delivered gifts for their family. It was the last thing the family
expected. The officers did not come to arrest them. They came to give.

Jesus's first coming was all about giving. *"For God so loved the world, that he
gave his only Son, that whoever believes in him should not perish but have eternal
life. For God did not send his Son into the world to condemn the world, but in
order that the world might be saved through him"* (John 3:16-17). Jesus came
to bring life to those who were dead in their sins. His presence on earth
provided the only way for mankind to have direct access to the Father.

Jesus' focus was on saving people. He knew that people would reject His
message. When they rejected Him, they also rejected the Father. Jesus
told His disciples, *"The one who hears you hears me, and the one who rejects
you rejects me, and the one who rejects me rejects him who sent me"* (Luke
10:16). To reject Jesus meant to reject the Father's provision for salvation.

The Father would not take this rejection lightly. At an appointed time,
God will step in and judge those who rejected His Son. God told Moses,
*"I will raise up for them a prophet like you from among their brothers. And I will
put my words in his mouth, and he shall speak to them all that I command him.
And whoever will not listen to my words that he shall speak in my name, I myself
will require it of him"* (Deuteronomy 18:18-19). God is not playing games. His
provision is our only hope. Those who reject Jesus face God's judgment.

In Christ Jesus you don't have to worry about this particular judgment.
Paul reminds us, *"There is therefore now no condemnation for those who are in
Christ Jesus"* (Romans 8:1). You are free from the curse of the Law. Sin no
longer dominates your life. You can live confidently in your spiritual
identity. Jesus took your judgment for sin on the cross. You have life!

Read: Open your Bible and read Romans 8:1-4.

Reflect: Prayerfully consider the following: Since Jesus took my
judgment for sin, how should that motivate me to spread His message?

Respond: As a result of these truths, what might need to change in my
attitude, beliefs, and actions? What steps do I need to take outwardly?

Listen and Speak

"For I have not spoken on my own authority, but the Father who sent me has himself given me a commandment—what to say and what to speak. And I know that his commandment is eternal life. What I say, therefore, I say as the Father has told me" (John 12:49-50).

The interpreter has a difficult job on his hands. He has to communicate the content and the passion of his client's words to the audience. This is no easy task. It requires great concentration and effort. His job is to listen attentively, and speak what was said in the language of the audience.

Jesus did not dispatch Himself to earth. He was sent by the Father with clear instructions to carry out His mission. This included the content and delivery of his communication. In other words, the Father told Him both what to say and how to say it. The Father was intimately involved in leading His Son. He wants to be intimately involved in leading you, too.

Jesus submitted Himself to the will of the Father to accomplish His divine mission. He reminds us, *"Truly, truly, I say to you, the Son can do nothing of his own accord, but only what he sees the Father doing. For whatever the Father does, that the Son does likewise" (John 5:19).* Jesus observed and listened to what the Father was doing around Him. He spoke to the people and took action to obey His every word. When the Father spoke, Jesus would speak. Independent of the Father's will, Jesus' actions would be unfruitful.

Jesus said, *"When you have lifted up the Son of Man, then you will know that I am he, and that I do nothing on my own authority, but speak just as the Father taught me" (John 8:28).* What if your life mirrored Jesus' words, *"I speak just as the Father taught me"*? How would that change your conversations and modify your schedule? We often say things we regret and do things we would rather not mention. Jesus is our model for active listening. How would practicing Jesus' model in these challenging areas change this?

The Father has much to say to you, even right now. Are you listening to His voice? Are you ready to respond? Listen and speak only after hearing from your Father. Letting God take the lead in the content and the words of your conversations can be truly electrifying. First listen, and then speak.

Read: Open your Bible and read John 8:47.

Reflect: Prayerfully consider the following: Am I listening to the Father before starting my conversations? What can I do to improve this today?

Respond: As a result of these truths, what might need to change in my attitude, beliefs, and actions? What steps do I need to take outwardly?

Perspective

"Now before the Feast of the Passover, when Jesus knew that his hour had come to depart out of this world to the Father, having loved his own who were in the world, he loved them to the end. During supper, when the devil had already put it into the heart of Judas Iscariot, Simon's son, to betray him, Jesus, knowing that the Father had given all things into his hands, and that he had come from God and was going back to God, rose from supper" (John 13:1-4).

Many passengers enjoy looking through their window as the plane flies above their city. They live almost every day of their lives looking at buildings, highways, and towns from a lower viewpoint, but the plane ride gives them an opportunity to see the bigger picture. They see how the different parts of their city all interconnect, and develop. It gives them a totally new perspective. Jesus always maintained the right perspective.

Jesus lived His life in light of the bigger picture, the divine story. His disciples primarily lived for the here and now. Jesus lived for eternity. He loved His disciples to the very end of His life. He loved Judas, who would betray Him for money. This eternal perspective produced an endless love.

Jesus knew that His time on earth was coming to an abrupt end. Jesus knew who He was, where He was going, and what still needed to be done. This is critical in order for you to live your life with a divine viewpoint. Do you know your identity right now as a believer? For starters, find every phrase in the New Testament that begins with *"in Christ"* and circle it. You can't think eternally if you don't know your spiritual identity in Christ.

God has given you everything you need to live the Christian life and produce spiritual fruit. With this in mind, you can love those who hate you, and serve them freely. Maintaining a lower perspective will become an obstacle to this goal. You can't love people fully if you are limited to your own viewpoint. You have to love them through God's eyes and God's heart. He loves your enemies. He loves those who steal from you and take advantage of you. Jesus was certain about where He was going. In Christ, this confidence is yours too. One day you will be with the Lord forever. Until that day, choose to live with eternal perspective.

Read: Open your Bible and read Matthew 5:44.

Reflect: Prayerfully consider the following: How can I maintain the right perspective with those who try to take things from my family and me?

Respond: As a result of these truths, what might need to change in my attitude, beliefs, and actions? What steps do I need to take outwardly?

Servant Leadership

*"He laid aside his outer garments, and taking a towel, tied it around his waist.
Then he poured water into a basin and began to wash the disciples' feet
and to wipe them with the towel that was wrapped around him.
He came to Simon Peter, who said to him, 'Lord, do you wash my feet?'
Jesus answered him, 'What I am doing you do not understand now,
but afterward you will understand' " (John 13:4-7).*

Working as a waiter in a restaurant is a great experience. You learn how to listen well and serve people. A good waiter can anticipate the needs of their customers and, stay one step ahead of the action. When customers have complaints, good waiters go above and beyond the call of duty to make things right. They must practice servant leadership to succeed.

In Jesus' day, servants were responsible for making guests feel welcome. This involved washing their feet, serving them food and creating a comfortable environment. Although Jesus was and is God, He purposefully took on the role of a servant. He humbled Himself and shocked the disciples with His actions. Jesus left the disciples almost speechless. Servant leadership practiced in our world today would shock many.

"You know that the rulers of the Gentiles lord it over them, and their great ones exercise authority over them. It shall not be so among you. But whoever would be great among you must be your servant, and whoever would be first among you must be your slave, even as the Son of Man came not to be served but to serve, and to give his life as a ransom for many" (Matthew 20:25-28).

Jesus basically told His disciples that their level of leadership would be determined by their capacity to serve others. A great leader is a true servant of the people. The greatest leaders are recognized by the magnitude of their service. Would people categorize you as a servant leader? Would they say that your actions are self-serving? How would they describe your character? Your leadership can only be great if you serve others in love. If you have never washed the feet of another person, look for an opportunity to do so this week. It is an amazing experience. It is something that you will never forget. Great leaders are first great servers. Servant leadership is promoted through humble service to others.

Read: Open your Bible and read Matthew 20:20-28.

Reflect: Prayerfully consider the following: Am I more concerned about titles and influence than I am about serving people in their area of need?

Respond: As a result of these truths, what might need to change in my attitude, beliefs, and actions? What steps do I need to take outwardly?

Clean

"Peter said to him, 'You shall never wash my feet.' Jesus answered him, 'If I do not wash you, you have no share with me.' Simon Peter said to him, 'Lord, not my feet only but also my hands and my head!' Jesus said to him, 'The one who has bathed does not need to wash, except for his feet, but is completely clean. And you are clean, but not every one of you.' For he knew who was to betray him; that was why he said, 'Not all of you are clean' " (John 13:8-11).

Keeping a patient clean after a major surgery is very important. But while wounds are still healing, the patient's range of motion is limited. They need someone else to carefully help lift their arms and legs to clean every part of their body. A careful and thorough sponge bath of that kind can be a humbling and even embarrassing experience. You have to fully depend on the strength and care of another to make sure you remain clean.

Jesus was modeling the heart of a leader—serving others and helping them become spiritually clean. He illustrated a spiritual principle: Spiritual purity requires spiritual washing. Paul wrote to Titus, *"He [Jesus] saved us, not because of works done by us in righteousness, but according to his own mercy, by the washing of regeneration and renewal of the Holy Spirit" (Titus 3:5).* Jesus is the One who cleanses us from all of our sins with His very own blood.

In Christ, you are clean. You were spiritually transformed at the time of your salvation. As you mature in Christ, you will sin, but the frequency of your sin should decrease. And when you sin, you must confess these sins to the Lord and be washed. Since Peter was already clean, Jesus only needed to wash his feet. In Christ, you are saved and totally washed:

"But if we walk in the light, as he is in the light, we have fellowship with one another, and the blood of Jesus his Son cleanses us from all sin. If we say we have no sin, we deceive ourselves, and the truth is not in us. If we confess our sins, he is faithful and just to forgive us our sins and to cleanse us from all unrighteousness" (1 John 1:7-9).

Since you have been cleansed, live a holy life. Live in the truth. Make your fellowship with God your number one daily priority. You don't have to live in guilt over the sins of your past. You are permanently forgiven in Christ. His blood has washed away your sins forever. Live clean. Be clean.

Read: Open your Bible and read Ephesians 5:26.

Reflect: Prayerfully consider the following: What can I do to help me remember God's Word more in order to live a life of holiness?

Respond: As a result of these truths, what might need to change in my attitude, beliefs, and actions? What steps do I need to take outwardly?

A Model for Blessing

"When he had washed their feet and put on his outer garments and resumed his place, he said to them, 'Do you understand what I have done to you? You call me Teacher and Lord, and you are right, for so I am. If I then, your Lord and Teacher, have washed your feet, you also ought to wash one another's feet. For I have given you an example, that you also should do just as I have done to you. Truly, truly, I say to you, a servant is not greater than his master, nor is a messenger greater than the one who sent him. If you know these things, blessed are you if you do them'" (John 13:12-17).

Getting stuck on a difficult math problem can be terribly frustrating. It can consume a significant amount of precious time and personal effort. When someone comes along with a simple explanation and an example to follow, everything changes. Having a good example to follow is priceless. In many areas of life, good examples help us unlock enormous possibilities.

Jesus wanted to leave an unforgettable picture in the minds and hearts of His disciples. He wanted to clarify their misconceptions regarding leadership and their relationship to each other. He wanted to show them what was required for God's blessings to flow through their lives. It was a moment they would never forget, a powerful challenge that convicted their hearts and challenged their selfish thinking. Do you want God's blessings?

Can you picture yourself serving others as Jesus did? Both cultural norms and past experience may make it very difficult. Maybe you are used to a different kind of leadership: giving orders for other people to follow rather than leading people by serving them. Jesus provides a new example to follow: a radical new paradigm for His followers to implement. The model Jesus left for you is a model for blessing. In other words, this kind of leadership produces great contentment. It will produce the right results. This kind of leadership will strengthen your team, and give them a deeper appreciation for you as their leader. Don't be afraid. Just do it.

Think about the impact this kind of leadership can have with your spouse, your children, and others whom you love. Help them find rest, cleansing, and encouragement. Be the model for blessing for generations to follow.

Read: Open your Bible and read John 15:14.

Reflect: Prayerfully consider the following: Do others see me as a servant leader? How can I obey God better in this area of my life?

Respond: As a result of these truths, what might need to change in my attitude, beliefs, and actions? What steps do I need to take outwardly?

Friend or Foe

"'I am not speaking of all of you; I know whom I have chosen. But the Scripture will be fulfilled, 'He who ate my bread has lifted his heel against me.' I am telling you this now, before it takes place, that when it does take place you may believe that I am he. Truly, truly, I say to you, whoever receives the one I send receives me, and whoever receives me receives the one who sent me'" (John 13:18-20).

Have you ever watched a movie with friends who have already sat through the entire film? They sit on the edge of their seats, tempted to tell you what's next. They warn you right before the next big scene, but they know they should not spoil the ending by leaking information beforehand.

The night of Jesus' arrest, however, He knew that it was important to give His disciples advance information on the identity of His betrayer. They would later reflect back on this moment to once again confirm that Jesus was the all-knowing God. Judas had spent three years with Jesus and the disciples. He had deceived everyone in the group except Jesus. When no one was looking, Judas negotiated deals for his own benefit and took money from the mobile ministry fund. Judas was a clever deceiver.

Judas was not a true brother. He was not a good friend, either. Judas fulfilled the prophecy, *"Even my close friend in whom I trusted, who ate my bread, has lifted his heel against me"* (Psalm 41:9). Have you ever been betrayed by a good friend? Have you ever had someone lie to your face, steal your property, or sow seeds of division to create trouble with others?

Jesus knows how you feel. Just as He encouraged His disciples, He wants to encourage you. As you remain faithful to the Lord, He will bless your life. Love Him more, and serve others unconditionally. The Lord will heal the wounds of betrayal and personal tragedy. Find your strength and your hope in the Jesus Christ. Let Him encourage you through every difficulty.

You are on a mission from God. Never let the actions of others discourage you from doing what God has called you to do. Keep your hope in the Lord. Remember the great promise of Isaiah, *"Even youths grow tired and weary, and young men stumble and fall; but those who hope in the Lord will renew their strength. They will soar on wings like eagles; they will run and not grow weary, they will walk and not be faint"* (Isaiah 40:30-31, NIV).

Read: Open your Bible and read I Samuel 30:6.

Reflect: Prayerfully consider the following: Have I allowed betrayal to discourage me? How can I renew my strength in the Lord today?

Respond: As a result of these truths, what might need to change in my attitude, beliefs, and actions? What steps do I need to take outwardly?

Truth in Love

"After saying these things, Jesus was troubled in his spirit, and testified, 'Truly, truly, I say to you, one of you will betray me.' The disciples looked at one another, uncertain of whom he spoke. One of his disciples, whom Jesus loved, was reclining at table at Jesus' side, so Simon Peter motioned to him to ask Jesus of whom he was speaking. So that disciple, leaning back against Jesus, said to him, 'Lord, who is it?' Jesus answered, 'It is he to whom I will give this morsel of bread when I have dipped it' " (John 13:21-26).

In our country, it is widely accepted to tell a lie to prevent others from "getting hurt." Shielding family and friends from painful truths is sometimes seen as preferable to speaking honestly about difficult realities. In the long-term, this approach can cause more damage than any good. It is much better to speak the truth in love rather than to postpone a difficult reality.

Jesus was about to reveal a difficult truth. One of His disciples was a complete fraud. Moreover, this disciple was about to commit his greatest act of treachery that very night. This was not easy to say or to accept. Jesus was completely aware of Judas' plans to betray Him. Jesus was deeply troubled. He loved Judas. Jesus shared His life and ministry with this man.

Jesus shows us how to expose a traitor, one who is living a complete lie. Jesus did not make an embarrassing scene to point out Judas' plans. He revealed Judas' true character in truth and in love. This was very personal for Jesus. Judas was not just anyone; he was Jesus' friend. And so this revelation was not made publically. It was a private dinner meeting with the disciples. It was first revealed to John, and later to the other disciples.

When exposing a lie, always confront others in truth and in love. What you say and how you say it is very important. Only get those involved who will be directly impacted by your course of action. Always deal graciously with people, even if they respond defensively. Picture yourself in their situation and adjust your approach to the way that you would want to be treated. Paul wrote, *"Therefore, having put away falsehood, let each one of you speak the truth with his neighbor, for we are members one of another. Be angry and do not sin; do not let the sun go down on your anger"* (Ephesians 4:25-26).

Read: Open your Bible and read Romans 12:19.

Reflect: Prayerfully consider the following: Have I tried getting even with others as a result of their betrayal? How can I change this attitude?

Respond: As a result of these truths, what might need to change in my attitude, beliefs, and actions? What steps do I need to take outwardly?

Head, Heart and Hands

"So when he had dipped the morsel, he gave it to Judas, the son of Simon Iscariot. Then after he had taken the morsel, Satan entered into him. Jesus said to him, 'What you are going to do, do quickly.' Now no one at the table knew why he said this to him. Some thought that, because Judas had the moneybag, Jesus was telling him, 'Buy what we need for the feast,' or that he should give something to the poor. So, after receiving the morsel of bread, he immediately went out. And it was night" (John 13:26-30).

We all make decisions. Decision-making is a process, and no two people make decisions in exactly the same way, every time. The pattern we follow speaks to our maturity in several areas of life, including our spiritual life. How you make decisions, and what resources you use to make your decisions, can make the difference between fruitfulness and fruitlessness.

As Judas persevered in his life of deceit, his decision-making process was filtered through an appetite for evil. After consistently submitting to evil over a period of time, a person becomes insensitive to its effect on others. They also become numb to sin's effect on their own lives. As Judas climbed the tower of evil one choice at a time, the ultimate act of wickedness was growing in his heart: the choice to betray the King of Kings. John wrote, *"During supper, when the devil had already put it into the heart of Judas Iscariot, Simon's son, to betray him"* (John 13:2). Judas' wicked thinking filled his heart.

Light and darkness oppose one another. Jesus reminds us, *"I am the light of the world. Whoever follows me will not walk in darkness, but will have the light of life"* (John 8:12). You cannot simultaneously walk in the Spirit and live a lie. You can't sin regularly and experience God's power. When left unchecked, your thoughts slowly cement themselves in your heart, and eventually, those desires will show themselves in what you say and do.

You need to pay close attention to what you read, what you see, and what you hear and say. When sin plants itself within your mind, your heart begins to absorb and grow these desires. In the course of time they will turn into actions. If you have a friend who is already considering taking steps in the wrong direction, warn them of the dangers ahead. Interrupt them in truth and in love. Plead with them to turn back to the Lord.

Read: Open your Bible and read Luke 22:53.

Reflect: Prayerfully consider the following: How has God delivered me from my struggle with sin and encouraged me to live in the light?

Respond: As a result of these truths, what might need to change in my attitude, beliefs, and actions? What steps do I need to take outwardly?

A New Commandment

"When he had gone out, Jesus said, 'Now is the Son of Man glorified, and God is glorified in him. If God is glorified in him, God will also glorify him in himself, and glorify him at once. Little children, yet a little while I am with you. You will seek me, and just as I said to the Jews, so now I also say to you, 'Where I am going you cannot come.' A new commandment I give to you, that you love one another: just as I have loved you, you also are to love one another. By this all people will know that you are my disciples, if you have love for one another"
(John 13:31-35).

The seated crowd waits expectantly. They stood in line for two hours before the doors were opened. Suddenly, a well-dressed man walks out and says, "The show is about to begin." This is followed up with a few important announcements. Everyone is listening attentively. No one wants to miss a single word. Excitement immediately fills the air until the electric moment when he finally says, "Let's start the show!" When Judas left the room, it marked the beginning of the end of Jesus' earthly ministry. From this point forward, Jesus revealed Himself as the suffering Messiah, the Savior, and the Lamb of God. Jesus magnified God's name through His anguish on the road to the cross. This intensifying pain reached an all-time high the next day when He hung on the cross at Calvary to carry our sins.

Jesus finalized His teaching that night with a new commandment. The disciples needed to serve one another as humble servants. They also needed to love one another as spiritual brothers in the family of God. Jesus was about to take His illustrations to a whole new level. His sacrificial death on the cross would illustrate how they should live and serve one another. It was summarized in one simple idea: self-sacrifice.

Jesus reversed His previous method of teaching. Now instead of modeling first what He wanted to teach them, He applied His teaching before illustrating how to do it. Surely they would look back and see how He loved them. But what Jesus would do on the cross would help them understand love in a totally new way. His act of love was unprecedented. How would others define the word love as it is lived out through your life? Would they say that it is the same self-sacrificing love demonstrated by your Savior? Jesus gave you a new commandment to apply every day.

Read: Open your Bible and read John 15:13.

Reflect: Prayerfully consider the following: Am I making regular, deliberate sacrifices to demonstrate my love and care for others?

Respond: As a result of these truths, what might need to change in my attitude, beliefs, and actions? What steps do I need to take outwardly?

Triple Denial

"Simon Peter said to him, 'Lord, where are you going?' Jesus answered him,
'Where I am going you cannot follow me now, but you will follow afterward.'
Peter said to him, 'Lord, why can I not follow you now? I will lay down my life
for you.' Jesus answered, 'Will you lay down your life for me? Truly, truly,
I say to you, the rooster will not crow till you have denied me three times' "
(John 13:36-38).

Every baseball player has the same opportunity to hit the ball into play. He may let the first pitch go by or he may come out swinging. He may hit a foul ball, or swing and miss a second time. After three strikes, however, the player is called "out" and forced to exit. Peter heard Jesus' message loud and clear. Jesus was leaving. He was moving on. Peter wanted to know where He was going so he could come along. In a moment of great passion, Peter declared his willingness to risk his life for the sake of Jesus. Despite that great passion, Jesus knew it was not yet Peter's time to die.

Although Peter had a mission to fulfill, he often reminds us of our own personal weaknesses. We take a stand and say, "This year I will give God more than ever before. I will take more risks, increase my generosity, and serve more in my local church." These kinds of goals are admirable, but the problem is that sometimes we don't make it past the first or second week without falling flat on our face. We become ashamed of how short we fall in our commitment to what we originally planned to do.

Many believers fall into this familiar cycle of despair. They run hard and they run fast, but they quickly run out of gas. It is the "all or nothing" approach. This leads to an unbalanced theology, no spiritual fruit, and unwise living. Be careful what promises you make to the Lord. Your relationship with Jesus is not just based on emotions. This is a spiritual relationship. He will tell you what sacrifices you need to make and when. Listen to His quiet voice. Peter would indeed go on to deny Jesus three times. Yet after this triple denial, Peter received something astonishing: triple grace. Even if you have denied Christ three times or more, it is not the end of the road. He wants to forgive you and make you whole, and nothing is beyond the reach of His grace. He can make all things well.

Read: Open your Bible and read John 18:25-27.

Reflect: Prayerfully consider the following: Am I faithful to Christ in my words and in my actions? Which of these need the most improvement?

Respond: As a result of these truths, what might need to change in my attitude, beliefs, and actions? What steps do I need to take outwardly?

I'll Be Back

"Let not your hearts be troubled. Believe in God; believe also in me. In my Father's house are many rooms. If it were not so, would I have told you that I go to prepare a place for you? And if I go and prepare a place for you, I will come again and will take you to myself, that where I am you may be also. And you know the way to where I am going" (John 14:1-4).

It's what every child wants to hear when mommy or daddy heads out to work: "I'll be back." These words paint a smile on a child's face. These words provide strong comfort when the children are not feeling well and encouragement when they don't understand why parents have to work in the first place. Confidence in the future gives them hope in the present.

Jesus was about to face an excruciating death. Instead of focusing on the trouble ahead, He focused on encouraging His men. He wanted them to remember that His words were true. There was nothing to fear. On the contrary, Jesus was leaving to make a special place for His followers to dwell with Him forever. The best part was that Jesus promised to return.

"For the Lord himself will descend from heaven with a cry of command, with the voice of an archangel, and with the sound of the trumpet of God. And the dead in Christ will rise first. Then we who are alive, who are left, will be caught up together with them in the clouds to meet the Lord in the air, and so we will always be with the Lord. Therefore encourage one another with these words" (1 Thessalonians 4:16-18).

Paul wrote these words to encourage the believers in Thessalonica. He wanted to give them hope by focusing their hearts on what lay ahead. Both Jesus and Paul focused on the promise yet to be fulfilled to encourage their disciples to continue God's work. This is what we all need to be reminded of. No matter how difficult life gets, one day, Jesus will be back. In light of what we may experience today, we can find renewed strength and hope.

Are you discouraged today because of your surroundings? Do things seem to get progressively worse lately rather than better? You are never alone. God is with you. The best is yet to come. One day all of your personal struggles and doubts will all make sense. One day Jesus will be back!

Read: Open your Bible and read 1 Corinthians 15:51-54.

Reflect: Prayerfully consider the following: Have I been down lately? How does the return of Christ for His people encourage my heart?

Respond: As a result of these truths, what might need to change in my attitude, beliefs, and actions? What steps do I need to take outwardly?

The Way

"Thomas said to him, 'Lord, we do not know where you are going. How can we know the way?' Jesus said to him, 'I am the way, and the truth, and the life. No one comes to the Father except through me. If you had known me, you would have known my Father also. From now on you do know him and have seen him' "
(John 14:5-7).

Tour guides often serve tourists from foreign countries; welcoming them and helping them discover new cultures, foods, places, and people groups. Certainly, reading about a country on the Internet has some value. But nothing compares, to having a tour guide show you the way. Exploring things through their eyes and personal experiences is priceless.

In the Upper Room, the disciples were looking for answers. Their friend was about to leave their presence. Thomas repeats the intent of Peter's original question, *"Where are you going?"* and adds another element, *"How can we know the way?"* Thomas in one sense was asking for a tour guide. The disciples knew neither the way nor the destination. Without a guide they were in trouble. Jesus makes one of His most profound statements to Thomas. He says that He is the way, He is the truth and He is the life. Jesus is salvation, the one who saves us and provides access to the Father. He is the Living Word of God. Everything Jesus says is truth.

In Jesus dwells eternal life. If you know Him, you have eternal life right now. If you know the Son, you already know the Father. Jesus does not simply offer one way among many. He is not simply one source of light and life. Your salvation is found in Him alone. Jesus is God in the flesh. He is the perfect representation of God the Father on earth. When you see Him work in your life, you see the loving heart of the Father in action.

Consider the pursuits of your life for a moment. Are you pursuing things through Christ's leadership? Are your plans and activities the result of listening to God's direction for your life? Secondly, are you doing everything with complete integrity? Don't expect God to bless deceit. God blesses your obedience to His Word. Lastly, are your plans and activities producing life in others? Can you see spiritual fruit? How is this impacting others? If Jesus is the way, let Him show you where to go next.

Read: Open your Bible and read 1 John 2:23.

Reflect: Prayerfully consider the following: Am I allowing Jesus to lead my life as His representative on earth? If not, what should I change?

Respond: As a result of these truths, what might need to change in my attitude, beliefs, and actions? What steps do I need to take outwardly?

Who's Authority?

"Philip said to him, 'Lord, show us the Father, and it is enough for us.' Jesus said to him, 'Have I been with you so long, and you still do not know me, Philip? Whoever has seen me has seen the Father. How can you say, 'Show us the Father'? Do you not believe that I am in the Father and the Father is in me? The words that I say to you I do not speak on my own authority, but the Father who dwells in me does his works. Believe me that I am in the Father and the Father is in me, or else believe on account of the works themselves' " (John 14:8-11).

Having healthy relationships with a group of close friends creates a unique bond. There are opportunities to celebrate life's successes and grieve together through personal losses. Without realizing it, these moments cement your relationship. You get to know one another at a much deeper level. These friends know you from the inside out. They love you deeply.

When the disciples saw Jesus they witnessed the Father in action. Jesus and the Father are one. Jesus dwells in the Father and the Father dwells in Him. When Jesus spoke, it was through the authority given by the Father. As God worked Jesus worked. The Father worked through the life of His Son in perfect synchronization. This process was made visible by the works Jesus performed. All of His works pointed people to the Father.

Philip was one of the first disciples called into the ministry. He had a long history with Jesus. Yet, Philip was totally unaware of the triune unity that existed between Father, Son, and Holy Spirit. Philip asked for another sign, a special revelation to prove Jesus' deity. Since Jesus was God, He could reveal the Father. Philip only needed to open his eyes to see Him clearly.

As a believer, God's Spirit lives within you. You don't need a sign from heaven or a special revelation to confirm this. God abides in you and you in Him. The question is, "Do my actions consistently reflect God's authority working through me?" If you are pointing people to the Father by what you say and do, God's in charge. If not, you are the one steering the ship. Here is the second question, "Are these works visible to others?" People desperately need to see the heart of the Father in every area of your life. Help them see the Father by submitting everything to Him.

Read: Open your Bible and read Matthew 7:15-20.

Reflect: Prayerfully consider the following: Do my activities make visible the love, unity, and authority of the Father? Am I getting in the way?

Respond: As a result of these truths, what might need to change in my attitude, beliefs, and actions? What steps do I need to take outwardly?

Pray BIG

"Truly, truly, I say to you, whoever believes in me will also do the works that I do; and greater works than these will he do, because I am going to the Father. Whatever you ask in my name, this I will do, that the Father may be glorified in the Son. If you ask me anything in my name, I will do it" (John 14:12-14).

Technology has changed the landscape of business. Many corporations have mobile employees who rarely visit the office. Through their laptops, iPads, or smart phones, they can access relevant information. Signing digital contracts and retrieving files from the Internet are now very common. Practices that are very common today were unthinkable not too long ago.

Jesus promised His disciples, *"But you will receive power when the Holy Spirit has come upon you, and you will be my witnesses in Jerusalem and in all Judea and Samaria, and to the end of the earth" (Acts 1:8).* Jesus was preparing His disciples for a global ministry. It would involve a much broader focus than what they had experienced. The disciples would not be alone in this new adventure. They would have the Holy Spirit to empower their witness.

We forget at times about Jesus' mission to reach all ethnic groups. So we stop praying for the lost and terminate our plans to reach them. We forget about the promise to do *"greater works than these"* because we are too busy feeling sorry for ourselves. We need to get up, pray hard, and watch God work through us. Jesus said, *"Ask, and it will be given to you; seek, and you will find; knock, and it will be opened to you" (Matthew 7:7).*

You have probably heard the phrase, "Think BIG" many times. The question is whether or not you "Pray BIG" as you "Think BIG"! Follow this thought. If God wants to expand His Kingdom through your life, you have to expand your thinking, too. Think bigger, much bigger! Look and pray for bigger opportunities! Pray, plan, and believe God for bigger doors to open for His eternal Kingdom! You have to take steps and do the work for these things to become a reality. God will give you the wisdom you need to reach more people. Pray Big and ask! *"If any of you lacks wisdom, let him ask God, who gives generously to all without reproach, and it will be given him. But let him ask in faith, with no doubting" (James 1:5-6).*

Read: Open your Bible and read 1 John 3:22.

Reflect: Prayerfully consider the following: Am I living a holy life? Are God's priorities my priorities? Do I want to see God do more within me?

Respond: As a result of these truths, what might need to change in my attitude, beliefs, and actions? What steps do I need to take outwardly?

Another Helper

"If you love me, you will keep my commandments. And I will ask the Father, and he will give you another Helper, to be with you forever, even the Spirit of truth, whom the world cannot receive, because it neither sees him nor knows him. You know him, for he dwells with you and will be in you. I will not leave you as orphans; I will come to you" (John 14:15-18).

Corporations have figured out the power of establishing mentoring programs. A seasoned executive selects a rising manager who has displayed executive potential. The executive meets with the manager regularly for coaching, problem solving, and instruction. The manager grows considerably and is better equipped to move up in the company. Preparing people for greater responsibility is not new. The disciples wanted Jesus to stay and establish His kingdom. Jesus had other plans. He was preparing them for His exit. Before making a promise, He reminded them that loving God and obeying His word are connected. John would later write: *"By this we know that we love the children of God, when we love God and obey his commandments. For this is the love of God, that we keep his commandments. And his commandments are not burdensome" (1 John 5:2-3).* Jesus wanted them to follow His Word. Their love would soon be tested.

When Jesus introduced the Holy Spirit, it would require some explaining. They must have thought, "How could the Holy Spirit be better than being with Jesus?" The Holy Spirit would be a permanent helper. He is the Spirit of truth. He would help the disciples distinguish between truth and error. John later wrote, *"When the Spirit of truth comes, he will guide you into all the truth, for he will not speak on his own authority, but whatever he hears he will speak, and he will declare to you the things that are to come" (John 16:13).*

Jesus described the Holy Spirit as a person. He is the third member of the trinity. The Holy Spirit is God. The Holy Spirit would reveal Himself to the disciples. They would know Him personally. The Holy Spirit is with every believer and in every believer. As God's child, you know the Holy Spirit. He is present with you and lives within you. He is a helper who never leaves you alone. You can lean on Him for direction. He wants to coach you into the image of Christ. Your life is powerless without Him. He wants to give you all the power you need. He is your personal helper.

Read: Open your Bible and read 1 Corinthians 6:19.

Reflect: Prayerfully consider the following: Am I relying on the Holy Spirit to empower me for God's work? What is He teaching me lately?

Respond: As a result of these truths, what might need to change in my attitude, beliefs, and actions? What steps do I need to take outwardly?

Love Reveals

"Yet a little while and the world will see me no more, but you will see me.
Because I live, you also will live. In that day you will know that I am in my Father,
and you in me, and I in you. Whoever has my commandments and keeps them,
he it is who loves me. And he who loves me will be loved by my Father,
and I will love him and manifest myself to him" (John 14:19-21).

Godly families can serve children from broken homes in many ways. When these children try to define what true love is, they have to look outside their home. Godly families can help them experience love the way God meant it to be. They can provide wise counsel and encourage these children. As a result, the love of God can be revealed in a visible way.

Love was revealed at the death, burial, and resurrection of Jesus. Although we were enemies of God, His mercy and grace overflowed towards us. Paul wrote, *"For if while we were enemies we were reconciled to God by the death of his Son, much more, now that we are reconciled, shall we be saved by his life" (Romans 5:10).* Since Jesus died, we died. Since Jesus lives, we now live. We live in Him and He lives in us. Jesus' life is revealed through us.

God loves you eternally. God loves you richly. He reveals His great love for you through His Son. God lives within you through His Spirit. As you love the Son you love the Father. As you follow the Son you follow the Father. Your love for God is demonstrated by keeping His Word. God reveals more of Himself to those who love Him and follow His Word.

Is the desire of your heart to love God more and follow His Word? Can you imagine what your life would be like if you walked closer to the Lord and experienced more of His presence? Spend a few minutes in holy imagination. What part of your character needs more of God's presence? What broken relationships require more time in personal prayer? What old habits need to stop? Who is waiting for you to love them more and meet their needs? What big decision is requiring you to step out in faith?

Be encouraged! God wants to reveal His purposes for your life. He is serious about leveraging your life to reach all people groups. You are a member of an eternal fellowship. Let God reveal Himself to you moment by moment. Love Him, obey Him, and listen to His voice. Love reveals.

Read: Open your Bible and read Romans 6:1-11.

Reflect: Prayerfully consider the following: This week, am I walking in newness of life? Am I drawing my daily strength and hope from the Lord?

Respond: As a result of these truths, what might need to change in my attitude, beliefs, and actions? What steps do I need to take outwardly?

The Teacher

"Judas (not Iscariot) said to him, 'Lord, how is it that you will manifest yourself to us, and not to the world?' Jesus answered him, 'If anyone loves me, he will keep my word, and my Father will love him, and we will come to him and make our home with him. Whoever does not love me does not keep my words. And the word that you hear is not mine but the Father's who sent me. These things I have spoken to you while I am still with you. But the Helper, the Holy Spirit, whom the Father will send in my name, he will teach you all things and bring to your remembrance all that I have said to you' " (John 14:22-26).

Do you recall the teacher who helped you break through your struggle with a very difficult subject? They explained things to you in a way that finally made sense. The examples they used were simple, yet profound. They went far beyond the call of duty in order to help every student learn. They created the right educational environment for every student to thrive.

Among other things, the Holy Spirit is your personal teacher. He will guide you into all truth. You can trust His instruction. He will protect you from false teaching. You can trust His warning signs. He will lead you in the right direction. You can trust His sovereignty. If the Holy Spirit is the teacher, you are His student. He will help you understand the deep things of God, and provide you with all spiritual discernment that is needed.

Just as the Holy Spirit taught the disciples, He continues to teach you. God is looking for people to be filled with the Holy Spirit and speak the words that flow from Him. The Holy Spirit is the Master Teacher. Paul wrote, *"And we impart this in words not taught by human wisdom but taught by the Spirit, interpreting spiritual truths to those who are spiritual"* (1 Corinthians 2:13).

It can be difficult for believers to accept the words of John, *"But you have been anointed by the Holy One, and you all have knowledge"* (1 John 2:20). Most of us feel inadequate when it comes to spiritual knowledge. The Holy Spirit fills this void. He has all knowledge and all power. You are complete in Christ. You lack nothing. Even when your memory fails, the Holy Spirit helps you remember what is needed for the moment. He lifts you up with God's promises. He challenges you with Christ's commands. The Holy Spirit knows what you need and He provides it. He is your teacher.

Read: Open your Bible and read Romans 5:5.

Reflect: Prayerfully consider the following: What is the Holy Spirit teaching me about His plans for my life? Am I hopeful about these plans?

Respond: As a result of these truths, what might need to change in my attitude, beliefs, and actions? What steps do I need to take outwardly?

True Peace

"Peace I leave with you; my peace I give to you. Not as the world gives do I give to you. Let not your hearts be troubled, neither let them be afraid. You heard me say to you, 'I am going away, and I will come to you.' If you loved me, you would have rejoiced, because I am going to the Father, for the Father is greater than I. And now I have told you before it takes place, so that when it does take place you may believe. I will no longer talk much with you, for the ruler of this world is coming. He has no claim on me, but I do as the Father has commanded me, so that the world may know that I love the Father. Rise, let us go from here" (John 14:27-31).

Those quiet, early morning moments are precious. You get up before everyone else and grab a cup of coffee. As you look around your kitchen, nothing is moving or making noise. You look out the window. Life seems to have paused. No cars are moving and no children are playing in the street. The neighbor's dog is still sleeping. These quiet times are so good.

There is a difference between God's peace and the world's peace. By themselves, people may experience temporary moments of rest and silence. God's peace and rest is eternal. The world's peace leaves you unsatisfied, incomplete, and wanting more. It has significant limitations. God's peace satisfies. His peace is abundant, and it has no limits. His peace is absolutely perfect. It satisfies your soul and refreshes your spirit.

Like the disciples, sometimes your heart is troubled, anxious and afraid. Unexpected challenges arrive without any warning. The news leaves you without words. This is a new experience for you and your family. Your mind begins racing and anxiety begins to grow in the process. Fear, uncertainty, and disbelief run circles around your head. You ask, "How could this be happening to me during this time? What do I do now?"

You have God's peace living within you. You need to allow His peace free rein to conquer and override all of your anxieties. The Apostle Paul wrote, *"And let the peace of Christ rule in your hearts, to which indeed you were called in one body. And be thankful"* (Colossians 3:15). God is still on the throne and God is still in control. Today, He knows exactly what you need. That's a reason to be thankful! Today, let His peace rule in your heart.

Read: Open your Bible and read Philippians 4:7.

Reflect: Prayerfully consider the following: Have I allowed worry to find a place in my heart? How can I let God's peace rule starting today?

Respond: As a result of these truths, what might need to change in my attitude, beliefs, and actions? What steps do I need to take outwardly?

Rich in Obedience

"What good is it, my brothers, if someone says he has faith but does not have works? Can that faith save him? If a brother or sister is poorly clothed and lacking in daily food, and one of you says to them, 'Go in peace, be warmed and filled,' without giving them the things needed for the body, what good is that? So also faith by itself, if it does not have works, is dead. But someone will say, 'You have faith and I have works.' Show me your faith apart from your works, and I will show you my faith by my works" (James 2:14-18).

There are certain things we expect to see. When we attend a wedding, we expect to see gifts for the bride and groom, dancing, and great celebration. When we attend large sporting events, we expect to see great athletes and many fans. When we attend a funeral, we see tears, family embracing, and close friends near by. These things are common. We expect to see them.

In the same way, when God transforms your life, He expects to see works of service. Works of service flow from a changed life. Since saving faith transforms your character, a changed character will produce good works, works of service. To be rich in obedience means to express your faith through your willingness to serve God through His church. Paul reminds us, *"For we are his workmanship, created in Christ Jesus for good works, which God prepared beforehand, that we should walk in them"* (Ephesians 2:10).

A lack of service points to a dead faith. Active service points to a living faith. What has changed in your character since accepting Christ as Savior? What does your service to God say about the vitality of your faith? Abraham served God through personal loss and sacrifice. He lost his family inheritance and left his country to serve God. Abraham was willing to sacrifice his son as an offering to God. His faith and his service to God worked together. Abraham's works of service perfected his faith.

What are you willing to lose or sacrifice for your faith to be perfected? Are you holding on to a dream where comfort and personal convenience rule? God has so much more planned for your life. He wants you to be rich in obedience. He wants you to serve others with your gifts, resources, talents, and abilities. This is how you prove your love for your Savior. This is how many people will come to know the Savior. Be rich in obedience.

Read: Open your Bible and read 1 Timothy 6:17-18.

Reflect: Prayerfully consider the following: Have I been focusing more on what I can gain and collect rather than how I can serve God's church?

Respond: As a result of these truths, what might need to change in my attitude, beliefs, and actions? What steps do I need to take outwardly?

The Source

"I am the true vine" (John 15:1).

New products can be both exciting and dangerous. They often represent the latest trends in the market. It may be a new software program, a great tool, or the latest personal gadget. Sometimes these products can replace what we have used for years. They have an enormous potential to disrupt the way we think and even our way of life, for the better or for the worse.

God is the source of all wisdom and spiritual satisfaction (John 15:1). Starting with Abraham, God planted the nation of Israel as a vine with the intent to make Him known and visible to the entire world. His desire was to connect all people to Himself through the nation of Israel. Israel failed repeatedly as a nation by disobeying God's Word, and, by extension, producing bad fruit: *"Yet I planted you a choice vine, wholly of pure seed. How then have you turned degenerate and become a wild vine?" (Jeremiah 2:21).*

God's heart has not changed. He still wants to connect people from all ethnic groups to Himself. God loves the entire world. God loves you. He still wants to produce something special, something with an eternal impact through your life. Today, however, God extends spiritual satisfaction and eternal life exclusively through His Son, Jesus. Jesus, the true vine, connects us to God. Jesus is the source. He said, *"I am the way, the truth, and the life. No one comes to the Father except through Me" (John 14:6).*

Jesus is eternal life. He is the living vine. Before you took your first breath, Jesus was intimately involved in the creation and fulfillment of God's plan for your life. You have been connected to the Life to deliver life. What a high honor! What a great privilege! You've been connected to the vine to deliver a continuous flow of love to others. As the true vine, Jesus connects you to the Father, the vinedresser, and provides what is needed to make God known and clearly visible to those who don't yet know Him.

Jesus is the true vine and you are His branch. You are not the vine; so don't try to be the vine. Be a good branch. As a branch, receiving a consistent flow of life-changing spiritual nourishment from the vine is your top priority. There is nothing more important for a branch to do.

Read: Open your Bible and read John 15:1-27.

Reflect: Prayerfully consider the following: Am I a good branch or am I fighting to be the vine? Am I allowing Jesus to be my source of satisfaction?

Respond: As a result of these truths, what might need to change in my attitude, beliefs, and actions? What steps do I need to take outwardly?

Personal Care

"I am the true vine and My Father is the vinedresser" (John 15:1).

Grandparents often have a special bond with their grandchildren. This connection is unique. The way they approach their grandchildren can be described with three simple words: love, care, and protection. They lavish these three things on their grandchildren. This relationship can be an important part of children's lives and help them mature in many ways.

The metaphor of John 15:1-11 will help you understand how the Christian life is supposed to work. God's plan is not complicated; it is simple, very simple. As the vinedresser, He is completely and intimately aware of every detail of your life. God knows what you are doing all of the time. He knows because He genuinely cares. He knows because He loves you.

God's love for you is unconditional. His plan for your life is a good one. He is the One who protects, manages, and cares for the vineyard. For this reason, He wants to produce the visible demonstration of His love through your life, as you receive spiritual nourishment from the vine. The vinedresser will make sure that all nourishment flows from the vine to the branches. As His precious branch, make sure you are ready to receive it.

God knows exactly what is needed for the vineyard to thrive and produce healthy fruit. He has a perfect plan ready to flow through your life. He knows what conditions generate the most fruit. Moreover, God knows how to cultivate the right environment for your life to flourish and produce high-quality fruit. His plan for your life will produce much fruit. Let Him care for you and show you the best way. God is very good at doing this.

God already simplified the process for your spiritual growth. Don't stress! Remember, your new source of satisfaction is not found in a program, an experience, an achievement, or in a material possession. Your new source of satisfaction is found in a person, Jesus Christ. He is the source of life.

Thank God for the work He has started and the fruit He will produce through your life. It takes time to get to know the vinedresser. God loves you. He truly cares for you. God will protect you and help mature you.

Read: Open your Bible and read John 15:1-11.

Reflect: Prayerfully consider the following: When was the last time I thanked God for His great power, protection, and care over my life?

Respond: As a result of these truths, what might need to change in my attitude, beliefs, and actions? What steps do I need to take outwardly?

Ready to Flow

"If anyone thirsts, let him come to Me and drink. He who believes in Me, as the Scripture has said, out of his heart will flow rivers of living water" (John 7:37-38).

Good wells provide an unlimited source of water. In ancient times, wells also served as social landmarks. There were certain times of the day when people would gather, talk, and draw water from the well. Since water was a daily need, relationships were often started and developed at the well.

Your search is over! As a believer, your complete spiritual satisfaction is already living within you—forever. Jesus Christ, the true vine, is also the only One who can quench your spiritual thirst. Now you can rest. Your spirit has finally found what it's been searching for. Jesus, the Eternal God, now lives within you. God's Spirit is ready to flow through your life like a rushing, mighty river. As you increase the receiving, God can increase the flowing. You are now designed to deliver life from the inside out.

In Christ, your life is a conduit of life for others! For this reason, you must allow His life to freely flow through you to others. Recognize that you are no longer the one living. Your "old self" was crucified with Christ. The "old you" is gone and the "new you" in Christ Jesus is here to stay. He now lives within you, and works through your life to deliver life to others.

The Apostle Paul wrote, *"I have been crucified with Christ; it is no longer I who live, but Christ lives in me; and the life which I now live in the flesh I live by faith in the Son of God, who loved me and gave Himself for me"* (Galatians 2:20). Jesus Christ paid for your sins with His own blood as He died on the cross. Your life does not belong to you any longer. In Christ Jesus, you are God's property, His very own special treasure; you belong to the Living God.

As you learn to receive a constant flow of spiritual nourishment from the vine, your life will be characterized by faith—one that trusts the vinedresser in every situation. You can't receive from the vine or please the vinedresser without faith. Did you know that your faith is a visible demonstration of your love for God? Your faith is revealed through your works of service to God, His church, and others. As God changes you from the inside out, your faith will grow and your good works will increase.

Read: Open your Bible and read Hebrews 11:6.

Reflect: Prayerfully consider the following: Am I regularly allowing God to change me from the inside out and serve others in the process?

Respond: As a result of these truths, what might need to change in my attitude, beliefs, and actions? What steps do I need to take outwardly?

Hazardous Connections

"Every branch in Me that does not bear fruit He takes away" (John 15:2).

Experienced electricians know the importance of establishing good connections when joining electrical wires together. They also know the potential hazards when inexperienced workers perform these connections. Short circuits, fires, and even explosions can result when faulty connections are made. Knowledgeable electricians will make the right connections.

Not every branch is rightly connected. Just because someone says, "I'm a branch," does not automatically make him or her a branch. Some are rightly connected to the vine, and others are not. On the outside, some branches may look, feel, and even smell like other healthy branches. Unless you're a vinedresser or a skilled gardener, you wouldn't easily notice the difference. This can be difficult to see. Similarly, some people who call themselves Christians are rightly connected to the vine, and others are not.

Those who aren't may say the right things, regularly attend church services, and even volunteer their time. You wouldn't notice the difference either, at least not immediately. The book of First John makes it clear; we can identify a true believer by the fruit of their life. Your purpose as a branch is to bear fruit—to make God visible to others by allowing the qualities of God to continuously flow through your life. John explains the difference:

"God is light and in Him is no darkness at all. If we say that we have fellowship with Him, and walk in darkness, we lie and do not practice the truth. But if we walk in the light as He is in the light, we have fellowship with one another, and the blood of Jesus Christ His Son cleanses us from all sin" (1 John 1:5-7).

Someone who claims to be a Christian, a follower of Jesus, but who does not produce fruit, is not really a true believer. Every branch that is truly connected to the vine will produce fruit. Every true Christian produces fruit, even if in very small amounts. When you are rightly connected to the vine, your life will change, and you will make God's presence visible to a dying world by producing fruit. God created you to produce good spiritual fruit. He created you to live in the light. Every true Christian is rightly connected in Christ. With this in mind, avoid hazardous connections.

Read: Open your Bible and read 1 John 2:19.

Reflect: Prayerfully consider the following: Am I rightly connected to Jesus Christ? Is my life regularly radiating more light than darkness?

Respond: As a result of these truths, what might need to change in my attitude, beliefs, and actions? What steps do I need to take outwardly?

Distractions

"Beware of false prophets, who come to you in sheep's clothing but inwardly are ravenous wolves. You will recognize them by their fruits. Are grapes gathered from thornbushes, or figs from thistles? So, every healthy tree bears good fruit, but the diseased tree bears bad fruit. A healthy tree cannot bear bad fruit, nor can a diseased tree bear good fruit. Every tree that does not bear good fruit is cut down and thrown into the fire. Thus you will recognize them by their fruits"
(Matthew 7:15-20).

Your letter is almost finished. Your cell phone rings just as you're about to begin writing the last paragraph. You press the ignore button and continue writing. Shortly after, a noisy news helicopter decides to hover over your home to get a good view of traffic. Next, your neighbor knocks forcefully on your front door. How can you ever finish with so many distractions?

In the Christian life there are multitudes of distractions. Sometimes these distractions will demand your full attention. However, as a branch, your primary responsibility is to stay focused on the Vine. Daily activities, people, and events work hard to shift your focus from the internal to the external, from the eternal to the temporary, and from the One who truly satisfies to those who can never satisfy. Do not get discouraged by the meaningless activity of other branches; you cannot control their behavior.

Don't let the behavior or condition of other branches take your focus away from the vine. Keep your full attention on Jesus. The Christian life is sourced through the vine not through other branches. The more you focus on the vine, the more visible God's attributes will be made known to others. As you intentionally allow the qualities of God to flow through you, He will produce life through your life. The good news is that *you* don't have to produce anything. Really…you don't. God is the producer.

You do, however, have to stay focused on the vine for His life to unreservedly flow through you. As a branch, your most critical role is simply to rest and receive from the vine! Jesus is the vine, your daily source for spiritual nourishment. Don't look for this nourishment in other branches, they can't supply it. Don't look for this nourishment in other activities, you won't find it. Don't get distracted. Stay focused on the vine.

Read: Open your Bible and read Colossians 3:2.

Reflect: Prayerfully consider the following: Am I allowing the temporal things of this life to distract me from the eternal?

Respond: As a result of these truths, what might need to change in my attitude, beliefs, and actions? What steps do I need to take outwardly?

Connected on Purpose

"And every branch that bears fruit..." (John 15:2).

As children are growing up they often say, "I can't wait until I'm bigger." This may mean reaching a certain height, weight, or being much older. They want to develop faster than the normal course of life will allow. They believe if they arrive much faster, all will be well and life will be perfect. They want greater challenges and more complex problems to solve.

The life of a branch is very simple. Your purpose as a branch is to bear fruit—to make God visible to others by allowing the qualities of God to continuously flow through your life. Connections are very important. Having the right connection to the vine is absolutely necessary in the production of spiritual fruit. As a branch, your purpose is to bear much fruit by making God visible to others. This is your primary mission.

The presence of the vinedresser is powerful. A continuous flow of spiritual fruit magnifies God's presence in this world and brings life-transformation to those who are connected to the wrong things. God's presence is the catalyst for eliminating the pain of this world. As His branch, your role is to allow His presence to flow through your life without any obstacles or restrictions. Your spiritual maturity is a progression, not a singular event. Spiritual growth is realized in your uninterrupted connection to the vine and through your consistent delivery of this fruit to others who need it.

In the Christian life, your spiritual maturity depends more on your consistency to receive from the vine, and release spiritual fruit than it does on any one-time event. The visible demonstration of God's love, the fruit, is not for you to produce, but to receive, celebrate, and release. As a branch, this is your role. As God's branch, this is your divine purpose.

But you may ask, "What does fruit look like?" You may even ask, "How do I know if I am producing the right kind of fruit?" Great questions! Here is just a sample of the fruit you are supposed to deliver to others on a daily basis: *"But the fruit of the Spirit is love, joy, peace, longsuffering, kindness, goodness, faithfulness, gentleness, self-control" (Galatians 5:22- 23).* Let God shape you and richly bless others through these spiritual qualities.

Read: Open your Bible and read Hebrews 12:3.

Reflect: Prayerfully consider the following: Am I choosing to allow discouragement to keep me from fulfilling the purpose God has for me?

Respond: As a result of these truths, what might need to change in my attitude, beliefs, and actions? What steps do I need to take outwardly?

Every Detail

"And every branch that bears fruit He prunes" (John 15:2).

Attention to detail is an important mark of a good leader, but this does not mean he has to be involved in every single decision. Instead, keeping the big picture firmly in mind, he coordinates the efforts of his team members as they work through these items and report back their findings. As he helps them understand what direction the team is going, they can make good decisions based upon his vision and established objectives.

Although God is all-powerful and all-knowing, He is intimately involved with every area of your life. Not only is God completely aware of your surroundings, He is also intimately involved with each and every step you take. The wisdom of the divine vinedresser allows Him to take care of His garden in a way that is beyond our capacity to understand or predict.

God is fully aware of every detail of your life. David wrote, *"O Lord, You have searched me and known me. You know my sitting down and my rising up; You understand my thought afar off. You comprehend my path and my lying down, and are acquainted with all my ways. For there is not a word on my tongue, but behold, O Lord, You know it altogether" (Psalm 139:1-4).* This level of involvement should lead us to an incredible confidence in our great Lord.

God knows us intimately, He watches over us, and He is intentionally involved with every detail of our lives. No matter how difficult life gets, remember that He knows exactly what you are experiencing. He knows your circumstances; He knows how things will affect you and your family; and He knows exactly what is needed to draw you closer to Him. The vinedresser has everything under control. The psalmist masterfully wrote, *"He counts the number of the stars; He calls them all by name. Great is our Lord, and mighty in power; His understanding is infinite" (Psalm 147:4-5).*

No matter what happens to the other branches, no matter how hard it rains or how others try to destroy the vine, He is in complete control. God knows what He is doing, so simply rest in Him. So during those restless nights, rest your hope in the Lord, He's got you covered. He is fully aware of what is happening to you and understands the challenges. He has experienced the pain. He knows the numbers. He knows every detail.

Read: Open your Bible and read Matthew 6:30.

Reflect: Prayerfully consider the following: Is my faith so shallow or small that I can't trust Almighty God to handle the details of my life?

Respond: As a result of these truths, what might need to change in my attitude, beliefs, and actions? What steps do I need to take outwardly?

Growing Pains

"And every branch that bears fruit He prunes, that it may bear more fruit"
(John 15:2).

Stretch marks are discouraging for teenagers. When the body grows faster than the skin can handle, these ugly marks appear on the body. Certain creams can help remove the marks, but usually not fast enough. Some of these marks may remain visible for many years. Some may never fade completely. In any delivery system, problems can be expected. Trucks run out of gas and get delayed in traffic, and delivery people may even take packages to the wrong address. In God's delivery system, problems sometimes arise not because you're doing something wrong but because you're doing something right. You might say, "That doesn't make any sense." If you understand the metaphor of John 15, it makes perfect sense, because problems can lead you to a greater level of intimacy with the vine.

When the branch begins to grow and produce fruit, it experiences new challenges. The branches start getting heavier and may shoot out in too many directions at once. Although this may sound good, it isn't at all. This additional weight has the potential to strain the branch. Excess greenery, beautiful though it is, can divert essential energy from the production of fruit. These factors can ultimately affect your connection back to the vine.

The vinedresser wants to produce an abundance of fruit through your life. For this reason, He will sometimes remove the excess from your life to keep you solidly connected to the vine and maximize your fruitfulness. This will require great discomfort on your part, but in the end, it will not compare to what He plans to do through your life. The vinedresser removes the excess from your life to strengthen your connection to the vine. Don't forget this key point. Your suffering has a divine purpose.

Spiritual growth often comes as we endure personal pain. Paul reminds us, *"Not only that, but we rejoice in our sufferings, knowing that suffering produces endurance, and endurance produces character, and character produces hope, and hope does not put us to shame, because God's love has been poured into our hearts through the Holy Spirit who has been given to us"* (Romans 5:3-5).

Read: Open your Bible and read Philippians 4:14.

Reflect: Prayerfully consider the following: Am I encouraging others through their pain? Am I ready to grow through personal pain?

Respond: As a result of these truths, what might need to change in my attitude, beliefs, and actions? What steps do I need to take outwardly?

Removing the Excess

"He prunes, that it may bear more fruit" (John 15:2).

Trimming hedges is never a one-time activity. In the rainy season, you may be trimming your hedges two to three times a month. If not, once a month may work well. Removing excess shrubbery takes considerable time. It takes the right equipment and the right skillset to get the job done right. The one doing the work determines exactly what needs to be cut.

At just the right time, the vinedresser steps into the vineyard of your life and clips away the excess shrubbery. This pruning process may be more than simply uncomfortable; it can be very painful. God will remove the excess from your life to draw you closer to the vine. The excess may be a prized possession, a job, savings, an event, a close friendship, or something else you hold dear. God has a purpose for everything He removes. He only removes what is absolutely necessary for you to produce more fruit.

God allows you to experience pain to further expand His presence here on earth. Don't try to figure it all out. He may decide to reveal His purpose for your pain, or He may not. Sometimes the only explanation we can find for what God removes from our lives is the comfort we're able to bring to others who experience a similar loss. Yet, there is good news—you can trust the vinedresser. God cares deeply and He knows what He is doing.

If we allow Him, God can also use our pain to bring great comfort and encouragement to others. Paul wrote, *"Blessed be the God and Father of our Lord Jesus Christ, the Father of mercies and God of all comfort, who comforts us in all our tribulation, that we may be able to comfort those who are in any trouble, with the comfort with which we ourselves are comforted by God" (2 Corinthians 1:3-4).* Will you let God use the pain in your life for His glory?

Although it can be extremely painful, difficult experiences can lead you to a greater level of fruitfulness. The less you have to weigh you down, the more fruit your life can deliver for the vinedresser. Don't allow yourself to get discouraged by the pruning process. Removing the excess is never pleasant for the branch. Be grateful to the Lord for His infinite wisdom, and rest fully in the fact that He has a purpose for everything He removes.

Read: Open your Bible and read John 15:1-11.

Reflect: Prayerfully consider the following: Do I trust God to remove anything He feels is necessary for my life to produce more fruit?

Respond: As a result of these truths, what might need to change in my attitude, beliefs, and actions? What steps do I need to take outwardly?

Secure

"You are already clean because of the word which I have spoken to you"
(John 15:3).

When you get ready to ride a fast rollercoaster, you want to make sure your body is as secure as possible. The reason for this is simple; not taking the necessary precautions can lead to serious injury or even death. Since you value your life, taking these extra measures is no problem at all.

At the moment of your salvation, your sins were forgiven and cleansed. You were grafted into the vine by the power of the Holy Spirit. Your attachment to the vine is totally secure. The very One who connected you guarantees this eternal connection. Paul wrote to the Ephesian believers, *"In Him you also trusted, after you heard the word of truth, the gospel of your salvation; in whom also, having believed, you were sealed with the Holy Spirit of promise, who is the guarantee of our inheritance until the redemption of the purchased possession, to the praise of His glory"* (Ephesians 1:13-14).

The vinedresser initiated your connection to the vine. Jesus said, *"My sheep hear My voice, and I know them, and they follow Me. And I give them eternal life, and they shall never perish; neither shall anyone snatch them out of My hand. My Father, who has given them to Me, is greater than all; and no one is able to snatch them out of My Father's hand"* (John 10:27-30). What does all this security really mean? It means that you can rest fully in the work of the vinedresser. You can trust His provision, protection, and eternal guarantee for your life. It means that you can focus on the presence of the vine and eliminate any worry or fear from your thinking. You are secure!

Paul wrote, *"For I am persuaded that neither death nor life, nor angels nor principalities nor powers, nor things present nor things to come, nor height nor depth, nor any other created thing, shall be able to separate us from the love of God which is in Christ Jesus our Lord"* (Romans 8:38-39). You are completely secure as a result of the finished work of Jesus Christ on the cross at Calvary. It is finished! Your eternal life is secure in Christ Jesus. If death is approaching, don't panic. Jesus overcame death. It no longer has power over your life. Death is simply a door into the next phase of your eternity.

Read: Open your Bible and read John 3:36.

Reflect: Prayerfully consider the following: Since I have eternal life right now in the Lord Jesus Christ, do I really need to fear dying?

Respond: As a result of these truths, what might need to change in my attitude, beliefs, and actions? What steps do I need to take outwardly?

Refill

"Abide in Me, and I in you" (John 15:4).

The gasoline station has one primary purpose: to refill your car with fuel to get you back on your journey. Your car will eventually burn all of this new gasoline and require more fuel for the ride. Every mile you drive brings you one mile closer to the next time you need to refill your vehicle.

Your connection to the vine is a growing, life-giving relationship. Your most important role as a branch is to continually remain in the vine and allow the vine to freely live in you. Remember, you can trust the vinedresser as He carries out His plan through the vine. Your continuous surrender to the desires of the vinedresser makes it possible for the vine to freely live through you. Surrendering actually represents your freedom.

Satan, the enemy, will aggressively oppose your spiritual surrender. He will use fear, doubt, and temptation to shift your thinking from surrender to dissatisfaction. He loves to deceive God's people by removing their focus from the vine. Satan wants you to seek satisfaction somewhere else. Here's the bottom line of all this opposition and distraction—Satan wants to destroy you (Genesis 3:1-5). For this reason, the process of spiritual surrender is a daily, moment-by-moment activity, not simply a one-time event. To experience the abiding life, let Jesus refill you continuously.

The apostle Paul later develops this idea with regards to our relationship with the Holy Spirit. He gives a very powerful command as he encourages believers to live wisely. Paul wants them to stop searching for external satisfaction, to stop being consumed by worldly living and temporary pleasures. He wants them to be constantly filled with God's Spirit. His command is both clear and direct, *"Be filled with the Spirit"* (Ephesians 5:18).

God wants you to be constantly filled with His Spirit. He wants you to get rid of your old way of living and allow His Son to guide your every thought, word, and action. When you allow God to replace the satisfaction you once found in the world with the life-giving satisfaction found in His Son, He can bring your life great freedom and contentment as you discover your new purpose for living. Don't just live your life; refill your spirit.

Read: Open your Bible and read 1 Peter 4:6.

Reflect: Prayerfully consider the following: Am I living in the Spirit? Am I daily going before God for Him to change me and fill me with His Spirit?

Respond: As a result of these truths, what might need to change in my attitude, beliefs, and actions? What steps do I need to take outwardly?

Spiritual Productivity

"Abide in Me, and I in you. As the branch cannot bear fruit of itself, unless it abides in the vine, neither can you, unless you abide in Me" (John 15:4).

Our culture loves to measure productivity. We have charts, graphs, and many other tools to help us quantify performance and assess efficiency. Measuring an employee's speed, efficiency, and quality of work is normal. It helps us establish standards for performance and forecast costs and profits. But in the spiritual world, spiritual productivity is measured very differently.

Total dependence on the vine always precedes spiritual productivity. A continuous surrender to the will of the vinedresser will naturally lead you to depend on Him fully, both for spiritual productivity and growth. A life characterized by continuous surrender and total dependence on the vine is the work of the vinedresser; then and only then can His work through your life thrive greatly. Spiritual productivity is relational, not mechanical.

As a branch, you must recognize your spiritual limitations. You can't produce the visible fruit of God's Spirit without being regularly connected to the vine. The focus of the Christian life is connectivity to the vine rather than activity for the vine. Your connectivity is what determines your activity. There is a direct relationship between dependence and fruit: as your dependence on the vine increases, the visible fruit of God's Spirit working through your life will increase as well. Don't focus on the fruit.

Focus your full attention on the vine. Ask God to increase your capacity to depend fully on Him. Total dependence involves resting securely in the vine and trusting in the complete care of the vinedresser. You are not required to manufacture a product, an experience, or an event. The vine, Jesus Christ, now lives within you. The vine produces everything needed to produce God's visible presence on earth. God's fruit through your life is produced from the inside out, and there is a direct relationship between dependence and fruit. Prayerfully dedicate your complete dependence on Jesus. Ask Him to help you trust His word as He directs your life each day.

"Incline your ear, O Lord, and answer me, for I am poor and needy. Preserve my life, for I am godly; save your servant, who trusts in you—you are my God" (Psalm 86:1-3).

Read: Open your Bible and read all of Psalm 86.

Reflect: Prayerfully consider the following: Am I depending on God as if He were my only hope? What new things have I learned about His ways?

Respond: As a result of these truths, what might need to change in my attitude, beliefs, and actions? What steps do I need to take outwardly?

The Provider

"I am the vine, you are the branches" (John 15:5).

Throughout history, there are many examples of great people who have crossed cultural, economic, and ethnic barriers to provide for the needs of others. These heroes do not always appear on the covers of national magazines, but their good work and their generosity are never forgotten.

Everything you need to live the Christian life is sourced and provided through the vine. There is no need to worry, fear, or lose sleep. God knows exactly what you need and when you need it. You can trust completely in His provision for your daily needs and let His word radically transform your old way of thinking. Before you can rest you have to trust:

"Be anxious for nothing, but in everything by prayer and supplication, with thanksgiving, let your requests be made known to God; and the peace of God, which surpasses all understanding, will guard your hearts and minds through Christ Jesus. Finally, brethren, whatever things are true, whatever things are noble, whatever things are just, whatever things are pure, whatever things are lovely, whatever things are of good report, if there is any virtue and if there is anything praiseworthy—meditate on these things" (Philippians 4:6-8).

Waiting for the provision of the vinedresser is another component of total dependence. You may need to undo old methods of life management techniques and begin new ones. When problems arise, strengthen your connection to the vine. Make asking and receiving from God your first priority, not your last resort. Be wise in your journey of faith, and *"Trust in the Lord with all your heart and lean not on your own understanding; in all your ways acknowledge Him and He shall direct your paths" (Proverbs 3:5-6).*

Replace worry, fear, and manipulation with trust, faith, and truthfulness. The vinedresser may occasionally shake your branch, but hold on for the ride. Remember who you're connected to—Jesus. Don't try to solve your problems without Him. Immediately invite Him to take full control of every situation and direct your steps right from the start. Trust Him, and you will be glad you did! Make a list of the things He has provided for you during this last month. You might be pleasantly surprised with the results.

Read: Open your Bible and read I Timothy 6:17.

Reflect: Prayerfully consider the following: How have I seen God provide richly for my family? Have I expressed gratitude to Him recently?

Respond: As a result of these truths, what might need to change in my attitude, beliefs, and actions? What steps do I need to take outwardly?

Replaced

"I have been crucified with Christ; it is no longer I who live, but Christ lives in me; and the life which I now live in the flesh I live by faith in the Son of God, who loved me and gave Himself for me" (Galatians 2:20).

Replacing things that break is not something most people look forward to. It is usually done out of pure obligation. It can be uncomfortable and very costly, sometimes taking more effort than what you planned for. But the new item is superior to what it replaces! This is even truer in the spiritual realm, when our lives are permanently replaced by the life of Christ.

Your spiritual transformation took place immediately at the moment of your salvation. Your old nature has been put to death and fully replaced with God's holy nature. Although you are the one breathing, you are no longer the one living. Jesus is the One living through your life. The more you let His life flow through you, the more productive you will be as a branch in connecting others to the vine. Remember, you've been changed.

Your *purpose for living* has been radically changed. You no longer live in the past or need to seek satisfaction from ungodly desires. Your purpose and satisfaction for living have been completely replaced. You now live by faith and not by sight. The more you let Jesus' life flow through you, the more productive and content you will be in connecting others to the vine.

The "old you" died and was buried; it has been replaced forever. You are free to discover God's unfolding purpose for your life by faith, as you abide in the vine and respond in obedience to His word. Although your spiritual transformation was instantaneous, the life-application of your conversion is a steady process. Are you living from the overflow of your new nature?

As you read through the Gospel of John, take time to pray, memorize scripture, and study each devotional carefully. Ask yourself this question, "How does my life need to change in light of this truth?" The answer is the life-application that you need to put into practice. Remember the words of Paul, *"All Scripture is breathed out by God and profitable for teaching, for reproof, for correction, and for training in righteousness, that the man of God may be complete, equipped for every good work" (2 Timothy 3:16-17).* Live by faith in Christ as you learn to apply God's Word in your life each and every day.

Read: Open your Bible and read Romans 6:6.

Reflect: Prayerfully consider the following: Since my old life has been replaced in Christ Jesus, what is my next step to grow spiritually?

Respond: As a result of these truths, what might need to change in my attitude, beliefs, and actions? What steps do I need to take outwardly?

Simplify

"I am the vine, you are the branches. He who abides in Me, and I in him, bears much fruit; for without Me you can do nothing" (John 15:5).

One characteristic of a genius is their ability to take a complex problem, break it down into stages, and deliver a practical solution. At times our desire to solve difficult problems brings out additional problems in the process for us to decipher. Life in the Spirit is simple, not complicated.

The most natural and productive activity for a branch is to abide in the vine. Without the vine, the branch cannot live, grow, or produce fruit. By itself, the branch can do NOTHING. You cannot fulfill your purpose without remaining in the vine. Be still. You were redeemed to remain in the presence of Jesus Christ. You must allow the vinedresser to remove all unnecessary attitudes, activities, and distractions to focus greater attention on the vine. You can't fulfill your purpose as a believer unless you receive from the vine and allow His life to regularly live and flow through your life.

As a branch, the energy and focus of your life must be radically simplified; receive, rejoice, and release. The more you simplify your daily relationship with Christ, the greater the potential to produce much fruit. Your life as a believer can make a huge difference when you do what you were created to do. You were redeemed to remain. As a branch, your "doing" is not about filling your schedule with more activities, events, and commitments. On the contrary, your "doing" involves reducing. In the Christian life, when you reduce you produce. When you don't reduce you can't produce.

The more you simplify your daily relationship with Christ, the greater the potential to produce much fruit becomes a reality. Here is the simplicity of the Christian life: your daily satisfaction and spiritual productivity is found in Jesus Christ. You were saved to experience complete satisfaction and daily spiritual nourishment in the vine. This is "the main thing." This is abiding. And in the Christian life, when you reduce you produce. Paul wrote, *"Not that we are sufficient in ourselves to claim anything as coming from us, but our sufficiency is from God" (2 Corinthians 3:5).* What do you need to reduce in your life to focus more carefully on the vine? Take steps to start reducing these activities. Abiding is the only way to be of any use to God.

Read: Open your Bible and read John 15:1-11.

Reflect: Prayerfully consider the following: What is the main thing I need to stop or adjust in my life to spend more time with the Lord Jesus?

Respond: As a result of these truths, what might need to change in my attitude, beliefs, and actions? What steps do I need to take outwardly?

The True Vine

"If anyone does not abide in Me, he is cast out as a branch and is withered; and they gather them and throw them into the fire, and they are burned"
(John 15:6).

It looks identical to the one in the department store, but the price is 70% less. You pick up and examine it very carefully. What a great deal! Or it would be, if it weren't a fake. There are many counterfeits in the world; it really does pay to check things out. You have to investigate claims before you can discover their true identity. There are many vines in the world of spiritual vineyards, but only one True Vine under the care of the master vinedresser. Jesus was actively involved in creation (John 1). He is the Beginning and the End, the Alpha and the Omega. Jesus is Eternal. He is the only true vine, and God's only solution to your sin problem.

Jesus is the Living Vine, the One who is the Life and delivers life to those who trust in Him. The crucified and risen Christ is God's only provision to completely satisfy the payment and penalty for your sins. Jesus is the True Vine; there is no other. All those who reject Him will face eternal separation from God. Peter told the religious leaders, *"This [Jesus] is the 'stone which was rejected by you builders, which has become the chief cornerstone.' Nor is there salvation in any other, for there is no other name under heaven given among men by which we must be saved"* (Acts 4:11-12).

Jesus died on the cross to connect you to God. He was buried, and on the third day, rose from the grave. Mohammed, Buddha, Confucius, and others have all died. Each one of them remains buried in the grave. Their teachings may have continued, but they did not produce eternal fruit nor connect others with the Father. These men were not the True Vine. They could not restore their own lives or produce new life for others.

Jesus' life produced life. You can't produce life if you are not the Life. Jesus is the Life and therefore, He can produce Life in you. Jesus said, *"I am the way, the truth, and the life. No one comes to the Father except through Me"* (John 14:6). Make a list of people you know that have not followed Jesus as Savior. Make it a point this week to pray for them by name and share these truths with them. Jesus is the hope of the world and the True Vine.

Read: Open your Bible and read Isaiah 42:6.

Reflect: Prayerfully consider the following: How can I creatively and effectively share with others this week the hope and promises of Jesus?

Respond: As a result of these truths, what might need to change in my attitude, beliefs, and actions? What steps do I need to take outwardly?

Conversations

"If you abide in Me, and My words abide in you, you will ask what you desire, and it shall be done for you" (John 15:7).

In general, there is a sharp distinction between the length of conversations of boys and girls. Typically girls love to talk and boys prefer action over conversation. Girls are highly relational. Boys tend to be very competitive. Bridging this social gap as they develop through life is quite a challenge.

Prayer has been described as the spiritual oxygen of the Christian life. There is a direct relationship between prayer and abiding. Prayer can bring you closer to God by helping you grow deeper in your daily fellowship and dependence on the vine. As you sharpen your focus on the things that matter most to God, He will guide you to pray in a way that magnifies His name by matching your desires with His desires. This is important. Your prayers are spiritually productive when they are aligned with God's word.

As a branch, you want to be productive in the way you invest your time. Your prayers are spiritually productive when they are aligned with God's Word. As you memorize God's Word and reflect on it throughout your day, something changes: you. The Word begins to change the way you think, process, and respond to your environment. This is a good change.

God's Word keeps you on the right track. Paul wrote, *"All Scripture is given by inspiration of God, and is profitable for doctrine, for reproof, for correction, for instruction in righteousness, that the man of God may be complete, thoroughly equipped for every good work" (2 Timothy 3:16-17)*. A regular study of God's Word and an open conversation about how it applies to every area of your life will lead you to productive spiritual conversations. When God's Word fills and directs your life, the vinedresser will respond to your prayers.

Prayer and personal application of God's Word should work together. Ask the Lord to search your heart for anything out of alignment with His Word. Confess it right away, and thank the Lord for His mercy and compassion. When you abide in Jesus Christ, God's Word abides in you. As you pray according to God's Word and in alignment with His will, God responds. God is waiting for your next conversation. Make it a good one.

Read: Open your Bible and read Matthew 6:9.

Reflect: Prayerfully consider the following: Since God is your Father, what kind of conversations do you think He is waiting for you to begin?

Respond: As a result of these truths, what might need to change in my attitude, beliefs, and actions? What steps do I need to take outwardly?

Be Rich

"On that day, when evening had come, he said to them, 'Let us go across to the other side.' And leaving the crowd, they took him with them in the boat, just as he was. And other boats were with him. And a great windstorm arose, and the waves were breaking into the boat, so that the boat was already filling. But he was in the stern, asleep on the cushion. And they woke him and said to him, 'Teacher, do you not care that we are perishing?' And he awoke and rebuked the wind and said to the sea, 'Peace! Be still!' And the wind ceased, and there was a great calm. He said to them, 'Why are you so afraid? Have you still no faith?' And they were filled with great fear and said to one another, 'Who then is this, that even the wind and the sea obey him?' " (Mark 4:35-41).

One of the things that bring us great stress is when we find ourselves in a situation that is beyond our ability to control. As a general rule, most of us do not plan to be in these kinds of situations. We avoid them like a plague. We prefer to remain in control. Being in a situation where we have no control over the final outcome is not something we generally pursue.

You can trust God with your destination and follow His leading. God takes care of the "where" and shows you the "how" at just the right time. Your part is to respond by faith and take the next step. You can be more of who God designed you to be, when you fear less and live by faith. To be rich in faith means spending personal time with Jesus moment-by-moment. If you follow God's direction, you will eventually find your destination.

The question you have to ask is, "Lord, what do you want me to do next?" In this journey, expect problems and completely depend on God to provide the solution. The disciples found themselves in a situation way beyond their ability to manage or control. There was not enough strength, money, resources, or protection to stop what appeared to be certain death. To live richly, you have to depend on Jesus for solutions rather than blame Him for your present circumstances; He is ready and able to help you.

Today, determine to believe in God's unlimited power and live with great expectancy. God's provision brings immeasurable peace and rest for your life. Do not fear. You can't simultaneously live with great fear and have great supernatural expectations. Be rich and trust God in all things.

Read: Open your Bible and read 2 Timothy 1:7.

Reflect: Prayerfully consider the following: What fears are holding back my service and ministry to those within my church and community?

Respond: As a result of these truths, what might need to change in my attitude, beliefs, and actions? What steps do I need to take outwardly?

The BIG Picture

"By this My Father is glorified, that you bear much fruit" (John 15:8).

Every good team knows the importance of listening to their coach. They want to please their coach and respond well to his instruction. It helps when he can communicate his plan with as few words as possible. A clear understanding of the game plan helps the team remember their mission and pull together. The goal of the branch is to produce an abundance of fruit to praise the name of the vinedresser. God wants to produce a generous amount of fruit through your life to magnify His name for all eternity. The goal of bearing much fruit is simply to give God greater glory through His work in your life. Keep this in mind: the greater the fruit the greater the glory. The goal is to bring God greater glory. This is His plan for your life.

An abiding life is one which receives a regular flow of spiritual nourishment from the vine, and intentionally delivers this life to others to bear much fruit. When you allow God to freely produce much fruit through your life, His name is glorified and made known to others. God wants your life to generously magnify His name. He wants you to be intentional about this.

God grafted you into His vineyard so your life would produce much fruit and glorify His name. Your life was designed to glorify God! In His infinite wisdom, He created you as His unique tool to make His light visible to others. Your gifts of speaking and serving others were specifically given to you to bring glory to His name. Use what God has given you to deliver His love to others. You are an instrument for God's purposes. Use your gifts!

Imagine the passion in Peter's heart as he writes this note to the early church family: *"As each one has received a gift, minister it to one another, as good stewards of the manifold grace of God. If anyone speaks, let him speak as the oracles of God. If anyone ministers, let him do it as with the ability which God supplies, that in all things God may be glorified through Jesus Christ, to whom belong the glory and the dominion forever and ever. Amen" (1 Peter 4:10-11).* Reflect on how you can use your speaking and ministry gifts to magnify God's name to others this week. The goal is to bear the fruit of God's character through your life. God is counting on you, so get started.

Read: Open your Bible and read Matthew 28:18-20.

Reflect: Prayerfully consider the following: Since making disciples is part of bearing much fruit, whom will you begin to develop in their faith?

Respond: As a result of these truths, what might need to change in my attitude, beliefs, and actions? What steps do I need to take outwardly?

More Fruit

"By this My Father is glorified, that you bear much fruit;
so you will be My disciples" (John 15:8).

Fruit is what you expect to find a few years after planting good seed in your garden. In time, you should expect a generous crop, not just enough to replace your original seed. This is the natural product of good water, rich soil, careful pruning, and great care. More fruit is wonderful indeed.

Your spiritual transformation is made evident by the fruit you deliver to others. A person who claims to be a Christian, but does not produce fruit, not even a small portion, is not a Christian. Fruit is the evidence of a transformed life and it should characterize your life as a believer. Fruit is evidence that you are rightly connected to the vine. As a branch, you should demonstrate the qualities which are characteristic of the vine.

These qualities are not developed all at once. It takes time to grow. You are an unfolding work of God. The vinedresser is more concerned with your consistency than with your speed. The goal of your transformation is the likeness of Jesus, being conformed into His very image. You have been transformed to be conformed into the image of Jesus Christ. Paul wrote, *"And we know that all things work together for good to those who love God, to those who are the called according to His purpose. For whom He foreknew, He also predestined to be conformed to the image of His Son" (Romans 8:28-29).* Today, let the vinedresser perform His good and perfect work in your life.

As a wise vinedresser, God begins to remove those areas of your life which are in direct opposition to His divine plan. He also begins to develop you through a variety of experiences, leading you to manifest the attributes of the vine to get through each one. Some seasons of life will be difficult to endure, and others pleasantly sunny or cool. Rest assured, each of these is designed for your spiritual transformation and growth. God never wastes an experience. Each one can produce more fruit and magnify God's name.

As His branch, how is the life of Jesus being reflected through your attitude and through your actions? What is He asking you to change? Is there a new way for you to produce more fruit that you have yet to consider?

Read: Open your Bible and read Romans 8:28-29.

Reflect: Prayerfully consider the following: Is there a difficulty in my life right now that God wants to use to produce more spiritual fruit?

Respond: As a result of these truths, what might need to change in my attitude, beliefs, and actions? What steps do I need to take outwardly?

As the Father Loved

"As the Father loved Me, I also have loved you; abide in My love" (John 15:9).

The love of a father is powerful and transformational. It infuses confidence, stability, and security into the life of their children and these are only a few of the benefits. There is a deep longing in our culture for strong, yet loving fathers to take their rightful place at home and within their communities.

With God, delivering love is very personal. Before He inspired His people to write about the characteristics of love, He decided to first demonstrate His love and model what love is supposed to look like. As the vinedresser, He is the author and the initiator of true love. God took the first step by sending His only Son to die on the cross for your sins. He did this to connect you with the only source of life-giving satisfaction (John 3:16).

Make no mistake: the love of the Father regarding the Son is powerful, perfect, and eternal. Likewise, the love that Jesus has for you is powerful, perfect, and eternal. His intimate relationship with the Father has always existed. Earlier, John wrote, *"In the beginning was the Word, and the Word was with God, and the Word was God. He was in the beginning with God. All things were made through Him, and without Him nothing was made that was made. In Him was life, and the life was the light of men"* (John 1:1-4).

Their communication has always been clear and uninterrupted. They shared complete knowledge, perfect unity, and infinite wisdom in every discussion. Jesus wants you to live in this very same love; a love that is unlimited in power, knowledge, wisdom, and unity. He wants you to receive this love from Him every moment of every day, and deliver this powerful, life-changing love to others. The love that Jesus has for you is great, perfect, and eternal. This love is not common. It is supernatural.

The world today needs to see this same love. They need to see how Jesus would respond in a given situation. People need to see the beauty of God's perfect presence unfolded through the lives of His people. They need to see a love that goes far beyond culture and political correctness; one that gives generously instead of takes, that sacrifices instead of demands, and serves willingly rather than burdens others. Such a love can only be divine.

Read: Open your Bible and read I John 4:18.

Reflect: Prayerfully consider the following: Am I loving others *"as the Father loved"*? Am I holding back my love for people because of my fears?

Respond: As a result of these truths, what might need to change in my attitude, beliefs, and actions? What steps do I need to take outwardly?

Love Perfected

"If you keep My commandments, you will abide in My love, just as I have kept My Father's commandments and abide in His love" (John 15:10).

No matter how great one's dreams may be to build a home, unless someone draws up the blueprints, nothing happens. The dream will never become a reality until action is taken. This reminds us of an important principle: when love is present, action follows. In the spiritual world, love is perfected by obedience—taking action according to God's Word.

Love and obedience are two sides of the same coin. Your love for God is demonstrated by, and perfected through, your obedience to His Word. Jesus modeled the beauty of perfect love through His obedience to the Father's commandments. He obeyed God's word 100% of the time. He did not compromise, neglect, or delay. He followed God wholeheartedly. When you don't obey you can't abide. Obedience is the gateway to living an abiding life. Love is perfected through obedience. Are you obedient?

Perfecting your love for God is simple, not complex. The famous slogan from Nike, "Just do it," reminded people to put on the right equipment and take immediate action. As you learn something new from God's Word, make it a habit to take immediate action. Never put off for tomorrow what God shows you to do today. Following God's Word is never dull. It is an exhilarating adventure! Don't neglect and overanalyze your obedience to God. Just do it! Obedience is the gateway to living an abiding life.

Whether the subject is prayer, giving, forgiveness, baptism, or something else, "just do it" and trust the vinedresser to work out the rest. He is worthy of your praise and worthy of your deepest confidence. As you practice God's word, your intimacy with the vine will grow deeper. Allow His love to grow and be perfected in you as you take the next step of faith.

"But be doers of the word, and not hearers only, deceiving yourselves. For if anyone is a hearer of the word and not a doer, he is like a man observing his natural face in a mirror; for he observes himself, goes away, and immediately forgets what kind of man he was. But he who looks into the perfect law of liberty and continues in it, and is not a forgetful hearer but a doer of the work, this one will be blessed in what he does" (James 1:22-25).

Read: Open your Bible and read Matthew 5:1-48.

Reflect: Prayerfully consider the following: What steps of love and obedience do I need to take today as a result of discovering these truths?

Respond: As a result of these truths, what might need to change in my attitude, beliefs, and actions? What steps do I need to take outwardly?

Love Grows

*"Love the Lord your God with all your heart and with all your soul
and with all your strength and with all your mind" (Luke 10:27).*

When living things grow, no one is surprised. It means that their internal systems are working well and doing their jobs. Healthy things grow. Growth is essentially the result of a natural process. You can often predict how much certain organisms will grow under controlled conditions.

In the Christian life, love is comprehensive. It is not limited, fractional, or temporary. God loves you with a perfect love. As you continue living an abiding life, your love for God and your love for others will grow. When God connected you to His Son at the moment of salvation, you became His child forever. This relationship was intentionally designed to grow.

Are you deliberately pursuing God? He wants you to love Him by pursuing Him with your total being. For this reason, He wants you to make loving Him your number one priority. Recognize that He is the One who has absolute control over everything. Since His provision for you through the vine can satisfy every need you have, there is no need to look elsewhere. You were designed to love and pursue Him. This is a critical part of your spiritual maturity. Good spiritual health and growth depend on it.

As you deepen your connection to the vine, you will grow in your love, passion, and appreciation for the vinedresser. Your capacity to love increases as you maintain a constant flow to and from the vine. In other words, uninterrupted fellowship feeds your spiritual growth. This is why it is so important to confess your sins right away; unconfessed sin will always interrupt your fellowship and prevent you from loving God with 100% of your heart, soul, strength, and mind. As you continue living an abiding life, your love for God and your love for others will grow and mature.

Remember the promise you have in Christ. *"If we confess our sins, he is faithful and just to forgive us our sins and to cleanse us from all unrighteousness. If we say we have not sinned, we make him a liar, and his word is not in us. What things have interrupted your fellowship with God in the past? Ask Him to guide you to avoid interruptions and stay in good fellowship" (1 John 1:9-10).* Don't let your love for God stop growing as a result of unconfessed sins.

Read: Open your Bible and read 1 John 1:9-10.

Reflect: Prayerfully consider the following: Am I allowing any sin to stop my love for God from flourishing and growing as He desires?

Respond: As a result of these truths, what might need to change in my attitude, beliefs, and actions? What steps do I need to take outwardly?

Full Joy

"These things I have spoken to you, that My joy may remain in you, and that your joy may be full" (John 15:11).

When a mother agonizes in labor for several hours to deliver her new baby, it is an exhausting experience. The pain she experiences is very real; yet all of this quickly fades the moment the new baby is in her arms. The joy of that moment surpasses the great pain caused by her labor. You were created to enjoy God's purposes for your life. That may sound a bit strange, but it's true. God created you for a greater purpose; and there is nothing dull or common about it. A strong characteristic of your life should be a heart filled with joy. You must believe that God's intentions for your life are pure and good. Almighty God has a good plan for your life (Philippians 1:6). You can trust Him wholeheartedly with your life.

God wants you to run the Christian race with a full tank. He wants you to persevere and finish strong. The uninterrupted presence of Christ flowing through your life is the power needed to live and finish strong. Jesus is your exclusive source for abundant satisfaction. Find the strength to live from the right source, as the wrong source will deplete you spiritually. David's source helped him persevere: *"Now David was greatly distressed, for the people spoke of stoning him, because the soul of all the people was grieved. But David strengthened himself in the Lord his God" (1 Samuel 30:6).*

All the spiritual resources you need are readily available for you to apply in your life right now. You don't have to go out and look for a temporary fix for satisfaction. You don't have to try buying more stuff to make you happy. All the satisfaction you'll ever need is already present within you. Regardless of your circumstances, you can have abundant joy right now!

If you have a real need, ask God and watch Him provide. He wants you to experience the joy found in living through the vine. Sometimes He will allow you to struggle, but trust Him; it is ultimately for your good. He loves you and has a purpose for every circumstance. Enjoy His presence at work within you. Jesus said, *"Until now you have asked nothing in My name. Ask, and you will receive, that your joy may be full" (John 16:24).*

Read: Open your Bible and read 1 John 1:4.

Reflect: Prayerfully consider the following: Is my joy full? If not, can it be that I am trying to find satisfaction in things, money, fame, or power?

Respond: As a result of these truths, what might need to change in my attitude, beliefs, and actions? What steps do I need to take outwardly?

Fight Club

"I say then: Walk in the Spirit, and you shall not fulfill the lust of the flesh. For the flesh lusts against the Spirit, and the Spirit against the flesh; and these are contrary to one another, so that you do not do the things that you wish" (Galatians 5:16-17).

Some people avoid intense arguments while others readily welcome them. Knowing that such conflicts lead to no good end, sidestepping them is often a good choice. When you grow up in a tough neighborhood, you learn how to fight well or run fast. But what do you do when faced with a spiritual attack? Are you supposed to fight? How should you respond?

Stand and let God fight! The Christian life is a daily battle. You will be attacked from many directions, but your greatest battle will originate from within. The desires of your flesh are in constant opposition to God's Word. They never rest and they never want to lose. They won't surrender, and they won't be completely satisfied. As a child of God, you already have the power to conquer your flesh. Let God fight for you.

Live to win. As you walk in the Spirit by living an abiding life, you will win the battle over your flesh. The power of God's Spirit is always far greater than the power of the flesh. You are not in a losing battle, you are in a war that has already been won. The power to win now lives in you. No matter what destructive habits or addictions defeated you in the past, the power to overcome now lives inside you. Abiding is the way you fight back.

Don't feel guilty. Don't beat yourself up when you sin and lose an individual battle. Confess your sins to the Lord, get back up, and stand. Let God fight your battles for you. When you try to fight your spiritual battles in your own strength, you lose. But when you stand and allow God's mighty power to fight through you, you are sure to win. You can be confident when God is doing the fighting. He can take care of your battles.

No matter what destructive habits defeated you in the past, the power to overcome now lives within you. Paul wrote, *"Finally, my brethren, be strong in the Lord and in the power of His might. Put on the whole armor of God, that you may be able to stand against the wiles of the devil"* (Ephesians 6:10-11).

Read: Open your Bible and read I Corinthians 10:13.

Reflect: Prayerfully consider the following: What are the three main battles that I have struggled with in the past? Why are they so tough?

Respond: As a result of these truths, what might need to change in my attitude, beliefs, and actions? What steps do I need to take outwardly?

Special Delivery

"But the fruit of the Spirit is love, joy" (Galatians 5:22).

You answer the doorbell and see a deliveryman on your doorstep. Before he even says a single word, you already know what he is going to deliver. The smell of pizza gives it away initially, but the uniform confirms it. People are waiting for your special delivery. What are you going to give them?

What you deliver is very important. As a Christian, demonstrating God's love to others is your most important delivery. Delivering God's love is an enjoyable and fulfilling experience. It is fulfilling to deliver what God designed you to deliver! If your delivery of God's love to others has stopped, it will negatively affect your relationship with the Lord. Your deliveries were meant to be an ongoing activity rather than a one-time event. You were designed to take God's love to others. Get started!

God shows His love to people in many different ways. Variety is a good thing. Without variety our lives would be very dull. Did you know that a variety of fruit glorifies God? Don't try to deliver God's love in exactly the same way others do. God created you the way you are for a reason. The methods of your delivery are often shaped by your personality, but the characteristics of love remain the same. When you are walking in the Spirit, abiding in Jesus, you will identify with the following characteristics:

"Love suffers long and is kind; love does not envy; love does not parade itself, is not puffed up; does not behave rudely, does not seek its own, is not provoked, thinks no evil; does not rejoice in iniquity, but rejoices in the truth; bears all things, believes all things, hopes all things, endures all things. Love never fails. And now abide faith, hope, love, these three; but the greatest of these is love"
(1 Corinthians 13:4-8).

It's not about you. Why? Simply put, love is about others. There is nothing selfish about it. Delivering a joyful love to others is about knowing God and making Him known. You don't produce this kind of love, because it can't be manufactured. God's love is received. As a branch, you simply receive God's love and deliver it to others with a cheerful spirit. It's about being a branch under complete submission to the vine and the plans of the vinedresser. You were uniquely designed to deliver God's love to others.

Read: Open your Bible and read 1 Corinthians 13:1-8.

Reflect: Prayerfully consider the following: Am I delivering a generous supply of love and joy to others? How can I do this more effectively?

Respond: As a result of these truths, what might need to change in my attitude, beliefs, and actions? What steps do I need to take outwardly?

Peace in the Storms

"But the fruit of the Spirit is love, joy, peace, longsuffering" (Galatians 5:22).

Stress has been linked as a contributing factor in heart disease, mental illness, insomnia, and other health challenges. It negatively accelerates specific health problems. People desperately need to experience peace. They need to find peace for their spirit and find rest for their soul.

The world desperately wants lasting peace but can't find it. God's infinite peace lives within every believer. The presence of Christ is ready to help you successfully navigate through the storms of life. You don't have to search for peace, because you already have it. As you find others defeated by the storms of life, point them to God's perfect refuge, His eternal peace, which is found in the person of Jesus Christ. Jesus said to His disciples, *"Peace I leave with you, My peace I give to you; not as the world gives do I give to you. Let not your heart be troubled, neither let it be afraid" (John 14:27).*

Anxiety should no longer control your thinking. As God's child, you can be confident of His provision in every area of your life. Develop the habit of seeking His provision for all of your needs. He is able, more than able, to take care of you. Likewise, He is more than able to take care of those around you. With each opportunity, boldly share how God has graciously provided for your needs. Paul wrote, *"Be anxious for nothing, but in everything by prayer and supplication, with thanksgiving, let your requests be made known to God; and the peace of God, which surpasses all understanding, will guard your hearts and minds through Christ Jesus" (Philippians 4:6-7).*

Don't be surprised if you find yourself in the middle of a perfect storm. The vinedresser may decide to place you right in the middle of a physical, relational, or financial crisis. Why would He do this? He may decide to use you to model the abiding life and serve as an encouragement to branches nearby. But don't worry, the Lord can deliver an abundance of fruit as He leads you through the storms of life. Paul wrote, *"I, therefore, the prisoner of the Lord, beseech you to walk worthy of the calling with which you were called, with all lowliness and gentleness, with longsuffering, bearing with one another in love, endeavoring to keep the unity of the Spirit in the bond of peace" (Ephesians 4:1-3).* You don't have to search for peace. You already have it.

Read: Open your Bible and read Matthew 6:25.

Reflect: Prayerfully consider the following: Am I being honest with God about my anxieties? What challenges have I not brought before Him?

Respond: As a result of these truths, what might need to change in my attitude, beliefs, and actions? What steps do I need to take outwardly?

Kindness, Goodness, and Faithfulness

"But the fruit of the Spirit is love, joy, peace, longsuffering,
kindness, goodness, faithfulness" (Galatians 5:22).

There are certain ingredients you look for before preparing a special meal. Whether you're following a recipe or operating with the instincts of a seasoned cook, you know the importance of finding exactly what you need. Every time you use these ingredients the right taste is guaranteed. It is a great feeling to know the predictability of the right ingredients.

You were designed to deliver kindness by helping others find rest. As a Christian, your life should be marked by kindness. Delivering kindness means removing the burdens others are carrying; it means simultaneously lightening the weights of life and giving others an opportunity to rest. We know that people are stressed and tired. Kindness also means showing mercy and favor to others, even when you don't think they deserve it. Jesus said, *"Come to Me, all you who labor and are heavy laden, and I will give you rest. Take My yoke upon you and learn from Me, for I am gentle and lowly in heart, and you will find rest for your souls" (Matthew 11:28-29).*

Check your motives. Your delivery is to be wrapped in purity. Every demonstration of God's love should be delivered with complete integrity. Integrity means being one, whole, or complete. There are no mixed messages, ulterior motives, or deceit. Every opportunity you have to deliver God's love is to be characterized by a pure heart. Even when you don't see immediate results, do it with moral excellence and let God take care of the results. Paul writes, *"And let us not grow weary while doing good, for in due season we shall reap if we do not lose heart. Therefore, as we have opportunity, let us do good to all, especially to those who are of the household of faith" (Galatians 6:9-10).* Do good to all and live in complete integrity.

Can your family, friends, neighbors and co-workers count on you? Or have you been known to say one thing and then do another instead? If so, that old behavior was not buried when Jesus moved into your life. Being faithful has a totally different look and feel. In Christ, you can live responsibly. You now have the capacity to deliver truth consistently. You no longer need to blame others for your actions. And in the process, you can teach believers around you what you have learned and obeyed (2 Timothy 2:2).

Read: Open your Bible and read John 8-11.

Reflect: Prayerfully consider the following: What are three ways that Jesus delivered kindness and goodness to others? How can I do likewise?

Respond: As a result of these truths, what might need to change in my attitude, beliefs, and actions? What steps do I need to take outwardly?

Gentleness and Self-Control

"But the fruit of the Spirit is love, joy, peace, longsuffering, kindness, goodness, faithfulness, gentleness, self-control. Against such there is no law. And those who are Christ's have crucified the flesh with its passions and desires. If we live in the Spirit, let us also walk in the Spirit. Let us not become conceited, provoking one another, envying one another" (Galatians 5:22-26).

The customer yells, "I'll have one more drink, Sam," as he drops his glass on the floor. He's a regular at the bar. Although gentle when sober, his lack of self-control transforms him after drinking for two hours. It is a difficult sight to see. His words and actions have become destructive.

Delivering gentleness is anything but normal. It isn't something we see every day. Often, we experience the exact opposite from those around us. Delivering gentleness involves humbling yourself before God and remaining submissive to His ways. Living an abiding life determines both the quality and the quantity of your delivery. Remember, the vine is the One who produces the fruit. James wrote, *"Therefore lay aside all filthiness and overflow of wickedness, and receive with meekness the implanted word, which is able to save your souls. But be doers of the word, and not hearers only, deceiving yourselves" (James 1:21-22).* Abiding in Christ is a significant prerequisite.

Delivering gentleness means leading instead of forcing, guiding instead of demanding, and being considerate instead of uncaring. Delivering gentleness involves receiving instructions cheerfully and maintaining the right attitude. It means demonstrating a caring spirit and taking the time to serve and help others. Paul reminds us, *"And be kind to one another, tenderhearted, forgiving one another, even as God in Christ forgave you" (Ephesians 4:32).* People need to know that you really care about them.

You cannot live an abiding life in Christ and lack self-control at the same time. When you are walking in the Spirit you will display and deliver self-control. You won't respond as others do. You won't participate in activities or conversations that destroy others or feed the desires of your flesh. Walking in the Spirit and exercising self-control work together. Gentleness and self-control are products of the Holy Spirit, not the flesh. Today, learn from God's Word and let him continue shaping your life.

Read: Open your Bible and read all of Galatians 5:1-26.

Reflect: Prayerfully consider the following: Where are gentleness and self-control lacking in my life? What is the root cause for this shortage?

Respond: As a result of these truths, what might need to change in my attitude, beliefs, and actions? What steps do I need to take outwardly?

Friends

*"This is my commandment, that you love one another as I have loved you.
Greater love has no one than this, that someone lay down his life for his friends.
You are my friends if you do what I command you. No longer do I call you
servants, for the servant does not know what his master is doing;
but I have called you friends, for all that I have heard from my Father
I have made known to you" (John 15:12-15).*

There was a time when tracking down old friends was very difficult. Doing so was an expensive and time-consuming endeavor. Along the way, many would get discouraged; constant obstacles forced them to stop searching. Today, old friends are no longer difficult to find. Technology has enabled us to inexpensively search and find old friends with the click of a mouse.

When you discover the characteristics of being God's friend, what you find is worth the pursuit. Jesus sets the example of true friendship by laying His life down for His friends. This is the greatest act of friendship—the greatest act of love. Jesus gave His life on behalf of the disciples to bring them into a permanent, life-giving relationship with the Father (1 Timothy 2:5). Jesus voluntarily died on the cross to give His friends eternal life.

Jesus loved His friends at all times. The disciples were much more than Jesus' students; they were His personal friends. If they ever felt the "not good enough" syndrome, being accepted as Jesus' friend erased this feeling right away. He loved them while they were watching Him minister to the people. He loved them when they asked ridiculous questions. He loved them when they behaved like immature men. Jesus even loved them when they all scattered and abandoned Him. He loved them until the very end.

Jesus wants you to love others as He has loved you. He wants you to be a good friend. He wants you to love people just as they are. He expects you to make personal sacrifices for their benefit. Jesus wants you to obey His commands without hesitation. Jesus wants this friendship to grow strong. His friendship means knowing the secrets of the Father. Jesus promises to let you know what the Father is doing around you. He promises to reveal God's will for your life. He promises to be with you and in you every moment of every day. Remember, you too are one His personal friends.

Read: Open your Bible and read James 2:23.

Reflect: Prayerfully consider the following: Since I am God's friend by faith in Christ Jesus, what does that say about how much God values me?

Respond: As a result of these truths, what might need to change in my attitude, beliefs, and actions? What steps do I need to take outwardly?

Go and Bear Fruit

"You did not choose me, but I chose you and appointed you that you should go and bear fruit and that your fruit should abide, so that whatever you ask the Father in my name, he may give it to you. These things I command you, so that you will love one another" (John 15:16-17).

Being picked last can be a painful experience for a young kid. The neighborhood kids get together to play a game of football. First, they have to pick teams. Usually the toughest kids rise to the call of captain. One-by-one they begin picking their teammates. The unproven kids are often picked last. This is never easy. Being someone's last choice is no fun at all. You were a part of God's first selection for His eternal team. What an honor and privilege! God selected you for Himself. You may have thought, "What can I possibly contribute to God's Kingdom? What gifts or experiences do I have that can serve His purposes?" The answers to those questions can be surprising. God selected you to be a part of His team. Now that you permanently belong to Him, He equips you for what's next.

In your selection, you have been *"appointed,"* or placed into His service. The idea has to do with being "set" or "placed" by God to do His work. This placement is your calling in life. In other words, God has uniquely ordained you to function in a specific area of ministry to produce spiritual fruit. Part of discovering your calling is recognizing your spiritual gifts. It involves knowing how they can be used to glorify God, serve His church, and reach the lost. You have been called to fulfill a specific mission through your local church. This is the reason God picked you for His team.

When you live your life the way God designed it for you to live, the fruit you produce for God will remain strong. There are no two branches exactly alike. What God has uniquely purposed for you to do can only be done by you. Sure, others can serve God, minister to others, and bear fruit. They have their place and you have your place. You have to discover and practice the unique spiritual function God has equipped you for. As you live out God's purposes for your life, you will begin to see Him answer prayers in alignment with His mission and your specific function. This is when everything comes together, when knowing and doing the will of God is synchronized. Get started today. Go and bear fruit.

Read: Open your Bible and read Romans 8:29-33.

Reflect: Prayerfully consider the following: Am I actively searching for God to use my gifts in my workplace and through His church to bear fruit?

Respond: As a result of these truths, what might need to change in my attitude, beliefs, and actions? What steps do I need to take outwardly?

Persecution Guaranteed

"If the world hates you, know that it has hated me before it hated you.
If you were of the world, the world would love you as its own; but because
you are not of the world, but I chose you out of the world, therefore the world
hates you. Remember the word that I said to you: 'A servant is not greater
than his master.' If they persecuted me, they will also persecute you.
If they kept my word, they will also keep yours" (John 15:18-20).

It's a phrase we have learned to expect from those who sell products and services: "Satisfaction guaranteed." Sales representatives first work through common problems we face every day. Next, they present their solution in a compelling way. Finally, they list every benefit, encouraging us to buy now. If we have doubts, they remind us, "Satisfaction guaranteed."

The Christian life is filled with promises—real promises. One of these promises is the reality of persecution. Persecution is not something we pray for. No one enjoys being mistreated, mocked, or pursued by others with harmful motives. There were people in Jesus' day that loved Him and others who deeply hated Him. Some would gladly receive every word He spoke while others criticized Him publically and spread malicious rumors.

Jesus wanted us to know that living for Him means enduring persecution. Since people hated Jesus and judged Him unfairly, they will do the same to you. Since people planted seeds of division regarding Jesus, they will do the same to you. Since people wanted to destroy Jesus' ministry and weaken His testimony, they will do the same to you. The attacks arrive because your faith is countercultural. It is in direct opposition to what people want.

Persecution is guaranteed to come. For this reason, get ready. Because of this, you need to be ready. Prepare yourself spiritually. Ask God to fill you with His spirit when challenged for your faith. Study God's Word, and know where to find answers for the most common objections to the faith. Remember the words of Peter on your adventure: *"But in your hearts honor Christ the Lord as holy, always being prepared to make a defense to anyone who asks you for a reason for the hope that is in you; yet do it with gentleness and respect, having a good conscience, so that, when you are slandered, those who revile your good behavior in Christ may be put to shame" (1 Peter 3:15-16).*

Read: Open your Bible and read 1 John 3:13.

Reflect: Prayerfully consider the following: Why should I not be surprised when others attack my faith? How can I give a better defense?

Respond: As a result of these truths, what might need to change in my attitude, beliefs, and actions? What steps do I need to take outwardly?

No Excuses

"But all these things they will do to you on account of my name, because they do not know him who sent me. If I had not come and spoken to them, they would not have been guilty of sin, but now they have no excuse for their sin. Whoever hates me hates my Father also. If I had not done among them the works that no one else did, they would not be guilty of sin, but now they have seen and hated both me and my Father. But the word that is written in their Law must be fulfilled: 'They hated me without a cause' " (John 15:21-25).

When police officers stop cars for speeding, the excuses they hear are endless. They might hear, "Officer, my car is new. I thought I was driving half that speed. I never speed!" Others insist, "This is my first time in this area. I was not aware of the signs. These signs are hard to see." When the officers come back with the ticket, their only reply is, "No excuses."

There is no justification for rejecting Jesus as Messiah, Savior, and Lord. Jesus' presence on earth indicted those who rejected Him. The hidden secrets of the Old Testament were revealed in the person of Jesus Christ. Jesus is the revelation of God. God's love for mankind was expressed completely as Jesus lived among the people. To reject Jesus and link His works with those of the devil was to reject God. This was inexcusable.

Is there a part of the Christian life that you hate? You may truly love God and serve Him to the best of your ability, but maybe there are certain portions of Scripture you choose not to follow. You may not consider this a complete rejection of your Lord, but it does affect your relationship in a profound way. There is no truth of God too small for you to fully obey. Your comprehensive submission to God's Word is the primary goal.

Consider the following questions: Are you being merciful and helping others when they find themselves in a mess? Are you taking steps to make peace with others when relationships are damaged? Have you allowed pride to stop you from obeying God? Are you allowing feelings to control your actions rather than God's truth? In your place of work, are you being salt and light in the way you speak and act? What about in your home? Don't make excuses; they don't work. Ask God and others for forgiveness when you have decided to act contrary to Jesus' commands. No excuses.

Read: Open your Bible and read Matthew 5:1-16.

Reflect: Prayerfully consider the following: Why is it so important to love God and follow His Word in every part of my life?

Respond: As a result of these truths, what might need to change in my attitude, beliefs, and actions? What steps do I need to take outwardly?

Get Ready

"But when the Helper comes, whom I will send to you from the Father, the Spirit of truth, who proceeds from the Father, he will bear witness about me. And you also will bear witness, because you have been with me from the beginning"
(John 15:26-27).

Many think of the game of tennis as strictly an individual sport. One opponent wins and the other loses. Even though doubles tennis may not be as popular, it is exciting to watch. These athletes combine their skills and synchronize their strategies to defeat their opponents. Each one has a specific role to play. They are no longer individual players, but one team.

God's plan to save people from an eternal Hell is a team effort. God's sovereignty is at work. His Spirit is on the move, and His people are ready for action. To reach people for Christ we have to work with and through the Holy Spirit. Are you ready? The Holy Spirit serves many functions; one in particular is giving witness to the Lord Jesus. The Holy Spirit will testify on behalf of Jesus. He will reveal the works and words of Jesus in a compelling way through creation, circumstances, and God's people.

Your part is just as important. God designed you to work with and through the Holy Spirit to share the message of Jesus with others. Letting others know about God's work of grace and mercy in your life is powerful. People can identify with your story. People can find hope as they hear about God's love revealed through your life. What you have received must be shared with those without Christ. Notice John's compelling testimony:

"That which was from the beginning, which we have heard, which we have seen with our eyes, which we looked upon and have touched with our hands, concerning the word of life—the life was made manifest, and we have seen it, and testify to it and proclaim to you the eternal life, which was with the Father and was made manifest to us— that which we have seen and heard we proclaim also to you, so that you too may have fellowship with us; and indeed our fellowship is with the Father and with his Son Jesus Christ" (1 John 1:1-3).

What about you? What are you waiting for to do your part in reaching others for Jesus Christ? The Holy Spirit is ready to help you reach your family and your friends. The time has come. Get ready and do your part.

Read: Open your Bible and read Romans 1:16.

Reflect: Prayerfully consider the following: Am I actively working with the Holy Spirit to share Jesus with others? If not, what am I afraid of?

Respond: As a result of these truths, what might need to change in my attitude, beliefs, and actions? What steps do I need to take outwardly?

Don't Stumble

"I have said all these things to you to keep you from falling away. They will put you out of the synagogues. Indeed, the hour is coming when whoever kills you will think he is offering service to God. And they will do these things because they have not known the Father, nor me. But I have said these things to you, that when their hour comes you may remember that I told them to you"
(John 16:1-4).

Do you have a tendency to trip over things? Some of us regularly crash into people or knock things over by mistake. Falling down as a result of not seeing a small object is no fun at all. It's both embarrassing and painful. We tell our kids as they walk, "Watch where you are going. Pay attention! Look both ways before crossing." Why? We don't want them to stumble.

Jesus did not want His followers to fall away from the faith. He wanted to warn them of what to expect to keep them from stumbling in their faith. Severe persecution has the ability to discourage believers severely in their faith. Jesus warned His disciples of being mistreated in the temple and removed from its presence. He warned them of the harsh rejection to come. Jesus wanted them to know that their very life would be at risk.

Jesus wanted His disciples to get ready. Things were about to change. He wanted them to keep their eyes and ears open. He did not want them to be surprised. He wanted them to stand firm in their faith until the end of their lives. Jesus wanted them to remember His words and hold on to His promises. The day was coming when people would begin to violently oppose His claims, because they did not know the Father (John 8:19).

Think through those times when you have been mocked or persecuted for your faith. What came to mind when you experienced this opposition? Did you remember the words of Jesus? When your faith is under attack, do not panic; do not respond in your flesh. Be aware of what is taking place around you. Let the Holy Spirit guide your thoughts and your words. Remember the words of Jesus. Let His words fill your mind and your heart. You are not fighting against people; you are fighting a spiritual battle. When persecution comes, respond with the power of the Holy Spirit. Let God speak through you. Don't get discouraged. Don't stumble.

Read: Open your Bible and read John 8:19.

Reflect: Prayerfully consider the following: Do I get angry with people when they challenge me for my faith? Do I stumble and sin as a result?

Respond: As a result of these truths, what might need to change in my attitude, beliefs, and actions? What steps do I need to take outwardly?

Your Advantage

"I did not say these things to you from the beginning, because I was with you. But now I am going to him who sent me, and none of you asks me, 'Where are you going?' But because I have said these things to you, sorrow has filled your heart. Nevertheless, I tell you the truth: it is to your advantage that I go away, for if I do not go away, the Helper will not come to you. But if I go, I will send him to you." (John 16:4-7).

When a football team plays at home, they have a competitive advantage: the home team doesn't have to get on a plane and spend several hours in travel; they do not have to sleep in a hotel far away from their families; they do not have to adapt to a new climate. This makes a big difference. The home team also has overwhelming support from their energetic fans.

Jesus wanted His disciples to know about their competitive advantage in the spiritual arena. During Jesus' ministry, the presence of God was with the disciples. This must have been an amazing experience for these men. Jesus' departure speech was therefore a moment of deep sadness rather than a time of expectancy. They must have thought, "Now we are in BIG trouble. Jesus is leaving us. It's over. We can't continue without Him." They did not understand how they could make things work without Him.

Before listening to the entire plan, the disciples choose to dwell on the present reality. Jesus was essentially telling them, "Listen brothers, I have to go to my Father. But I won't leave you alone. Something new and better is about to happen. Someone will come and help you do my work. But if I don't leave, I can't send Him to you." Although they did not fully understand the implications, they continued to listen to their Lord.

In the book of Acts, both the disciples and the people witnessed the coming of the Helper, *"Being therefore exalted at the right hand of God, and having received from the Father the promise of the Holy Spirit, he has poured out this that you yourselves are seeing and hearing" (Acts 2:33).* The coming of the Holy Spirit gives all believers the competitive advantage in the spiritual realm. You are never alone. God's Spirit fills you and promises to teach you all things. The Spirit of the Living God lives within you. You don't need to live in sadness or in deep resentment. You have *the* advantage.

Read: Open your Bible and read John 7:37-39.

Reflect: Prayerfully consider the following: Am I allowing the power of the Holy Spirit to transform my sadness, anger, and resentment?

Respond: As a result of these truths, what might need to change in my attitude, beliefs, and actions? What steps do I need to take outwardly?

The Persuader

"And when he comes, he will convict the world concerning sin and righteousness and judgment: concerning sin, because they do not believe in me; concerning righteousness, because I go to the Father, and you will see me no longer; concerning judgment, because the ruler of this world is judged" (John 16:8-11).

Buying a new car can be a stressful endeavor. When it comes time to negotiate the final price, the intensity of the sale increases; unexpected charges are added, and you begin feeling the financial pressure. The manager is usually called in when you decide to decline the current offer. The manager will work hard to persuade you to accept the present deal. He may give you coupons for future oil changes, or reduce the price even more. His job is to persuade you with the facts and close the deal.

Jesus explained some of the core functions of the Holy Spirit. The Holy Spirit will help people see the reality of their sin in the light of God's Word. Regardless of the culture, the Holy Spirit shows people their true spiritual condition. He helps them see how short they fall of God's holy standard, the Ten Commandments. The Holy Spirit persuades people to repent as they discover their inability to be right with God on their own terms.

The Helper reminds the lost of the only unpardonable sin: rejecting Jesus as Savior and Lord of all. He convinces people of the perfect righteousness found only through Jesus Christ. He clearly presents Jesus as God's solution to their sin problem. He shows them how Jesus' substitutionary death on the cross paid the total price for their sins. With great power, the Comforter helps people find the Way, the Truth, and the Life. He provides every living person with an opportunity to know God personally.

The Holy Spirit warns people of the eternal judgment to come. He communicates this warning through God's people, technology, nature, circumstances, and other means. Like a good prosecutor, He develops a strong case that contains an abundance of evidence. He urges people to act now. He pleads with them to turn from their sin and turn to God. The urgency is to help others avoid the final judgment. This is the day when those who reject Jesus as Savior will be judged by their works. Be faithful in telling others about Jesus and His salvation. Let the Holy Spirit persuade.

Read: Open your Bible and read 2 Corinthians 4:4.

Reflect: Prayerfully consider the following: What can I do today to connect those who are lost with Jesus? How can I help them see Him?

Respond: As a result of these truths, what might need to change in my attitude, beliefs, and actions? What steps do I need to take outwardly?

Revealing What's Next

"I still have many things to say to you, but you cannot bear them now. When the Spirit of truth comes, he will guide you into all the truth, for he will not speak on his own authority, but whatever he hears he will speak, and he will declare to you the things that are to come. He will glorify me, for he will take what is mine and declare it to you. All that the Father has is mine; therefore I said that he will take what is mine and declare it to you" (John 16:12-15).

Tutoring programs are extremely helpful as you work your way through tough subjects. Tutors help you in a very personalized way. They help you work through homework assignments, unanswered questions, and a host of other challenges faced by most students. One of the reasons for their effectiveness is their ability to adapt to match your learning style and pace.

The Holy Spirit is the perfect tutor. He reveals God's will for your life at a pace you can understand. He is not trying to add more stress. He is trying to help you depend on His power to do God's work. The Holy Spirit knows when you need more preparation and experience. He knows when you are ready to take your next test. Like a master tutor, He knows you and understands how you think, making adjustments to help you grow.

The Father, Son, and Holy Spirit always function as one. The Holy Spirit does not carry out His own agenda. What He hears from heaven He speaks. Part of what the Spirit hears pertains to your future. What has God designed for your family? What career choice is He waiting for you to pursue? What area of ministry in your church did He equip you to do? The Holy Spirit wants to reveal these things to you. He wants you to know God's plan and start taking action to fulfill your destiny.

God is painting a beautiful portrait of your life. You have to listen to the Holy Spirit to know what colors He wants to use next. He will remind you of Jesus' words and reveal His plans one step of obedience at a time. The evidence of you aligning yourself with God's plan is simple—Jesus is glorified. He is glorified when you have daily personal time with God. His name is exalted when you tell others about His Son. God is revealed to others when you take the next step of faith and trust Him more. The Holy Spirit will gently reveal God's plan for you to understand and take action.

Read: Open your Bible and read James 1:22.

Reflect: Prayerfully consider the following: Am I listening to the Holy Spirit? What truth is He revealing that I need to follow today?

Respond: As a result of these truths, what might need to change in my attitude, beliefs, and actions? What steps do I need to take outwardly?

A Little While

"'A little while, and you will see me no longer; and again a little while, and you will see me.' So some of his disciples said to one another, 'What is this that he says to us, 'A little while, and you will not see me, and again a little while, and you will see me'; and, 'because I am going to the Father'?' So they were saying, 'What does he mean by 'a little while'? We do not know what he is talking about.' Jesus knew that they wanted to ask him, so he said to them, 'Is this what you are asking yourselves, what I meant by saying, 'A little while and you will not see me, and again a little while and you will see me'?" (John 16:16-19)

Fireworks are used to celebrate the anniversary of a country, the start of a new year, and other special occasions. As these small rockets scream into the sky, they release beautiful streams of temporary lights and sounds. Some have multiple layers of lights released only seconds apart. But you have to pay close attention, since their effects are only for a little while.

Jesus knew where He came from and where He was going. His time with the disciples was coming to an end. Jesus was slowly preparing them for His departure to the Father when He said, *"I will be with you a little longer, and then I am going to him who sent me"* (John 7:33). His investment in the disciples would now be given an opportunity to yield spiritual fruit. The time for the disciples to live by the power of the Holy Spirit was near. This is what Jesus promised and this is what He expected (John 15:1-11).

Are you living your life in the power of the Holy Spirit? Do you focus more on the comforts of life rather than the indwelling presence of God? Do you have a sense of urgency regarding spiritual things? Think of those whom you influence every day. Imagine if your doctor told you, "You only have one month to live." What would you change to maximize the "little while" that remains? Suddenly, making more money or holding onto old grudges is no longer a priority. Your time is short. You have to get ready.

Your life on earth is only for a "little while." You cannot waste time. The disciples did not understand the big picture. This led to arguments regarding positions of influence among them. Make every decision with an eternal perspective. Take deliberate steps to restore and heal broken relationships. Your life is temporary, but your impact can be eternal.

Read: Open your Bible and read James 4:14.

Reflect: Prayerfully consider the following: Are my actions, attitudes, and plans reflecting a temporary or an eternal impact on people?

Respond: As a result of these truths, what might need to change in my attitude, beliefs, and actions? What steps do I need to take outwardly?

From Sadness to Gladness

"Truly, truly, I say to you, you will weep and lament, but the world will rejoice. You will be sorrowful, but your sorrow will turn into joy. When a woman is giving birth, she has sorrow because her hour has come, but when she has delivered the baby, she no longer remembers the anguish, for joy that a human being has been born into the world. So also you have sorrow now, but I will see you again, and your hearts will rejoice, and no one will take your joy from you. In that day you will ask nothing of me. Truly, truly, I say to you, whatever you ask of the Father in my name, he will give it to you. Until now you have asked nothing in my name. Ask, and you will receive, that your joy may be full" (John 16:20-24).

It happens every minute of every day. After hours of agony and pain, a pregnant mother delivers a new baby into this world. Every ounce of energy is used to convert the physical and emotional distress into a new opportunity for life to thrive. The change from severe struggle to great celebration is truly amazing. It is a day that a mother will never forget.

Jesus recognized the temporary sadness involved when a friend decides to leave. He wanted the disciples to focus more on the reality of His eternal resurrection than on his temporary departure. This was the reason for His illustration of the woman giving birth. Yes, there would be sadness, but what was coming would replace their sadness with joy. The disciples would see Jesus again. Jesus spent many days after His resurrection encouraging His team to finish God's work in the power of the Holy Spirit.

The resurrection would transform mourning and hopelessness into celebration and hope. This joy would remain with the disciples for the rest of their lives. It would renew their faith, transform their prayer life, and help them accomplish their eternal mission. Is that not what the resurrection has done for your life? You were once without hope and living in despair; your sins were catching up to you; you found yourself living for temporary gains and pleasures, but Jesus changed everything.

Today, you can pray according to God's perfect will and receive what He has promised to deliver. God listens when His children pray. You can live with a joy that overflows from your heart. You no longer have to live in the pain caused by others or yourself. Smile, you can be glad now.

Read: Open your Bible and read Nehemiah 8:17.

Reflect: Prayerfully consider the following: Are joy and gladness a visible part of my life? Do I focus more on my personal challenges than on Jesus?

Respond: As a result of these truths, what might need to change in my attitude, beliefs, and actions? What steps do I need to take outwardly?

Rich in Generosity

"Jesus sat down opposite the place where the offerings were put and watched the crowd putting their money into the temple treasury. Many rich people threw in large amounts. But a poor widow came and put in two very small copper coins, worth only a few cents. Calling his disciples to him, Jesus said, 'Truly I tell you, this poor widow has put more into the treasury than all the others. They all gave out of their wealth; but she, out of her poverty, put in everything—all she had to live on' " (Mark 12:41-44).

Everyone is asking you to give financially. You hear it on the radio and watch compelling stories on television. They make presentations at your place of work and some even knock at your door. In one form or another, the question they all asking is, "Would you give generously to this cause?" But how does a disciple of Jesus define true generosity? It means keeping less of what you have and giving sacrificially to advance God's purposes.

Here is the main idea: to give more, you have to keep less. Jesus carefully contrasted the giving of the rich with the sacrifice of the poor widow. The rich gave out of their abundance and some of what they had left over. They gave large gifts, but it cost them very little—there was no sacrifice on the part of the rich. It was not an act of faith, and it did not reflect their total dependence on God. These people were not rich in generosity.

The poor widow gave out of her extreme poverty. She gave God all that she had. She only gave two small coins, but it cost her everything she had to live on. She sacrificed everything to give to God. Without question it was an act of faith. It reflected her complete dependence on God. Your giving is a clear indicator of your true spiritual maturity. We focus too much on how much we give. God is paying attention to the percentage we keep. Have you ever asked, "How much of God's money should I keep for myself? How much do I really need to live on? When you trust God and give generously to His work, He will provide for all of your needs.

Consider these questions: Am I giving God the first 10% of my income? Am I giving faithfully to support local and global missions? Am I giving spontaneously to help those in need? Am I giving sacrificially to multiply God's work? Am I giving by faith? Am I rich in generosity towards God?

Read: Open your Bible and read Luke 6:38.

Reflect: Prayerfully consider the following: Do the words faithful, obedient, and generous describe my giving towards God?

Respond: As a result of these truths, what might need to change in my attitude, beliefs, and actions? What steps do I need to take outwardly?

The Father Loves You

*"I have said these things to you in figures of speech. The hour is coming when
I will no longer speak to you in figures of speech but will tell you plainly
about the Father. In that day you will ask in my name, and I do not say
to you that I will ask the Father on your behalf; for the Father himself loves you,
because you have loved me and have believed that I came from God.
I came from the Father and have come into the world, and now
I am leaving the world and going to the Father" (John 16:25-28).*

It was a long day for little Marie. Many hours were spent playing outside,
watching television, and singing nursery rhymes. Most children went home
for the day, but Marie's dad works late. She was very tired. But when her
dad walked through the door, everything changed. Marie raced towards
her daddy and wrapped her arms around his legs. No matter what
happened earlier, she knew her daddy loved her and was coming soon.

Jesus was reiterating one of His previous lessons. The lessons regarding
the Father were difficult for the disciples to understand. What they
believed about God would be tested and expanded. Earlier Jesus taught,
*"Whoever has my commands and keeps them is the one who loves me. The one
who loves me will be loved by my Father, and I too will love them and show
myself to them" (John 14:21, NIV).* We can see the love of the Father
expressed throughout the entire Bible. When you love the Son you love
the Father also. God intended to reveal Himself through Jesus Christ.

Think through the implications of this next statement. God loves you!
God really loves you! You need to let this fact settle in your heart right
now. God loves you. He is your Father and you are His child. You are
God's friend. Like a good father, God will never leave or abandon you.
His presence lives within you at all times. You can call Him Father. He is
the One who sustains you and He provides for all of your needs.

Since the Father lives within you, His love abides in you wherever you go.
Be confident in God's love for you. You can be certain that He is ready to
pick you up and hold you close when pressures of life overwhelm you.
You don't have to fear your circumstances or worry about tomorrow.
Rest securely in God's presence. The Father himself loves you.

Read: Open your Bible and read John 14:21.

Reflect: Prayerfully consider the following: Am I resting in my Father's
presence? Am I totally depending on Him to provide for my needs?

Respond: As a result of these truths, what might need to change in my
attitude, beliefs, and actions? What steps do I need to take outwardly?

The Overcomer

"His disciples said, 'Ah, now you are speaking plainly and not using figurative speech! Now we know that you know all things and do not need anyone to question you; this is why we believe that you came from God.' Jesus answered them, 'Do you now believe? Behold, the hour is coming, indeed it has come, when you will be scattered, each to his own home, and will leave me alone. Yet I am not alone, for the Father is with me. I have said these things to you, that in me you may have peace. In the world you will have tribulation. But take heart; I have overcome the world' " (John 16:29-33).

Every young boy has dreams of becoming a superhero. Watching masked men display extraordinary strength as they fight off evil villains is worth every minute of their time. The thought of possessing great strength and serving those in danger is thrilling. Some even have their own special superhero name picked out. Becoming a superhero would be a dream come true. Anything less than being a superhero would be rather boring.

Without Christ and before the coming of the Holy Spirit, the disciples were anything but superheroes. Some might say they acted more like fearful children than mature disciples. Jesus predicted their reaction to the persecution that would soon follow. The disciples would run away right in the middle of their first major spiritual test. They would abandon Jesus in the process and leave their Master alone. But Jesus was never really alone. When everyone scattered, the Father was present with Jesus.

The word *"tribulation"* carries the idea of pressure that is coming together. You cannot escape the pressures of life. Although some difficulties are only seasonal, they still impact your life. Expect spiritual pressures and problems as you grow in your faith. Jesus said this would come so get ready. In Christ, you are an overcomer. Meditate on Paul's words:

"Who shall separate us from the love of Christ? Shall tribulation, or distress, or persecution, or famine, or nakedness, or danger, or sword? No, in all these things we are more than conquerors through him who loved us. For I am sure that neither death nor life, nor angels nor rulers, nor things present nor things to come, nor powers, nor height nor depth, nor anything else in all creation, will be able to separate us from the love of God in Christ Jesus our Lord" (Romans 8:35, 37-39).

Read: Open your Bible and read 1 Corinthians 4:9.

Reflect: Prayerfully consider the following: Do I speak as a defeated person or an overcomer in Christ? What message am I sending to others?

Respond: As a result of these truths, what might need to change in my attitude, beliefs, and actions? What steps do I need to take outwardly?

Knowing God

"When Jesus had spoken these words, he lifted up his eyes to heaven, and said, 'Father, the hour has come; glorify your Son that the Son may glorify you, since you have given him authority over all flesh, to give eternal life to all whom you have given him. And this is eternal life, that they know you the only true God, and Jesus Christ whom you have sent' " (John 17:1-3).

Do you enjoy finding the right solution to a tough problem that demands many days to figure out? It may require more time and resources than what you first expect. It may stretch you intellectually and emotionally. You may even encounter new problems along the way, but none of this is bothersome. Why? Knowing the right solution is your great motivator.

Before Jesus, God was not someone who was easy to understand. God revealed Himself through the prophets, but most people did not know Him intimately. The Father chose to reveal Himself through His Son. Jesus explained, *"All things have been handed over to me by my Father, and no one knows the Son except the Father, and no one knows the Father except the Son and anyone to whom the Son chooses to reveal him" (Matthew 11:27).* Jesus came to reveal the Father and to help people know the Father personally.

The great mystery people are trying to solve is, "What is eternal life and where can I find it?" More than a destination, eternal life is relational. You find eternal life in a Person, not in a destination. It's about knowing God and knowing Jesus Christ personally. Knowing God is eternal life. This is what it's all about. Eternal life is about knowing God intimately through His Son Jesus Christ. For this reason Jesus gave His life. He died for you to know the only true God. Isaiah writes, *"Out of the anguish of his soul he shall see and be satisfied; by his knowledge shall the righteous one, my servant, make many to be accounted righteous, and he shall bear their iniquities" (Isaiah 53:11).*

God wants you to know the truth about Him. Rather than hide and remain an unsolved mystery, God wants to reveal more of Himself to you personally. God chose you to reveal the hidden mysteries found in Jesus Christ. Just as Jesus glorified God through the overflow of His relationship with the Father, the Father is ready to use your life in the same way to change lives. Start celebrating. Keep pursuing your Savior. Know God.

Read: Open your Bible and read Jeremiah 9:23-24.

Reflect: Prayerfully consider the following: Do I celebrate the fact that I know God and understand His ways with others? What am I waiting for?

Respond: As a result of these truths, what might need to change in my attitude, beliefs, and actions? What steps do I need to take outwardly?

Finish the Work

"I have glorified You on the earth. I have finished the work which You have given Me to do" (John 17:1-4).

Finish God's work through your life! We all love a great finish as in a good movie. The intensity of a final scene can move people physically and emotionally. There is nothing like a great finish. God loves to watch a great finish in the lives of His people. He loves to see lives transformed by His awesome power. He loves to see relationships healed and marriages restored. God loves to see forgiveness demonstrated and mercy distributed through His people. He loves to see His great work accomplished through your life. God wants to see you finish strong.

God wants you to finish the work He chose for you to do. He wants you to persevere and make a difference in the lives of those around you. He wants you to finish well. Paul wrote to Timothy, *"I have fought the good fight, I have finished the race, I have kept the faith. Finally, there is laid up for me the crown of righteousness, which the Lord, the righteous Judge, will give to me on that Day, and not to me only but also to all who have loved His appearing"* (2 Timothy 4:7-8). You are in a race that only you can run.

The vinedresser is counting on you to deliver and get the job done. He is invested heavily in your life and He is looking forward to a generous return. Remember, the enemy wants to destroy your life. He doesn't want you to finish the work. He will do everything he can, and even use other branches to discourage you along the way. Don't get sidetracked…finish the work. Stay focused. Don't get discouraged…finish the work. John wrote, *"He [Jesus] who is in you is greater than he who is in the world"* (1 John 4:4).

Living an abiding life is the way to end well and finish God's great work. It's spending time with Jesus and responding to His instructions moment-by-moment. This is the key to glorifying God and fulfilling His purposes for your life. Spend time thanking God for helping you finish His work through your life. Continue studying God's Word and receiving from His Son each and every day. Let God finish His great work through you, through abiding. This is how He designed you to grow in your faith. This is how He desires for you to live day-by-day and moment-by-moment. Finish the work!

Read: Open your Bible and read 1 Peter 2:17.

Reflect: Prayerfully consider the following: Am I finishing what God is asking me to do? Am I persevering in my love and service to others?

Respond: As a result of these truths, what might need to change in my attitude, beliefs, and actions? What steps do I need to take outwardly?

You Belong to God

"And now, Father, glorify me in your own presence with the glory that I had with you before the world existed. I have manifested your name to the people whom you gave me out of the world. Yours they were, and you gave them to me, and they have kept your word. Now they know that everything that you have given me is from you. For I have given them the words that you gave me, and they have received them and have come to know in truth that I came from you; and they have believed that you sent me" (John 17:5-8).

There is a strong sense of responsibility when you own an item of great value. Instinctively, you take great care of what you own. If maintenance is required, no one needs to force you to make the investment. You take measures to protect what you have and manage it well. You do what you can to make your property thrive, last longer, and increase in significance.

You are infinitely valuable to God. Jesus left the perfect presence of the Father to claim you as His own. He gave up the glory of heaven to purchase you with His very own blood. God chose you for Himself. Paul wrote, *"Blessed be the God and Father of our Lord Jesus Christ, who has blessed us in Christ with every spiritual blessing in the heavenly places, even as he chose us in him before the foundation of the world, that we should be holy and blameless before him. In love he predestined us for adoption as sons through Jesus Christ, according to the purpose of his will"* (Ephesians 1:3-5).

Jesus summarizes the dominant characteristics of His property. First, you were chosen as God's property. Although this may be difficult to understand, God chose you to be His before you were created. The fact that you trusted Jesus for your salvation proves God's ownership. Second, you follow God's Word. This does not mean you never sin again. But it does mean that sin no longer controls your life. You now live by faith in the power of the Holy Spirit. You belong to a holy God.

Third, you know and believe the truth revealed through Jesus. You believe in His life and accept His salvation. You receive what He has to give you. You are confident in the perfect work of Jesus on the cross. You share His great love with others. You accept God's authority and submit to His will for your life. Why do you do all of this? It's simple. You belong to God.

Read: Open your Bible and read Romans 14:8.

Reflect: Prayerfully consider the following: Do I live as I belong to God or to another owner? Recently, how is God asking me to serve Him?

Respond: As a result of these truths, what might need to change in my attitude, beliefs, and actions? What steps do I need to take outwardly?

Divine Security

"I am praying for them. I am not praying for the world but for those whom you have given me, for they are yours. All mine are yours, and yours are mine, and I am glorified in them. And I am no longer in the world, but they are in the world, and I am coming to you. Holy Father, keep them in your name, which you have given me, that they may be one, even as we are one. While I was with them, I kept them in your name, which you have given me. I have guarded them, and not one of them has been lost except the son of destruction, that the Scripture might be fulfilled" (John 17:9-12).

Watching the security team responsible for protecting the President is impressive. Before attending large gatherings, security officers spend days preparing for his arrival. They secure buildings, detour traffic, and close buildings as necessary. Their main priority is to protect the President at all costs. They prepare for his every move to minimize any abrupt surprises.

Jesus prayed for God's protection over your life. He personally asked the Father to watch over you. Jesus understood the threats and challenges that come when you choose to follow Him. Knowing that God watches over you should help you rest in His protection. It should also help you accept things when great difficulties come your way. God continues to watch over you when persecution or personal struggles arrive. He watches you closely. He is aware of the loss and understands the cost.

Jesus also prays for unity among God's people. Knowing the power found in love and unity, Jesus prays for believers to live in one accord. He wants them to genuinely love one another and live in harmony with one another. Think through the relationships that you have with other believers. Do you regularly try to help people with opposing views find a solution? Do you take action when a believer has been mistreated or taken advantage of by another believer? God wants you to be involved in protecting other believers. He also wants you to protect the love and unity of His church.

The power to protect believers and help them live in unity comes from God. You have a role to play in each of these areas. You are responsible for others. Helping people grow spiritually involves protecting them from danger. It also involves helping them take steps for peace with others.

Read: Open your Bible and read Romans 8:38-39.

Reflect: Prayerfully consider the following: Am I confident in God's protection over my life? Am I pursuing love, peace, and unity with others?

Respond: As a result of these truths, what might need to change in my attitude, beliefs, and actions? What steps do I need to take outwardly?

Set Apart

"But now I am coming to you, and these things I speak in the world, that they may have my joy fulfilled in themselves. I have given them your word, and the world has hated them because they are not of the world, just as I am not of the world. I do not ask that you take them out of the world, but that you keep them from the evil one. They are not of the world, just as I am not of the world. Sanctify them in the truth; your word is truth" (John 17:13-17).

The goalkeeper on a soccer team has the responsibility of keeping the opposing team from getting the ball into the goal. He can use any part of his body to stop his opponents from scoring. If needed, he can call on his teammates for additional reinforcement. To win the game, the goalkeeper must stay alert and protect his goal at all costs. This is his main priority.

In anticipation of the opposition to come, Jesus prayed for the protection of His disciples. Attacks from the enemy were only a matter of time. Jesus reminded them earlier, *"Blessed are you when people hate you and when they exclude you and revile you and spurn your name as evil, on account of the Son of Man"* (Luke 6:22)! Count on being hated, ignored, and mistreated by others as a result of your faith. Be alert and ready to stand against Satan's personal attacks on you and your family. God's grace will be with you.

Jesus prayed that the Father would *"keep them from the evil one."* The *"them"* in this prayer includes you, too. God is the One who protects you from personal attacks by Satan. He is in charge. You never have to face an attack that God is not fully aware of. Rest assured, He is at work. Paul wrote, *"But the Lord is faithful. He will establish you and guard you against the evil one"* (2 Thessalonians 3:3). You are on the winning team. God regularly blocks Satan and his team from scoring destructive points on your life.

Jesus concludes, *"Sanctify them in the truth; your word is truth."* The word *"sanctify"* means to be "made holy" or "set apart" for God's purposes. Knowing, loving, and obeying God's Word is what keeps you in spiritual shape to live well. It is what gives you the power to resist your enemies. It gives you the strength needed to endure the most difficult opposition. Paul affirmed, *"The Lord will rescue me from every evil deed and bring me safely into his heavenly kingdom"* (2 Timothy 4:18). You have been set apart for God.

Read: Open your Bible and read 1 John 5:18.

Reflect: Consider the following: Am I committed to knowing, loving, and obeying God's Word? Am I resting in God's power to fight my battles?

Respond: As a result of these truths, what might need to change in my attitude, beliefs, and actions? What steps do I need to take outwardly?

Perfectly One

"As you sent me into the world, so I have sent them into the world. And for their sake I consecrate myself, that they also may be sanctified in truth. I do not ask for these only, but also for those who will believe in me through their word, that they may all be one, just as you, Father, are in me, and I in you, that they also may be in us, so that the world may believe that you have sent me. The glory that you have given me I have given to them, that they may be one even as we are one, I in them and you in me, that they may become perfectly one, so that the world may know that you sent me and loved them even as you loved me" (John 17:18-23).

Supermarkets have changed drastically over the years. Grocery stores used to sell only food and a basic array of household items. Today, the new wave of supermarkets sell tires, clothes, health and tax services, computers, phones, and more. Their goal is to meet all of their customers' needs by making these essential items available in one shopping experience.

The idea of perfect unity is not a new one. It started in eternity past with the Father, Son, and Holy Spirit. Jesus wants the church today to be similarly unified. He wants us to function as one church. In a supermarket, departments do not compete against one another. They work together to serve their customers. The church has to work as one body to better serve the lost world and reach people for Jesus. The greater the unity, the greater the eternal impact for God's Kingdom. We have to work together.

Jesus prayed for the church to function as one for the world to believe the message of the gospel. Division in a church affects the ability to reach people. It brings confusion and keeps them away. When we practice being perfectly one, people will understand God's love. This will show evidence of Jesus' divinity and relationship with the Father. There is great power in unity. Consider the multiplicative effect of being perfectly one with other believers. If you do your part in helping the church pursue unity as one, it will not only change you, it will change your church. And when it ultimately transforms your church, this change will positively impact believers for generations to come. It will create a powerful heritage within your ministry. Build relational bridges. Help others become perfectly one.

Read: Open your Bible and read Romans 12:5.

Reflect: Prayerfully consider the following: Why do you think becoming perfectly one as a church is such a powerful witness for Jesus Christ?

Respond: As a result of these truths, what might need to change in my attitude, beliefs, and actions? What steps do I need to take outwardly?

Make Him Known

"Father, I desire that they also, whom you have given me, may be with me where I am, to see my glory that you have given me because you loved me before the foundation of the world. O righteous Father, even though the world does not know you, I know you, and these know that you have sent me. I made known to them your name, and I will continue to make it known, that the love with which you have loved me may be in them, and I in them" (John 17:24-26).

Buying a home before it is built is common in rapidly growing areas. Watching the construction team prepare the land and lay the foundation builds great anticipation. Homeowners often visit the job site weekly to take pictures and start dreaming of this new phase in their lives. The parents can't wait, and the kids are ready to finally have their own rooms.

If you were given a chance to watch a five-minute video of God's throne and the beauty of heaven, it would radically change your prayer life. Since Jesus came from heaven, He knew what it was like. Jesus was glorified with the Father in heaven. The angels gave Him the honor that was due from eternity past. It was a glorious scene. The Righteous Father expressed His love for the Son and the Son did likewise. It was beyond what mere words can describe. Jesus was ready for His disciples to join Him in this glory.

God is preparing an eternal home for His children (Matthew 25:34). The main attraction is not the home, but those who will be present. The presence of the Father, Son and Holy Spirit is the heart of this special place. God wants you to make His name known. The reason is simple: people need to be saved from their sins and experience this eternal fellowship.

This loving fellowship with the Father, Son, and Holy Spirit starts when we accept Jesus as Savior. Paul wrote, *"For this reason I bow my knees before the Father, from whom every family in heaven and on earth is named, that according to the riches of his glory he may grant you to be strengthened with power through his Spirit in your inner being, so that Christ may dwell in your hearts through faith—that you, being rooted and grounded in love, may have strength to comprehend with all the saints what is the breadth and length and height and depth, and to know the love of Christ that surpasses knowledge, that you may be filled with all the fullness of God" (Ephesians 3:14-19).* Make Him known.

Read: Open your Bible and read Ephesians 3:1-19.

Reflect: Prayerfully consider the following: Is God challenging my heart to know more about His love and make Him known to others?

Respond: As a result of these truths, what might need to change in my attitude, beliefs, and actions? What steps do I need to take outwardly?

The Place

"When Jesus had spoken these words, he went out with his disciples across the brook Kidron, where there was a garden, which he and his disciples entered. Now Judas, who betrayed him, also knew the place, for Jesus often met there with his disciples" (John 18:1-2).

What is your favorite part of God's creation? Do you enjoy mountaintops, quiet rivers, oceans, or large lakes? There is something about nature that helps us relax, reflect, and refocus. Sitting on the shore of a great ocean or walking through a beautiful garden is a great reminder of God's power and His undeniable wisdom. Such places can help quiet your heart and listen for God's voice. They can serve to draw you closer to the risen Savior.

Jesus and His disciples were moments away from Judas' betrayal. It was a night none of them would soon forget. This particular garden had been a common meeting place for Jesus and His disciples. It was a place that represented intimate fellowship with the Savior. It was no doubt a place associated with teaching, prayer, and brotherly love. When the disciples had questions, it was a safe place for them to ask. It was a place to help them break away and rest from the growing demands of the people.

For your spiritual growth to thrive, you also need to regularly make time to talk with your Lord and Savior. But this practice is not only for your personal renewal. It is also an opportunity to invite others to join you from time to time. Luke tells us, *"And he came out and went, as was his custom, to the Mount of Olives, and the disciples followed him" (Luke 22:39).* Jesus not only sought solitude for Himself to fellowship with the Father, but He also invited His disciples to join Him during His spiritual journey. He wanted them to personally see and experience this activity. It would serve as a catalyst for their growth. Do others often join you in prayer?

The place you choose is not as important as the Person whom you plan to meet. Connecting with God and enjoying His fellowship is the goal. Find a place in your home and a place within your city for spiritual retreats. You may retreat daily at home and weekly or monthly elsewhere. As you discover these special places, invite others to join you to grow with you.

Read: Open your Bible and read Mark 14:32.

Reflect: Prayerfully consider the following: What does this verse teach me about spiritual leadership? Who should I invite to join me in prayer?

Respond: As a result of these truths, what might need to change in my attitude, beliefs, and actions? What steps do I need to take outwardly?

I Am He

"So Judas, having procured a band of soldiers and some officers from the chief priests and the Pharisees, went there with lanterns and torches and weapons. Then Jesus, knowing all that would happen to him, came forward and said to them, 'Whom do you seek?' They answered him, 'Jesus of Nazareth.' Jesus said to them, 'I am he.' Judas, who betrayed him, was standing with them. When Jesus said to them, 'I am he,' they drew back and fell to the ground"
(John 18:3-6).

Hunting down criminals on the run is a complicated and costly pursuit. News agencies flash pictures of the vigilante and plead with their viewers to report anyone who matches the description. City and state police officers are placed on high alert. They inform the local community. They work longer hours than normal and increase the intensity of their search. When the criminal is finally captured, the entire team celebrates together.

Jesus knew that His friend Judas would betray Him. It was a fulfillment of prophetic scripture: *"Even my close friend in whom I trusted, who ate my bread, has lifted his heel against me"* (Psalm 41:9). Judas and his team of hunters pursued Jesus as they would a notorious criminal. Some scholars believe hundreds of soldiers may have been involved in the plot. This involved great planning and craftiness on the part of Judas and his team. His betrayal was wickedly intentional. He was determined to destroy his good friend. He was now face-to-face with public enemy number one.

Jesus did not try to run from the situation. He stepped forward and spoke first. Jesus knew they came to arrest Him. It was time for Him to finish His special mission. When Jesus said, *"I am he,"* the power behind His words knocked the entire team of soldiers and officers to the ground like a bowling ball knocking down all of the pins in the alley. Jesus responded with heavenly authority, referring to Himself by one of the Old Testament names of the God of Israel: *"I am"* (c.f. Exodus 3:14, John 10:7; 11:25; 15:1).

Have you ever been betrayed by a good friend? It is a painful experience and often difficult to talk about. Matthias was later chosen by God to replace the void left by Judas' absence. In the same way, God will find others to fill the void left by friends who abruptly move out of your life.

Read: Open your Bible and read John 17:12.

Reflect: Prayerfully consider the following: Am I a good friend to others? How can I better love, protect, and encourage my friends?

Respond: As a result of these truths, what might need to change in my attitude, beliefs, and actions? What steps do I need to take outwardly?

Stop Fighting

"So he asked them again, 'Whom do you seek?' And they said, 'Jesus of Nazareth.' Jesus answered, 'I told you that I am he. So, if you seek me, let these men go.' This was to fulfill the word that he had spoken: 'Of those whom you gave me I have lost not one.' Then Simon Peter, having a sword, drew it and struck the high priest's servant and cut off his right ear. (The servant's name was Malchus.) So Jesus said to Peter, 'Put your sword into its sheath; shall I not drink the cup that the Father has given me?' " (John 18:7-11).

Unusual health problems sometimes call for special diets designed to help patients avoid problem foods or balance their internal systems over time. The patients always have a choice in the matter. They can choose to accept their condition and submit to these strict diets or ignore the clear warning signs, keep fighting, and refuse to change any eating habits at all.

Surrounded by a multitude of soldiers and officers, the disciples reached their maximum stress levels. It was hard enough to hear Jesus say He was going to the Father. It would be fine to see Him leave on a heavenly chariot. Being arrested by a mob was not part of their thinking, especially at the hands of their trusted friend Judas. How do a group of guys who are not yet filled with the Holy Spirit react to such a hostile situation? For Peter, the answer was to draw his sword and start fighting right away.

Jesus had promised earlier to care and protect His disciples (John 17:2). He was not about to go back on His promise. Although it may have been the last thing on Peter's mind, God's will was being carried out right in the middle of an intimidating situation. Peter wanted to fight for Jesus and protect Him from false imprisonment. Yet there was no need to fight. God was doing His perfect work. Jesus was right where He needed to be.

Is God telling you today, "Put away your sword"? Rather than accepting God's will in an area of your life, are you trying to fight it away? If God is working, why are you still fighting? Your reluctance to submit to God's will can hurt not only you, but also those around you. God is not intimidated by your situation. He may have you exactly where He needs you to be. If you submit to His will, others may come to know the Savior through this very difficult test. Put your sword away. Submit to God and stop fighting.

Read: Open your Bible and read Matthew 26:39.

Reflect: Prayerfully consider the following: Am I fighting to submit to God's will for a particular area of my life? Why am I fighting this battle?

Respond: As a result of these truths, what might need to change in my attitude, beliefs, and actions? What steps do I need to take outwardly?

Expedient

"So the band of soldiers and their captain and the officers of the Jews arrested Jesus and bound him. First they led him to Annas, for he was the father-in-law of Caiaphas, who was high priest that year. It was Caiaphas who had advised the Jews that it would be expedient that one man should die for the people"
(John 18:12-14).

Physical training is not something everyone enjoys. But when you are a member of a sports team, you have no choice. Imagine being part of a competitive team where only one athlete trains. He is the only one who eats healthy and experiences soreness in his muscles. Only he spends four hours a day in the gym working hard. Does this sound ridiculous to you?

When the religious leaders had Jesus arrested, they may have had a similar thought in mind. The people of Jerusalem were making considerable noise regarding the claims of Jesus. Some said that He was the promised Messiah, while others said His origin was demonic in nature. The crowds were divided, and so were the religious leaders. Pressure from all angles threatened their personal and professional security. They needed to act.

Caiaphas had advised and prophesied that one man, Jesus, should die for the people. It was a brilliant idea. Why should the religious leaders lose their position, their power, and their people over one guy who claimed to be God? Why should everyone suffer? Why should they lose so many people over this matter? It was better to sacrifice one for all than to sacrifice the multitudes. It was indeed the perfect plan to solve the issue.

Jesus suffered and died so that you might have eternal life. The author of Hebrews reminds us, *"He did not enter by means of the blood of goats and calves; but he entered the Most Holy Place once for all by his own blood, thus obtaining eternal redemption" (Hebrews 9:12, NIV).* As Jesus carried the weight of all of our sins, He paid the price with His very own blood. More than Caiaphas could ever imagine, it truly was expedient for Jesus to die. He was the only one who had the power to secure our eternal redemption. Peter wrote, *"For Christ also suffered once for sins, the righteous for the unrighteous, that he might bring us to God, being put to death in the flesh but made alive in the spirit" (1 Peter 3:18).* Jesus' death brings you to God.

Read: Open your Bible and read Matthew 27:1-2.

Reflect: Consider the following: Is it easy for me to see God's hand at work, even when people are planning to use me for their personal benefit?

Respond: As a result of these truths, what might need to change in my attitude, beliefs, and actions? What steps do I need to take outwardly?

Special Access

"Simon Peter followed Jesus, and so did another disciple. Since that disciple was known to the high priest, he entered with Jesus into the courtyard of the high priest, but Peter stood outside at the door. So the other disciple, who was known to the high priest, went out and spoke to the servant girl who kept watch at the door, and brought Peter in. The servant girl at the door said to Peter, 'You also are not one of this man's disciples, are you?' He said, 'I am not.' Now the servants and officers had made a charcoal fire, because it was cold, and they were standing and warming themselves. Peter also was with them, standing and warming himself" (John 18:15-18).

It can happen when you least expect it: you are at a large sporting event with your family, and you bump into an old friend in the hallway. After so many years, he still remembers you. He has a special pass that gives you and your family a unique opportunity to walk on the field. His credentials give him special access to meet the players. You can touch the field with your hands and run around on it with your kids. Special access is great.

The Bible describes John as someone who was very personable. Two characteristics that stand out in his life are relational and dependable. John knew people and he knew them well. It is no surprise that he connected with a variety of people. John knew the powerful high priest of Jerusalem. We don't know all of the details involved regarding their relationship.

What we do know is that John was no stranger to the high priest. That relationship gave John special access to the events that followed. It also provides Peter with an incredible opportunity to enter this restricted area and see Jesus up close. Sadly, instead of standing strong with Jesus, Peter squandered his special access by denying that he knew the Lord Jesus at all.

Has God given you special access to be in the presence of influential people and speak on His behalf? Are you speaking or remaining silent? Have you ever found yourself in a place or in a position and wondered, "How did I get here? I don't deserve to be here. Why am I here?" God will give you access to people and events so you can proclaim the message of Jesus. It is not a right. Special access is a high privilege. Make the most of it!

Read: Open your Bible and read Mark 14:54.

Reflect: Prayerfully consider the following: Do you follow Jesus at a safe distance? Is it difficult for you to easily relate to others and connect?

Respond: As a result of these truths, what might need to change in my attitude, beliefs, and actions? What steps do I need to take outwardly?

Nothing to Hide

"The high priest then questioned Jesus about his disciples and his teaching. Jesus answered him, 'I have spoken openly to the world. I have always taught in synagogues and in the temple, where all Jews come together. I have said nothing in secret. Why do you ask me? Ask those who have heard me what I said to them; they know what I said.' When he had said these things, one of the officers standing by struck Jesus with his hand, saying, 'Is that how you answer the high priest?' Jesus answered him, 'If what I said is wrong, bear witness about the wrong; but if what I said is right, why do you strike me?' Annas then sent him bound to Caiaphas the high priest" (John 18:19-24).

It's hard to tell when a con artist is telling the truth and when he is lying. They are very good at practicing deceitfulness. They have mastered the art of deception so well that they can look you straight in the face and tell you the biggest lie imaginable without revealing their dishonesty. They pride themselves in carefully hiding the truth and manipulating good people.

Jesus did not come to deceive, but to save. He spoke openly about the Father and about His own mission here on earth. He did not form a secret society to communicate His message. He was the chief spokesman. Jesus taught the way because He was the Way. He spoke the truth because He was the Truth. Jesus spoke about the life because He was the Life. Jesus is the full revelation of God the Father on earth. Both in word and in deed, He came to reveal the Father's love. There was nothing for Him to hide.

Jesus' response to the high priest leads us to ask a penetrating question. What would others say is the message you regularly communicate? Would they say that your message is consistent wherever you go? Is the way you talk at church the way you talk with your co-workers? Do your family and friends all hear the same message? What exactly are you trying to say?

Jesus practiced integrity. He was the same wherever He went. People knew what He was about. They knew what He stood for even if they did not agree with His teachings. His message was clear and His life backed it up 100%. What about you? Does your life back up your message? Are you hiding a practice that would bring shame to yourself and to your Lord?

Read: Open your Bible and read Ephesians 4:25.

Reflect: Prayerfully consider the following: Am I sharing with others all that I know about God? Do my message and my behavior always match?

Respond: As a result of these truths, what might need to change in my attitude, beliefs, and actions? What steps do I need to take outwardly?

Cold Denials

"Now Simon Peter was standing and warming himself. So they said to him, 'You also are not one of his disciples, are you?' He denied it and said, 'I am not.' One of the servants of the high priest, a relative of the man whose ear Peter had cut off, asked, 'Did I not see you in the garden with him?' Peter again denied it, and at once a rooster crowed" (John 18:25-27).

The witness declares, "There is no mistake. This man is the one I saw that night. I am certain he committed this crime." Although only a few sentences long, the testimony of the witness makes an impact on the jury. As evidence piles up, the prosecution has established the burden of proof. The jury delivers their final decision—guilty as charged.

There was no mistaking Peter among the twelve disciples. How could anyone forget this impulsive character? While in the garden during his last confrontation with the soldiers, he chopped off a man's ear. This kind of news spread quickly, especially after Jesus healed the wounded man. After Peter denied Jesus a third time, He began to curse and swear to mask his true identity. Have you denied knowing Jesus recently? When Peter heard the rooster crow a second time, he began to weep as he remembered the prophecy of Jesus regarding his upcoming triple-denial (Mark 14:72).

God is fully aware of your character. He knows when you remain faithful and He knows when you pretend to be someone who you are not. He can see right through you each time. When people challenge you for your faith, does fear take over? Do you send mixed messages to protect your job or to keep relationships comfortable? You have to be authentic in order to be effective. Don't be a stumbling block. Be completely truthful.

When Jesus begins to shine through your life, others will notice. The way you talk and the way you act will be different than before you met Christ. But make no mistake: your faith will be tested. Don't coldly deny Jesus as Peter did—three times in one cold evening. When pressure from others begin to squeeze you, make sure that what comes out of you is the truth. Determine now to acknowledge Jesus in every situation. Visualize yourself defending your faith before the tests even begin. Don't deny your Savior.

Read: Open your Bible and read Mark 14:72.

Reflect: Prayerfully consider the following: Does it break my heart when I am not faithful to the Lord? Do I quickly seek His mercy and forgiveness?

Respond: As a result of these truths, what might need to change in my attitude, beliefs, and actions? What steps do I need to take outwardly?

The Pretenders

"Then they led Jesus from the house of Caiaphas to the governor's headquarters. It was early morning. They themselves did not enter the governor's headquarters, so that they would not be defiled, but could eat the Passover. So Pilate went outside to them and said, 'What accusation do you bring against this man?' They answered him, 'If this man were not doing evil, we would not have delivered him over to you.' Pilate said to them, 'Take him yourselves and judge him by your own law.' The Jews said to him, 'It is not lawful for us to put anyone to death.' This was to fulfill the word that Jesus had spoken to show by what kind of death he was going to die" (John 18:28-32).

When you buy a ticket to watch a modern play, you expect to see professional performers hard at work after practicing for several months to perfect their skills and deliver an outstanding show. The night of the performance, they expertly apply makeup and wear carefully chosen costumes to express the personality of their characters. They pretend to be someone who they are not. This is what you would expect them to do.

Jesus was preparing His disciples for the big show when He took them aside and said, *"See, we are going up to Jerusalem. And the Son of Man will be delivered over to the chief priests and scribes, and they will condemn him to death and deliver him over to the Gentiles to be mocked and flogged and crucified, and he will be raised on the third day"* (Matthew 20:18-19). This must have been confusing for the disciples. Jesus was talking about respectable representatives of Jewish social and religious groups. How could these guardians of justice and truth condemn their only Messiah?

The chief priests and the scribes were more concerned about ritual impurity than they were about the guilt of premeditated murder. They were more concerned about following minor details of the law than keeping God's two greatest commandments—loving God and loving others. They wanted to use their influence to force the Roman authorities to deliver Jesus to His death. Are you more concerned with keeping the small details of your life in order rather than pursuing personal holiness, worship, and loving others? Are you pretending to be religious to get your way in a particular matter? Stop doing this! Live through your true identity. Be real and refuse to follow the example of the pretenders.

Read: Open your Bible and read Matthew 26:59-63.

Reflect: Prayerfully consider the following: Do I seek justice over personal gain? Do I choose to follow God's Word, even when I suffer?

Respond: As a result of these truths, what might need to change in my attitude, beliefs, and actions? What steps do I need to take outwardly?

Personal Examination

*"So Pilate entered his headquarters again and called Jesus and said to him,
'Are you the King of the Jews?' Jesus answered, 'Do you say this of your own
accord, or did others say it to you about me?' Pilate answered,
'Am I a Jew? Your own nation and the chief priests have delivered
you over to me. What have you done?'" (John 18:33-35).*

To increase international exposure and display their great originality, many countries are developing their own "Seven Wonders" for all to come and see. These unique sites often reflect the beauty of history, nature, and man-made creations. It is one thing to watch them on your computer, and another to visit them in person. A personal examination is always better.

Pilate was performing a personal examination regarding the curiosity surrounding Jesus. Since the chief priests and the scribes delivered Jesus to Pilate, he knew the Jews were pursuing the death of Jesus by crucifixion. What Pilate could not fully understand was the reason behind the strong charges brought against Him. If Jesus were the King of the Jews, it would make no difference to Pilate. He was not the least bit interested in Jewish political life. Pilate wanted to examine Jesus himself and find answers.

Pilate heard the serious accusation from the Jews loud and clear. He was being accused of blasphemy after claiming to be the King of the Jews, the Promised Messiah. Pilate was still unclear as to why this charge generated so much controversy among the people. When he looked at Jesus' physical appearance, it must have made him laugh deep inside. Amazingly, Jesus did not defend His claims of deity. He was not there to argue or to persuade Pilate to let Him go free. Jesus willingly submitted Himself to His destiny.

In the course of their conversation, Jesus put Pilate on the spot and asked directly who Pilate believed Him to be. Christ was leading Pilate to examine His claims for Himself. Pilate mocked this approach. He was not interested at all in Israel's political plans or in their Messiah. All he wanted to know was what Jesus had done to deserve a death sentence. Jesus invited a personal response, but Pilate purposely maintained his distance. Like so many, Pilate did not want to make his conversation with Jesus a personal one. Unfortunately this reality is all too common in our culture.

Read: Open your Bible and read Luke 13:5.

Reflect: Prayerfully consider the following: Am I helping others make Jesus' invitation a personal one? How can I improve my approach?

Respond: As a result of these truths, what might need to change in my attitude, beliefs, and actions? What steps do I need to take outwardly?

An Eternal King

"Jesus answered, 'My kingdom is not of this world. If my kingdom were of this world, my servants would have been fighting, that I might not be delivered over to the Jews. But my kingdom is not from the world.' Then Pilate said to him, 'So you are a king?' Jesus answered, 'You say that I am a king. For this purpose I was born and for this purpose I have come into the world—to bear witness to the truth. Everyone who is of the truth listens to my voice.' Pilate said to him, 'What is truth?' (John 18:36-38).

Watching epic battles of good versus evil makes you want to stand up and shout, "Start fighting men!" Soldiers executing a surprise plan of attack leave us on the edge of our seats. The suspense is beyond what words can describe. We absolutely love to see good rise and triumph over evil. When good kings defeat their enemies, everyone stands up and cheers.

The prophet Daniel wrote, *"I saw in the night visions, and behold, with the clouds of heaven there came one like a son of man, and he came to the Ancient of Days and was presented before him. And to him was given dominion and glory and a kingdom, that all peoples, nations, and languages should serve him; his dominion is an everlasting dominion, which shall not pass away, and his kingdom one that shall not be destroyed"* (Daniel 7:13-14). Jesus is the Eternal King. His Kingdom will pursue and conquer all other kingdoms. Jesus has all authority and power. He will reign forever. He will destroy His enemies.

Yet none of that was apparent to Pilate when Jesus stood before him. Jesus did not look like a King. He did not have an army ready to fight and rescue Him from death. Pilate may have thought that Jesus was a creative lunatic or an unusual deceiver, but certainly not a King. What Pilate did not know was that Jesus' Kingdom was spiritual in nature rather than physical. Jesus revealed His purpose to Pilate by making His presence known to others. Jesus came to fulfill and to bear witness of the truth of the gospel. Jesus made it clear that those who pursue truth find truth through His voice. Truth is a person. Jesus is the truth. Pilate had ears, but he could not hear the truth about Jesus. Can you imagine the Eternal King standing before you? There are so many people today who try to avoid spiritual conversations. They want to avoid the personal implications.

Read: Open your Bible and read 1 John 4:6.

Reflect: Prayerfully consider the following: Am I worried more about how people will respond to Jesus or where they will spend their eternity?

Respond: As a result of these truths, what might need to change in my attitude, beliefs, and actions? What steps do I need to take outwardly?

No Guilt

"After he had said this, he went back outside to the Jews and told them, 'I find no guilt in him. But you have a custom that I should release one man for you at the Passover. So do you want me to release to you the King of the Jews?' They cried out again, 'Not this man, but Barabbas!' Now Barabbas was a robber"
(John 18:38-40).

"Not guilty" can be one of the most liberating phrases for a defendant to hear. It represents the final ruling after a period of weeks, months, or even years of waiting. Everyone on the defense team celebrates enthusiastically. The case is finally closed. No more meetings and interviews are required. The defendant is free to leave the courtroom and enter society once again.

It was obvious to Pilate that Jesus was an innocent man. He may have had his doubts regarding Jesus' mental health since He was claiming to be the King of Israel, but there was no question regarding His innocence. Jesus was not breaking any Roman law. He was not trying to overthrow the government. Jesus was only stating the truth about who He was. Jesus was and is the Promised Messiah. He is Lord, Savior and King of Kings.

What is most amazing in this story is the fact that Pilate found Jesus not guilty of any crime, but decided to leave His fate in the hands of the people. More specifically, Pilate gave the Jews a choice to release the innocent Jesus or a notorious robber, Barabbas, according to their customs. Barabbas was a severe threat to the safety of Jerusalem. He was arrested and thrown into prison for causing a rebellion within the city and murdering at least one person (Luke 23:19). These are not minor crimes. Barabbas was a hard core criminal who deliberately hurt people and opposed the law.

Why would the people refuse to stand up for the truth? Why choose a known murderer over a man completely innocent of all charges? Isaiah writes, *"He was despised and rejected by men; a man of sorrows, and acquainted with grief; and as one from whom men hide their faces he was despised, and we esteemed him not"* (Isaiah 53:3). Pilate placed the responsibility of Jesus' fate in the hands of an angry mob. He had the authority and the responsibility to stand up for the truth, but He chose not to do so. Pilate was guilty of practicing injustice. Do you practice injustice?

Read: Open your Bible and read Matthew 27:24.

Reflect: Prayerfully consider the following: Do I compromise truth and justice when pressured to do so? What fears push me to compromise?

Respond: As a result of these truths, what might need to change in my attitude, beliefs, and actions? What steps do I need to take outwardly?

Circus of Pain

"Then Pilate took Jesus and flogged him. And the soldiers twisted together a crown of thorns and put it on his head and arrayed him in a purple robe. They came up to him, saying, 'Hail, King of the Jews!' and struck him with their hands"
(John 19:1-3).

When the circus comes to town, both children and parents get very excited. There are certain things they have come to expect over the years. They begin imagining clowns squirting water, elephants standing on two feet, and fearless acrobatics displayed above the crowds. Who could ever forget the sugary taste of cotton candy and glazed caramel apples? The circus does a great job of entertaining us and creating positive memories.

When Jesus was delivered to Pilate's men, he entered the Circus of Pain. It was an environment where evil flourished and pain was expected. Jesus was severely whipped by these men. They did not hold back at all. They were determined to brutally punish Jesus and mock Him as King. One soldier after another took turns to humiliate and tear apart the Savior. Isaiah wrote, *"I gave my back to those who strike, and my cheeks to those who pull out the beard; I hid not my face from disgrace and spitting"* (Isaiah 50:6).

Even as they ripped out His flesh with a whip of thorns, Jesus did not fight the Circus of Pain. It was a bloody scene. There was too much violence to watch. Jesus accepted this unmerciful savagery with unusual humility. He did not speak one word in protest. This was an important part of God's sovereign plan. The soldiers wove a crown of thorns to mock Jesus' claim as King. They placed the crown on the head of our Savior, piercing His flesh with its wicked thorns. The pain must have been excruciating to bear.

To add insult to injury, the soldiers placed a robe of royal purple on Jesus. Jesus was mocked for His position as King, seemingly stripped of His authority and ridiculed for His lack of power. Since no one intervened to honor or protect Jesus' kingdom, the soldiers gleefully continued their satanic mockery, slapping Jesus with their bare hands as they continued to ridicule their prisoner. Never before had they hosted a King like Jesus in the Circus of Pain. This was a day these soldiers would not soon forget.

Read: Open your Bible and read Isaiah 53:5.

Reflect: Prayerfully consider the following: Do I often think about the brutality endured by Jesus to pay for my sins? Have I thanked Him lately?

Respond: As a result of these truths, what might need to change in my attitude, beliefs, and actions? What steps do I need to take outwardly?

Emotional Displays

"Pilate went out again and said to them, 'See, I am bringing him out to you that you may know that I find no guilt in him.' So Jesus came out, wearing the crown of thorns and the purple robe. Pilate said to them, 'Behold the man!' When the chief priests and the officers saw him, they cried out, 'Crucify him, crucify him!' Pilate said to them, 'Take him yourselves and crucify him, for I find no guilt in him' " (John 19:4-6).

Mannequins are visual displays with a purpose. They help shoppers see how the latest fashion designs look on a person's body. You may find a mannequin wearing a swimsuit, fitness clothing, or a new wedding dress. They do not explain what the style is supposed to communicate. They do not solicit your business. The mannequins only display the designs.

Pilate was trying to strike an emotional chord with the angry mob. It was a live political negotiation. Having Jesus introduced to the Circus of Pain was a good way to start. Jesus' body was a living display of the Roman marks of cruelty and shame. His body was ripped open and bleeding as He stood before the large crowd. Pilate used Jesus as a living display to reinforce His innocence. Surely this would make people change their minds. Surely this would give them a change of heart to reconsider. Pilate's plan failed fast.

The people raised their voices and shouted, *"Crucify him, crucify him!"* Can you imagine hearing all of these voices in one accord shouting at the top of their lungs to crucify their Messiah? The response appears to have really shocked Pilate. It was unbelievable. The people were reacting irrationally. They were not fair or even remotely truthful in their undeserved brutal condemnation of Christ. They were deliberately dismissing the obvious to get their own way. They elevated their hatred above the law, abandoning all pretenses of justice, mercy and grace. The people wanted Jesus dead.

Regardless of his own opinion, Pilate had to make a choice. If he protected Jesus, Pilate risked endangering his position. Reports of uncontrollable crowds and protests would reach the ears of higher authorities. Pilate might be demoted as a result. If Pilate turned Jesus over to the people, the growing mob would crucify Jesus, but eventually they would calm down and go home. The cost to protect Pilate's world was the life of one man, Jesus.

Read: Open your Bible and read 1 Peter 2:22.

Reflect: Prayerfully consider the following: Am I truthful in every situation? Do I try to manipulate people or act deceitfully in some way?

Respond: As a result of these truths, what might need to change in my attitude, beliefs, and actions? What steps do I need to take outwardly?

Superstitions

"The Jews answered him, 'We have a law, and according to that law he ought to die because he has made himself the Son of God.' When Pilate heard this statement, he was even more afraid. He entered his headquarters again and said to Jesus, 'Where are you from?' But Jesus gave him no answer. So Pilate said to him, 'You will not speak to me? Do you not know that I have authority to release you and authority to crucify you?' Jesus answered him, 'You would have no authority over me at all unless it had been given you from above. Therefore he who delivered me over to you has the greater sin' " (John 19:7-11).

Superstitions are found in every culture. When you think through most of them, you will find their logic to be very strange and undeniably funny. Here are a few examples: a rabbit's foot will bring you good luck; it is bad luck to walk under a ladder or cross the path of a black cat; never deny a pregnant woman what she wants; and be careful not to break a mirror.

Superstitions existed in Jesus' day as well. When claimed to be the *"Son of God,"* this title carried spiritual, political, and authoritative implications. The Jews focused primarily on the spiritual implications, and the pagans focused on a bizarre mix of spiritual and authoritative implications. Referring to Jesus as the *"Son of God"* pointed to a divine origin. If Jesus was from heaven, Pilate was in big trouble. He had just finished severely punishing Jesus. Pilate displayed Jesus before the people for his own personal gain.

Pilate was not concerned with Jewish law. Yes, Jesus' radical claim clearly made Him guilty of blasphemy according to the Law (Leviticus 24:16). But there is another implication Pilate likely considered: if Jesus is the *"Son of God,"* we have to honor and serve Him. Crucifying a god in this culture was unthinkable. It would create more problems for the people, especially for those directly responsible such as Pilate and the Jewish leaders.

Pilate asked, *"Where are you from?"* He does not seem to be asking about the city He came from. Rather it appears he wanted to know from what part of the heavenly world He originated. Pilate was afraid. He did not expect an encounter with the gods when he planned his appointments earlier that morning. Jesus explained that real authority could not be manufactured because it is given from above. Jesus is from above.

Read: Open your Bible and read John 18:30.

Reflect: Prayerfully consider the following: Am I helping to clarify who Jesus is to those whom I know and meet? Do I have strange superstitions?

Respond: As a result of these truths, what might need to change in my attitude, beliefs, and actions? What steps do I need to take outwardly?

Self-Preservation

"From then on Pilate sought to release him, but the Jews cried out, "'If you release this man, you are not Caesar's friend. Everyone who makes himself a king opposes Caesar.' So when Pilate heard these words, he brought Jesus out and sat down on the judgment seat at a place called The Stone Pavement, and in Aramaic Gabbatha" (John 19:12-13).

Every good judge will do his best to make sure prospective jurors can remain impartial throughout the entire trial. The judge and the attorneys will probe each juror to see if the details surrounding their case trigger a response from the juror that may dispose them to make an unfair decision. One biased juror can negatively affect the final outcome of the trial.

Pilate was torn emotionally. He genuinely wanted to release Jesus. He must have wrestled with the question, "Do I protect my personal interests and aspirations or do I protect the innocent?" He had to make a decision. If he took a stand for the truth, it would cost him his career. With the mob growing in anger, it may have even cost him his life. This anger would surely lead to violence. It had to be one or the other, but not both. Pilate listened closely to the angry crowd. He had to make a decision right away.

Pilate was afraid of the negative personal consequences that came with fighting for the truth. Not being Cesar's friend would mean opposing the entire Roman government. Since Jesus was a King, the Jewish leaders painted Him as a direct threat to Rome. If Pilate released Jesus, he would be responsible for continuing this rebellion towards Cesar. This fear created by the Jewish leaders was very real for Pilate. It was stronger than his fear of divine retribution from the gods for his self-preserving actions.

Here is true wisdom, *"The fear of man lays a snare, but whoever trusts in the Lord is safe"* (Proverbs 29:25). When you are afraid of people, trouble follows. Caring more about what others will say or do as opposed to what God will say or do is a painful trap. Moses commanded his leaders, *"You shall not be partial in judgment. You shall hear the small and the great alike. You shall not be intimidated by anyone, for the judgment is God's. And the case that is too hard for you, you shall bring to me, and I will hear it"* (Deuteronomy 1:17). Be just in your decisions. Ask godly people for help when needed.

Read: Open your Bible and read 1 Samuel 15:1-35.

Reflect: Prayerfully consider the following: What can I learn from Saul's life regarding wanting the approval of people rather than God's approval?

Respond: As a result of these truths, what might need to change in my attitude, beliefs, and actions? What steps do I need to take outwardly?

Who's Your King?

"Now it was the day of Preparation of the Passover. It was about the sixth hour. He said to the Jews, 'Behold your King!' They cried out, 'Away with him, away with him, crucify him!' Pilate said to them, 'Shall I crucify your King?' The chief priests answered, 'We have no king but Caesar.' So he delivered him over to them to be crucified" (John 19:14-16).

Watching the inauguration of a high official such as a president or a king is memorable. The new leader is given an opportunity to speak before the people and cast his vision for the future. Millions of dollars are spent to honor this new leader. Extravagant parties, unprecedented entertainment, new celebrities, and high honors from officials are all part of the package.

It was an eventful day in Jerusalem. Barabbas, the notorious criminal, was being released from prison. Jewish families were slaughtering lambs in preparation for the Passover. And Pilate was about to make the biggest mistake of his life. It was near six in the morning and Jesus was exhausted from lack of sleep and an abundance of torture. After much internal deliberation, Pilate decided to give the people what they want. He contemplated this decision, but eventually he took the easy way out.

Jesus is brought before the people. Pilate raises his voice and says, *"Behold your King!"* The intensity and the demands continued. The people wanted Jesus crucified immediately. They wanted Him dead. Pilate, amazed by their stubbornness, responded, *"Shall I crucify your King?"* Pilate was perplexed. Jesus was obviously the King of Israel. The people were not interested in a King from heaven. They were very comfortable with their lives in submission to Caesar. They insisted, *"We have no king but Caesar."* This must have broken Jesus' heart. It was a true statement. God was not their King. They appointed their own King and rejected God.

Who is your King? The answer to this question can be seen in the person or thing that has complete authority over your life. In other words, it is what you submit to in every decision. What controls your decisions controls you. What influences you to do what you do or say what you say? What is the primary factor in your decision-making process? If God is indeed King in your life, He will rule and direct every area of your life.

Read: Open your Bible and read Genesis 49:10.

Reflect: Prayerfully consider the following: Does my obedience to God reflect His rule over my life? Is there a specific area that He is not ruling?

Respond: As a result of these truths, what might need to change in my attitude, beliefs, and actions? What steps do I need to take outwardly?

Lifting Weights

"So they took Jesus, and he went out, bearing his own cross, to the place called The Place of a Skull, which in Aramaic is called Golgotha. There they crucified him, and with him two others, one on either side, and Jesus between them" (John 19:17-18).

Fitness trainers assess a person's physical strength, body fat, and endurance before starting an exercise program. They do this to find the right starting point for the trainee. Training is designed to increase in resistance as the trainee makes progress. Adding excessive weight or resistance too quickly can injure the trainee. When this happens, all training comes to a stop.

Jesus' body was weak from the beatings and torture He had received at the hands of the Romans. For this reason, He was unable to carry His cross very far on His own. When He reached the city gate, He was unable to carry it any further. The cross was randomly given to a bystander named Simon to carry up to Golgotha, which was outside the walls of the city. The author of Hebrews writes, *"And so Jesus also suffered outside the city gate to make the people holy through his own blood"* (Hebrews 13:12, NIV).

Although Jesus was unable to physically carry His own cross, He was able to carry the total weight of our sin as He hung on the cross at Calvary. Only Jesus was able to lift the weight of our sin. For this reason, God speaks through Isaiah and says, *"Therefore I will divide him a portion with the many, and he shall divide the spoil with the strong, because he poured out his soul to death and was numbered with the transgressors; yet he bore the sin of many, and makes intercession for the transgressors"* (Isaiah 53:12). On the cross, Jesus paid the full price for our sins. Although He knew no sin, He became sin for us. The Lamb of God suffered and died to make us holy.

Peter wrote, *"For Christ also suffered once for sins, the righteous for the unrighteous, that he might bring us to God, being put to death in the flesh but made alive in the spirit"* (1 Peter 3:18). The weight of your sin was supernaturally cancelled out on the cross. Since Jesus suffered and died, your sins died, too. You are not a prisoner of sin any longer. Jesus died to bring you to God. He was nailed to a cross to remove the power of sin over your life. He carried the weight of all your sins. Stop lifting weights.

Read: Open your Bible and read Luke 23:26.

Reflect: Prayerfully consider the following: Am I still carrying the weight of my sins? What do I need to confess to remove these weights?

Respond: As a result of these truths, what might need to change in my attitude, beliefs, and actions? What steps do I need to take outwardly?

The King of the Jews

"Pilate also wrote an inscription and put it on the cross. It read, 'Jesus of Nazareth, the King of the Jews.' Many of the Jews read this inscription, for the place where Jesus was crucified was near the city, and it was written in Aramaic, in Latin, and in Greek. So the chief priests of the Jews said to Pilate, 'Do not write, 'The King of the Jews,' but rather, 'This man said, I am King of the Jews.' Pilate answered, 'What I have written I have written'" (John 19:19-22).

Investing in advertising is very expensive. Many hours are spent planning, designing, and producing the final product. What is more expensive is when you don't double-check your work and advertise something with the wrong information. This is both painful and costly. It is not surprising for people to get angry when their work is measured by one costly mistake.

As Jesus hung on the cross, a sign was placed above His head to indicate His crime: *"Jesus of Nazareth, The King of the Jews."* Pilate boldly stood against the religious leaders. He must have smiled as he wrote this title in three different languages—Greek, Latin and Aramaic. The common people spoke Greek, the Romans spoke Latin, and the Jews spoke Aramaic. Pilate deliberately mocked the Jews. He wanted everyone to read the accusation.

Not surprisingly, the chief priests and the religious leaders were furious. Pilate was not budging on his position. What difference would it make? Jesus was going to die. The Jews did not care. They had invested too much time, effort, and money. They were determined to protest. In their minds, Jesus was a liar, a demon, or a lunatic. Jesus being recognized as *"The King of the Jews"* was blasphemy for this group. This time, their protest did not work. Pilate was disgusted with their hatred towards Jesus, an innocent man. He refused to edit the "misprint" for their benefit.

Consider for a moment what gets you angry. When people say things about Jesus and His church that are not true, does this make you angry? When they try to pass on false information regarding your Savior, do you stand up and speak out? Do you help them understand what church is really about? The world does not need another obnoxious Christian. But it does need more bold witnesses for Christ who live to serve their King.

Read: Open your Bible and read Psalm 1:1-3.

Reflect: Prayerfully consider the following: How can meditating more on God's Word help me better defend and serve my Lord and King?

Respond: As a result of these truths, what might need to change in my attitude, beliefs, and actions? What steps do I need to take outwardly?

The Hour of Darkness

"So also the chief priests, with the scribes and elders, mocked him, saying, 'He saved others; he cannot save himself' " (Matthew 27:41-42).

It was an unusually dark hour. Marked by unbelief, torture and defeat, it was a time of great confusion and sorrow. For the disciples, it was a moment in time that would seem to stand still for a while. The final chapter in the life and ministry of Jesus, their friend, was coming to an abrupt end. It was the moment many of the religious leaders hoped for. It was their hour of triumph. Victory was near. Total conquest was certain. It was almost time to celebrate. This self-proclaimed rabbi and messiah would finally get what He deserved for blaspheming their God: death.

The death of Jesus would come about deceitfully, forcefully, and violently. It would give evidence to the great presence of evil and the lack of true spirituality in the hearts of men. The cross was the recognized symbol for death for the worst of criminals. When someone hung on a cross they did not survive. No matter how strong a person was there was no escaping the fury of the cross. The cross meant the death of a criminal was certain.

The cross is one of the cruelest forms of death known to mankind. It was built for a criminal, but on it hung our Savior and King. The Pharisees were correct in their conclusion. Jesus was unable to simultaneously save His life and save us from our sins. It was either one or the other. If He saved His life from the punishment of our sins, we would be lost today.

Jesus voluntarily offered His life as a permanent sacrifice for your sins. This is exactly what a Savior is supposed to do. Jesus suffered so that you might live with Him and in Him forever. Jesus endured the hour of darkness to release you from an oppressive spiritual darkness that you cannot escape alone. His hour of darkness and unbelievable anguish would ultimately turn into your eternity of light and unspeakable joy. The hour of darkness was difficult, but temporary. The resurrection was glorious and eternal.

"Looking to Jesus, the founder and perfecter of our faith, who for the joy that was set before him endured the cross, despising the shame, and is seated at the right hand of the throne of God" (Hebrews 12:2).

Read: Open your Bible and read Matthew 27:41-54.

Reflect: Consider the following: How would my life be today if I remained in darkness? What areas need to die today for Christ to live?

Respond: As a result of these truths, what might need to change in my attitude, beliefs, and actions? What steps do I need to take outwardly?

Military Games

"When the soldiers had crucified Jesus, they took his garments and divided them into four parts, one part for each soldier; also his tunic. But the tunic was seamless, woven in one piece from top to bottom, so they said to one another, 'Let us not tear it, but cast lots for it to see whose it shall be.' This was to fulfill the Scripture which says, 'They divided my garments among them, and for my clothing they cast lots' " (John 19:23-24).

The rules of the game of marbles are simple. The field of play is a circle drawn in the dirt. The objective is to knock at least one marble outside of the circle. If you do, you continue playing. If you don't, the next player has a chance to do the same. When children play marbles with their friends, it is not to fulfill Biblical prophecy, but to have fun and win more marbles.

On the cross, Jesus was in agony. His life on earth was coming to an end. It was one of the darkest hours of mankind. The Lamb of God was being offered up as a sacrifice for all men. A few soldiers personally witnessed the Savior suffer on the cross up close. One would think that the cruelty of the cross would have changed their hearts. One would think it would have produced great compassion for their fellow man, but it did not. Jesus was just another criminal. His death made no difference to them at all.

The game played by the soldiers that dark afternoon was a fulfillment of Psalm 22:18. These military games were part of God's plan all along. It was not uncommon for executioners to claim the property of their victims. Jesus died once for all, including the soldiers who surrounded Him. Before these soldiers claimed their property, Jesus cried out, *"Father, forgive them, for they know not what they do" (Luke 23:34).* The chief priests, the scribes, Pilate, the angry mob and the soldiers were all included in this prayer. Jesus knew these things would happen. He was ready to forgive freely.

When Jesus' tunic was presented, they played games to see who would win this prize. The tunic was his inner clothing. It was his most valuable piece of clothing. Has someone ever tried taking advantage of you or someone that you love? Has someone recently taken something valuable from your possession? If others have played games with what is important to you, you are not alone. Do as Jesus did. Forgive them freely for their actions.

Read: Open your Bible and read Psalm 22:18.

Reflect: Prayerfully consider the following: How do I respond when others play games with what I value? Do I always forgive them freely?

Respond: As a result of these truths, what might need to change in my attitude, beliefs, and actions? What steps do I need to take outwardly?

Your Presence

*"So the soldiers did these things, but standing by the cross of Jesus
were his mother and his mother's sister, Mary the wife of Clopas,
and Mary Magdalene. When Jesus saw his mother and the disciple whom
he loved standing nearby, he said to his mother, 'Woman, behold, your son!'
Then he said to the disciple, 'Behold, your mother!' And from that hour
the disciple took her to his own home" (John 19:24-27).*

Nothing speaks louder of your love for others than your presence does, especially when people are experiencing great personal sorrow. Standing by them can make all the difference in the world. Nothing can replace your presence. It is priceless. It communicates love and genuine concern. It provides strength and hope to the hurting. Your presence is powerful.

When Mary and Joseph brought Jesus to the temple, *"Simeon blessed them and said to Mary his mother, 'Behold, this child is appointed for the fall and rising of many in Israel, and for a sign that is opposed (and a sword will pierce through your own soul also), so that thoughts from many hearts may be revealed'" (Luke 2:34-35).* Mary knew this day would arrive. It would be a day of sorrow and a day of incredible pain. This was the destiny of her son and Savior.

Mary had experienced incredible joy when the angel first announced God's plan for her life. It was a great honor to serve God as His vessel of honor. She welcomed the opportunity to be used by Him. Now this same woman would have to watch her cherished son, who had been beaten beyond recognition, suffer and die as a criminal. There was nothing Mary could do to stop the cruelty. It was a sight that no mother would ever wish to see.

Even during His greatest pain, Jesus took time to care for His mother. He appointed John to be responsible for her care. Jesus knew John very well. Along with Peter and James, John was one of Jesus' personal friends. He knew John was very trustworthy. He knew John would do a good job in providing for His mother's future needs. There was no doubt as to John's continued commitment to step up and serve Mary and the others. What about you? Can people depend on you to be present and willing to serve when tragedy arrives? Are you someone who is available to help others walk through their darkest hours? Your presence really makes a difference.

Read: Open your Bible and read Romans 12:15.

Reflect: Prayerfully consider the following: Do I stand nearby when others are hurting the most? How can I make myself more available?

Respond: As a result of these truths, what might need to change in my attitude, beliefs, and actions? What steps do I need to take outwardly?

You Will Be With Me

"One of the criminals who were hanged railed at him, saying, 'Are you not the Christ? Save yourself and us!' But the other rebuked him, saying, 'Do you not fear God, since you are under the same sentence of condemnation? And we indeed justly, for we are receiving the due reward of our deeds; but this man has done nothing wrong.' And he said, 'Jesus, remember me when you come into your kingdom.' And he said to him, 'Truly, I say to you, today you will be with me in Paradise' " (Luke 23:39-43).

Hiking up a mountain can be an intimidating experience for a child. The overwhelming size of the mountain and the unfamiliar paths can frighten even the bravest of children. When a father holds the hand of his child and says, "Don't worry, you will be with me" the child can relax and continue upward. The promise and presence of the father makes all the difference.

In the darkest of hours and under the most excruciating pain, Jesus reached out and changed a life. Two criminals shared the crucifixion with Jesus that afternoon. These two criminals were guilty as charged. Maybe they were good friends with the notorious Barabbas. They were receiving what they deserved: death. There were no more appeals and no more trials. These men were in their final hours. There was no way out and they all knew it.

It is interesting to see how people respond in their final hours. When they are faced with the reality of death, what they say at those final moments is usually highly personal and very important to them. It can reveal their greatest fears, hopes, and insecurities. The first criminal, like the religious leaders, rejected Jesus and mocked His claim as Messiah. The first criminal was a complete rebel, even during his final hours of life. There was no repentance, no faith, no sense of guilt or shame, and no salvation.

The second criminal was the complete opposite. He feared God and recognized his own sin. He was not a rebel in his final hours. He knew that his life was hopeless. He believed in Jesus as Messiah. He knew that Jesus was a just man and wanted to be a part of Jesus' Kingdom. He wanted Jesus to remember him. What a humble, but powerful statement. Jesus offered living hope to this dying criminal, *"Today you will be with me in Paradise."* As a believer, Jesus is always with you. He now lives within you.

Read: Open your Bible and read John 14:20.

Reflect: Prayerfully consider the following: Since Jesus lives in me, am I ever alone? What does this say about my purpose and hope for living?

Respond: As a result of these truths, what might need to change in my attitude, beliefs, and actions? What steps do I need to take outwardly?

"It is Finished!"

"After this, Jesus, knowing that all was now finished, said (to fulfill the Scripture), 'I thirst.' A jar full of sour wine stood there, so they put a sponge full of the sour wine on a hyssop branch and held it to his mouth. When Jesus had received the sour wine, he said, 'It is finished,' and he bowed his head and gave up his spirit"
(John 19:28-30).

"Time flies when you are having fun" is a well known phrase. The core idea is very simple: when you do things that are very enjoyable, life seems to move much faster. These are special moments. We want them to continue without interruption as long as possible. When you are not having a pleasant time, however, life seems to almost stop and stand still. The minutes feel like hours and the hours feel like multiple days.

After what scholars believe was a three-hour period of pure agony on the cross, Jesus was ready to give up His Spirit and die physically. Even in the last few minutes of His life, Jesus fulfilled prophetic scripture (Psalm 22:15; 69:21). Jesus had earlier refused to accept a mixture of wine (mingled with myrrh) that was designed to reduce the pain of the cross (Matthew 27:34). He did not try numbing the reality before Him. Instead, He voluntarily endured God's full wrath over sin's penalty. The sour wine Jesus received to drink on the cross was supposed to help Him endure more torture.

Earlier, Jesus prayed to the Father, *"I have glorified You on the earth. I have finished the work which You have given Me to do"* (John 17:4, NKJV). On the cross at Calvary Jesus finished His perfect work of divine redemption. He completed His heavenly mission. Every prophecy about Jesus' first coming as a suffering servant was fulfilled. Jesus fulfilled God's promises. He died in our place. Jesus paid the full price for all of our sins. His amazing, substitutionary death provided the way for us to experience salvation.

What do you do when the pains of life are too much for you to handle? Are you willing to endure great difficulties, even when the reason behind these challenges is unjust? God wants you to finish what He has started in your life. His plan is not necessarily for you to take the easy road through life. Sometimes He simply wants you to trust Him for more strength and wisdom. Make it a point to finish your mission. It is your destiny.

Read: Open your Bible and read Philippians 1:6.

Reflect: Prayerfully consider the following: Am I intentional about finishing what God has purposed for me to do with my gifts and abilities?

Respond: As a result of these truths, what might need to change in my attitude, beliefs, and actions? What steps do I need to take outwardly?

The Day of Preparation

"Since it was the day of Preparation, and so that the bodies would not remain on the cross on the Sabbath (for that Sabbath was a high day), the Jews asked Pilate that their legs might be broken and that they might be taken away. So the soldiers came and broke the legs of the first, and of the other who had been crucified with him" (John 19:31-32).

Celebrating Thanksgiving in the United States is a favorite family tradition. Many hours are invested in preparation for this great occasion. A few days before, holiday schedules are adjusted, flights are booked and road trips begin. For those hosting this special dinner in their home, numerous preparations are made to make sure everything looks and tastes wonderful.

Jesus died on the Jewish Day of Preparation. The Friday before the Passover involved getting everything ready to help God's people remember His magnificent deliverance from Egypt. It was a day traditionally filled with much activity among the Jews as they prepared for the annual Passover celebration. This particular Day of Preparation had special significance. This Passover, Jesus became the Passover Lamb. He became our sacrifice.

Breaking the legs of the two criminals would prevent them from pushing their bodies up to take another breath. It was a cruel way to expedite their sentence. The Romans were comfortable with leaving people on the cross until their death. The Jews were very serious about their laws. Leaving a man to die over the Sabbath would negatively impact the land.

The Law said, *"And if a man has committed a crime punishable by death and he is put to death, and you hang him on a tree, his body shall not remain all night on the tree, but you shall bury him the same day, for a hanged man is cursed by God. You shall not defile your land that the Lord your God is giving you for an inheritance"* (Deuteronomy 21:22-23). The hypocrisy of the Jews was astounding. They deliberately murdered Jesus and broke God's Law in the process. At the same time they went to great pains to keep every other small detail of the Law. Make sure you approach times of celebration and worship with a pure heart. God sees and knows our hearts. You can't pretend to be holy and pure when you purposely disobey God's Word.

Read: Open your Bible and read Ephesians 1:4.

Reflect: Prayerfully consider the following: Am I trying to live a pure and holy life? What scriptures do I tend to ignore or oppose the most?

Respond: As a result of these truths, what might need to change in my attitude, beliefs, and actions? What steps do I need to take outwardly?

Pierced

"But when they came to Jesus and saw that he was already dead, they did not break his legs. But one of the soldiers pierced his side with a spear, and at once there came out blood and water. He who saw it has borne witness— his testimony is true, and he knows that he is telling the truth—that you also may believe. For these things took place that the Scripture might be fulfilled: 'Not one of his bones will be broken.' And again another Scripture says, 'They will look on him whom they have pierced' " (John 19:33-37).

Investigators try to block off public access to a crime scene as quickly as possible. They don't want anything or anyone to contaminate their investigation. They have to get everything right the first time. Careful attention to detail is critical. Once the investigators have collected sufficient evidence, they can begin to build a case based on their findings.

The death of Jesus was filled with great evidence to prove His claims as the Messiah and Savior. The evidence is overwhelmingly clear. For the Jew who is seeking to know the truth, he can find the evidence in God's Word. The psalmist wrote as he looked ahead at the death of the Messiah, *"Dogs surround me, a pack of villains encircles me; they pierce my hands and my feet"* (Psalm 22:16, NIV). By the time Jesus' body was pierced, he was already dead. If a person who is alive is pierced only blood flows out of their body. If a dead person is pierced, both blood and water flow from their body.

The fulfillment of scripture continues, *"I can count all My bones. They look and stare at Me"* (Psalm 22:17, NKJV). None of Jesus' bones were broken on the cross. The psalmist writes, *"He protects all his bones, not one of them will be broken"* (Psalm 34:20, NIV). Once again we see the messianic prophecies unfolding in the life and death of Jesus. Bones not being broken is significant in these prophecies because they refer to the bones of the Passover lamb. *Numbers 9:12* reads, *"They shall leave none of it until the morning, nor break any of its bones; according to all the statute for the Passover they shall keep it."* On the cross, Jesus was the perfect sacrifice for our sins.

Think about the evidence of your faith. Is it visible to others? Can people look back on stories that you have shared from the Bible? When trouble pierces your life, does the Spirit take the lead? What exactly comes out?

Read: Open your Bible and read Revelation 1:7.

Reflect: Prayerfully consider the following: What would others say is the most visible evidence in my life regarding my faith in Jesus Christ?

Respond: As a result of these truths, what might need to change in my attitude, beliefs, and actions? What steps do I need to take outwardly?

A Personal Burial

"After these things Joseph of Arimathea, who was a disciple of Jesus, but secretly for fear of the Jews, asked Pilate that he might take away the body of Jesus, and Pilate gave him permission. So he came and took away his body. Nicodemus also, who earlier had come to Jesus by night, came bringing a mixture of myrrh and aloes, about seventy-five pounds in weight. So they took the body of Jesus and bound it in linen cloths with the spices, as is the burial custom of the Jews. Now in the place where he was crucified there was a garden, and in the garden a new tomb in which no one had yet been laid. So because of the Jewish day of Preparation, since the tomb was close at hand, they laid Jesus there"
(John 19:38-42).

Funerals and burials have a way of capturing our attention. When it involves someone we care deeply about it forces us to stop and reflect. Life at times seems to accelerate quickly. We are reminded how short life is in the presence of the dead. We are impacted greatly when present at the burial of a dear friend or family member. It moves us profoundly. Two very prominent men were responsible for burying the Lord Jesus. Joseph and Nicodemus were religious, civic, and political leaders. They were part of the elite seventy-one member Sanhedrin group that ruled Israel. More important than their external similarities, both men had a genuine passion for God (John 3:1-2; Luke 23:51). Both men had unsettled hearts and were searching for the Lord God. They sincerely wanted to find God's Kingdom.

Being rich, they probably paid for all of the cloths, ointments, and spices traditionally used for burial. Great care was practiced throughout this process. The psalmist wrote, *"All Your garments are scented with myrrh and aloes and cassia, out of the ivory palaces, by which they have made You glad"* (Psalm 45:8, NKJV). This was a slow and careful procedure. It is one thing to attend a funeral and another to actually prepare the body for burial.

Imagine what Joseph and Nicodemus were thinking as they wrapped the body of their Savior. What thoughts would fill your mind? The deep wounds in His flesh might remind you of the torture He endured for you. The holes in His scalp might cause you to look ahead at the eternal crown He will soon wear. Perhaps the spices remind you of the beauty of the coming resurrection and how this spiritual victory will change everything.

Read: Open your Bible and read Luke 23:51.

Reflect: Prayerfully consider the following: Am I really searching for God and making personal adjustments to find His perfect will for my life?

Respond: As a result of these truths, what might need to change in my attitude, beliefs, and actions? What steps do I need to take outwardly?

Breaking News

"Now on the first day of the week Mary Magdalene came to the tomb early, while it was still dark, and saw that the stone had been taken away from the tomb. So she ran and went to Simon Peter and the other disciple, the one whom Jesus loved, and said to them, 'They have taken the Lord out of the tomb, and we do not know where they have laid him.' So Peter went out with the other disciple, and they were going toward the tomb. Both of them were running together, but the other disciple outran Peter and reached the tomb first" (John 20:1-4).

Breaking news travels very fast these days. Within seconds, the headline is communicated through social media and other media outlets. Electronic news subscriptions allow many to receive instant alerts directly on their phones and tablets. Information has never moved so fast. Receiving instant summaries and updates of the major news stories has never been simpler.

Back in the days of Jesus, information did not travel quite as fast. When Mary Magdalene discovered the empty tomb, she was not able to text or tweet Peter and the other disciples. The breaking news regarding the empty tomb was delivered the old fashioned way, in person. Mary did not walk back slowly with the information. Mary chose to run and deliver the news as fast as possible. She could not keep this news to herself.

Mary was in a panic. She did not expect to see an empty tomb. John outlined her two major concerns. First, she believed that Jesus' body was stolen. "Someone is responsible for this," she must have thought. Second, she believed Jesus' body was lost. Mary may have cried as she shared her story. Surely there was a sense of urgency and despair in her voice. Peter and John were equally shocked by what they heard. They responded by racing to the tomb to check things out for themselves. It was a story that was beyond belief. It was a big story that required further investigation.

What would you consider breaking news in your life today? What is God doing that others must know about right away? Consider the large stones dividing death and life in your spiritual journey. How has God removed you from a destructive habit? How has He turned your family around? What has He changed about your character? This is a BIG deal. Don't keep this story undercover. This is breaking news! Tell someone today!

Read: Open your Bible and read Matthew 28:2.

Reflect: Prayerfully consider the following: What stones has God rolled away from my heart recently? How has this directly changed my attitude?

Respond: As a result of these truths, what might need to change in my attitude, beliefs, and actions? What steps do I need to take outwardly?

An Empty Tomb

"And stooping to look in, he saw the linen cloths lying there, but he did not go in. Then Simon Peter came, following him, and went into the tomb. He saw the linen cloths lying there, and the face cloth, which had been on Jesus' head, not lying with the linen cloths but folded up in a place by itself. Then the other disciple, who had reached the tomb first, also went in, and he saw and believed; for as yet they did not understand the Scripture, that he must rise from the dead. Then the disciples went back to their homes" (John 20:5-10).

Have you had a "light bulb moment" recently? This is when you finally understand something after many weeks or even months of careful analysis and study. The moment often comes unexpectedly. With great synergy, everything comes together quickly. You were not planning for things to happen this way, so you celebrate the milestone and look back in wonder.

When John and Peter approached the tomb of Jesus, the "light bulb moment" would begin to come together. Up to this point they had been with Jesus without knowing Jesus. They struggled with His teachings regarding His great suffering and death to come. They did not know how to connect the messianic prophecies. Jesus later rebuked His disciples by saying, *"'O foolish ones, and slow of heart to believe all that the prophets have spoken! Was it not necessary that the Christ should suffer these things and enter into his glory?' And beginning with Moses and all the Prophets, he interpreted to them in all the Scriptures the things concerning himself"* (Luke 24:25-27).

John paused and took a good look before entering the tomb. He carefully scanned and stared at the contents. Peter stepped right in and started looking around. They both noticed how things were organized and folded neatly. Jesus did not leave in a hurry. There was neither a fight nor any struggle to get out of the tomb. The "light bulb moment" was quickly unfolding. Peter and John were beginning to connect the dots. They would soon be able to believe in the resurrection. They were beginning to understand what Jesus meant. The purpose of the cross was becoming clear. It was transformational. It was far beyond anything they might have hoped or expected. The tomb was empty because Jesus has risen. They did not yet realize that death has been conquered. The Messiah lives.

Read: Open your Bible and read Luke 9:44-45.

Reflect: Prayerfully consider the following: What has the resurrection meant to me personally? When did I really understand its significance?

Respond: As a result of these truths, what might need to change in my attitude, beliefs, and actions? What steps do I need to take outwardly?

Overwhelmed

"But Mary stood weeping outside the tomb, and as she wept she stooped to look into the tomb. And she saw two angels in white, sitting where the body of Jesus had lain, one at the head and one at the feet. They said to her, 'Woman, why are you weeping?' She said to them, 'They have taken away my Lord, and I do not know where they have laid him.' Having said this, she turned around and saw Jesus standing, but she did not know that it was Jesus"
(John 20:11-14).

Programs that describe the lives of missing children are difficult to watch. If you have children, watching the parents of the missing child speak can bring tears to your eyes. You identify with their role and sense part of their pain. Some parents find themselves looking out the window, weeping in complete despair and praying for their child to return home safely.

The empty tomb shook Mary to the core of her being. This was not a moment for silent grieving. Mary outwardly expressed her great pain and sadness. Her heart was broken and her hope was lost. By this time Peter and John had returned home. Mary decided to stay. Luke gives us a few more details to help us, *"While they were perplexed about this, behold, two men stood by them in dazzling apparel. And as they were frightened and bowed their faces to the ground, the men said to them, 'Why do you seek the living among the dead? He is not here, but has risen. Remember how he told you, while he was still in Galilee, that the Son of Man must be delivered into the hands of sinful men and be crucified and on the third day rise' "* (Luke 24:4-7).

Mary was unable to recognize the powerful presence of God's messengers standing right in front of her. The angels were not wearing designer jeans and a trendy shirt. The Bible describes their wardrobe as *"dazzling apparel."* You could not mistake these guys for average men. Even worse, she was not able to recognize the presence of her Savior. How could she overlook all of this? Mary was too overwhelmed with grief to notice. Her deep sadness kept her from seeing the reality of God's presence and from recognizing God's promises. This can happen to you if you are not careful. Life's problems and pain can totally consume you to the point that you are unable to recognize God's promises or experience His powerful presence.

Read: Open your Bible and read Luke 24:16.

Reflect: Prayerfully consider the following: What is God leading me to change to experience a particular promise and see His presence at work?

Respond: As a result of these truths, what might need to change in my attitude, beliefs, and actions? What steps do I need to take outwardly?

Transactional or Personal

"Jesus said to her, 'Woman, why are you weeping? Whom are you seeking?'
Supposing him to be the gardener, she said to him, 'Sir, if you have carried him
away, tell me where you have laid him, and I will take him away.' Jesus said
to her, 'Mary.' She turned and said to him in Aramaic, 'Rabboni!'
(which means Teacher). Jesus said to her, 'Do not cling to me, for I have
not yet ascended to the Father; but go to my brothers and say to them,
'I am ascending to my Father and your Father, to my God and your God.'
Mary Magdalene went and announced to the disciples, 'I have seen the Lord'
—and that he had said these things to her" (John 20:15-18).

Companies are taking steps to help their executives better understand
their corporate culture and values. They want to make sure these
executives have the right perspective when making important decisions.
Serving customers and working with frontline staff are all necessary in this
process. Knowing what their employees and customers experience will
only make them stronger. Although Jesus was Mary's Lord and Savior she
didn't recognize Him that morning. Mary knew Jesus personally yet her
response was far from personal. Jesus asked Mary two direct questions.
It appears that Mary did not even listen to His questions. She responded
out of the overflow of her grief. Have you ever responded this way?

Jesus asked, *"Why are you weeping?"* and *"Whom are you seeking?"* but Mary
was focused on the "Where?" instead. Can you relate to Mary's response?
Jesus' questions were very personal. She quickly changed the conversation
from personal to transactional. Mary's primary intention was to find the
dead body. Had she stopped for a moment to consider the questions Jesus
was asking, she would have seen that her sorrow was totally unnecessary.

When Jesus called Mary's name, she suddenly recognized Him as her dear
friend, loving Teacher, and precious Lord. The conversation changed from
transactional to personal again. In Aramaic, *"Rabboni"* means "my Lord"
and in Hebrew it means "teacher." Jesus was both. Apparently Mary
grabbed Jesus, probably His feet, and would not let go of Him. She did not
want to let Jesus out of her sight. She wanted Him to permanently stay,
but that was not God's plan. Jesus would soon return again to the Father.

Read: Open your Bible and read John 10:27.

Reflect: Prayerfully consider the following: Is my relationship with God
personal or impersonal and transactional? Can I recognize His voice?

Respond: As a result of these truths, what might need to change in my
attitude, beliefs, and actions? What steps do I need to take outwardly?

Go and Tell

"So they departed quickly from the tomb with fear and great joy, and ran to tell his disciples. And behold, Jesus met them and said, 'Greetings!' And they came up and took hold of his feet and worshiped him. Then Jesus said to them, 'Do not be afraid; go and tell my brothers to go to Galilee, and there they will see me' " (Matthew 28:8-10).

It can happen to us when we least expect it and in the most unusual way. A friend from our past recognizes us while we stand in line at the local grocery store. They immediately walk up to us and say, "Hello." You are surprised, but very pleased to see them. The next few minutes are spent sharing photos, contact information, and taking sufficient time to catch up.

When Mary and her sister planned to visit the tomb of Jesus, they were in for a big surprise and an unexpected greeting. *"But the angel said to the women, 'Do not be afraid, for I know that you seek Jesus who was crucified. He is not here, for he has risen, as he said. Come, see the place where he lay'"* (Matthew 28:5-6). The angel's announcement of the risen Christ filled their hearts with great joy. The angel commanded them to *"go and tell"* the disciples the good news. All of what Jesus had promised was unfolding. Jesus was not dead. He was alive! It was now time to sing and celebrate!

Now these two women were moving fast to get the message of the risen Christ to the disciples. Without advance notice, Jesus met them on their journey with a heavenly "Hello." If they were shocked when they saw the angel, their hearts must have stopped when they saw their risen Lord.

They were commanded twice to *"go and tell"* the other disciples about the good news of the resurrection. Pay close attention to their response. Immediately these two women bowed down, grabbed Jesus' feet and worshipped their Savior. Their first response was to worship their Lord. Jesus accepted their worship and challenged them to tell the disciples where He could be found. It was an unexpected greeting with a very predictable command, *"go and tell."* What is God asking you to *"go and tell"* to others? Your worship of God is what fuels your passion to tell others about the risen Savior. There are times when your next step of obedience is to tell others about what you have seen, read, and heard about Jesus.

Read: Open your Bible and read Matthew 28:1-20.

Reflect: Consider the following: What adjustments do I need to make in my daily worship? Who is God telling me to *"go and tell"* about Jesus?

Respond: As a result of these truths, what might need to change in my attitude, beliefs, and actions? What steps do I need to take outwardly?

Spiritual Peace

"On the evening of that day, the first day of the week, the doors being locked where the disciples were for fear of the Jews, Jesus came and stood among them and said to them, 'Peace be with you.' When he had said this, he showed them his hands and his side. Then the disciples were glad when they saw the Lord. Jesus said to them again, 'Peace be with you. As the Father has sent me, even so I am sending you.' And when he had said this, he breathed on them and said to them, 'Receive the Holy Spirit. If you forgive the sins of any, they are forgiven them; if you withhold forgiveness from any, it is withheld' " (John 20:19-23).

Mischievous boys love to scare their big sisters. They hide in the dark and grab their sister's feet while roaring like a hungry bear. They find enthusiasm in placing dead lizards and frogs near the front door. Watching their sister scream and jump in the air is priceless for them. Experience will keep the big sister on high alert and cause her to be more guarded.

It had only been a few days since Jesus was crucified. The disciples were without their leader. They were scared and on high alert. They forgot what Jesus had told them earlier, *"Peace I leave with you; my peace I give to you. Not as the world gives do I give to you. Let not your hearts be troubled, neither let them be afraid"* (John 14:27). It's difficult to remember things when you are scared for your life. Imagine sitting in a room and wondering whether the next knock on the door will be a friend or an executioner.

Jesus' work on the cross was necessary for us to have spiritual peace. Paul wrote, *"Therefore, since we have been justified by faith, we have peace with God through our Lord Jesus Christ"* (Romans 5:1). If Jesus is our Savior, we have God's peace living within us. His physical and bodily resurrection proves that He is Messiah and Lord. Jesus appeared to His disciples to settle their hearts and encourage them in their mission. He promised to give the disciples the Holy Spirit to equip and empower them for this great work.

In the same way the Father sent Jesus, the Lord commissioned His men for their special assignment. As Jesus' disciple, you have a specific mission to accomplish in the power of the Holy Spirit. Do not be afraid of the opposition. God lives within you. He promises to equip and empower you for this assignment. Discover your specific mission and start moving!

Read: Open your Bible and read Luke 24:47-49.

Reflect: Prayerfully consider the following: Am I connecting God's eternal peace with my personal mission? Is fear holding me back?

Respond: As a result of these truths, what might need to change in my attitude, beliefs, and actions? What steps do I need to take outwardly?

Physical Evidence

"Now Thomas, one of the Twelve, called the Twin, was not with them when Jesus came. So the other disciples told him, 'We have seen the Lord.' But he said to them, 'Unless I see in his hands the mark of the nails, and place my finger into the mark of the nails, and place my hand into his side, I will never believe.' Eight days later, his disciples were inside again, and Thomas was with them. Although the doors were locked, Jesus came and stood among them and said, 'Peace be with you.' Then he said to Thomas, 'Put your finger here, and see my hands; and put out your hand, and place it in my side. Do not disbelieve, but believe.' Thomas answered him, 'My Lord and my God!' Jesus said to him, 'Have you believed because you have seen me? Blessed are those who have not seen and yet have believed' " (John 20:24-29).

Most of us want to see some kind of evidence to back up a story when it sounds too good to be true. We might put on an imaginary detective hat and begin to ask questions that would help us uncover the truth. We do not want to be critical, but we want to use common sense. Thomas must have put on his detective hat when he heard about Jesus' appearing. He was not moved by their story nor was he influenced by their strong presentation. Thomas wanted physical evidence to prove their claims.

Think about the last testimony you heard from another believer. Did you immediately believe what they said? Did you doubt their entire story? Was your response to what they said encouraging or discouraging? Did you crush their spirit or deliver greater hope? Without question, you should investigate miraculous claims and stories of faith. It would be foolish to believe everything you hear without testing it. But today, God works in ways that are different from what you are used to or comfortable with.

Isaiah wrote, *"For my thoughts are not your thoughts, neither are your ways my ways, declares the Lord. For as the heavens are higher than the earth, so are my ways higher than your ways and my thoughts than your thoughts"* (Isaiah 55:8-9). God's Word is filled with great stories of faith and miracles. Seek to understand how God is writing a story of grace in the lives of others. Your story may not be all that exciting just yet. You may want to see even more physical evidence. God may simply be asking you to trust Him even more.

Read: Open your Bible and read Mark 16:14.

Reflect: Prayerfully consider the following: How can I encourage others more in their faith? What doubts keep me from taking steps of faith?

Respond: As a result of these truths, what might need to change in my attitude, beliefs, and actions? What steps do I need to take outwardly?

Believe and Live

"Now Jesus did many other signs in the presence of the disciples, which are not written in this book; but these are written so that you may believe that Jesus is the Christ, the Son of God, and that by believing you may have life in his name"
(John 20:30-31).

It has to be one of the most awkward moments for a conference facilitator to experience. After hearing the speaker talk for thirty minutes, the subject matter increases in complexity. Frustrated, one participant yells out, "I'm lost. What exactly are you talking about? What's the big idea? Your lecture is not clear to me at all." Silence fills the air in the room.

When John wrote his account of the story of Jesus, he wanted to make sure everyone understood the main purpose of his book. John wanted people to believe in Jesus and find life in His name. The stories and examples he includes, by inspiration from the Holy Spirit, point to this overall theme. John wanted to make it clear that everlasting life is found in Jesus. He was not trying to complicate this reality. He wanted to be clear.

God wants everyone to have eternal life through His Son, Jesus Christ. *"For God so loved the world, that he gave his only Son, that whoever believes in him should not perish but have eternal life. For God did not send his Son into the world to condemn the world, but in order that the world might be saved through him. Whoever believes in him is not condemned, but whoever does not believe is condemned already, because he has not believed in the name of the only Son of God"* (John 3:16-18). John wants you to believe this truth. He wants you to experience real life through Jesus Christ. Jesus is the hope of the world.

The evidence of John's testimony is sufficient for you to believe in Jesus. John wrote skillfully about the Messiah, the Son of God. Notice John's profound simplicity as he quotes his Master's words, *"Truly, truly, I say to you, whoever hears my word and believes him who sent me has eternal life. He does not come into judgment, but has passed from death to life"* (John 5:24). John's passion is to make the message of Jesus clear. He wants you to know Jesus personally. John wants you to know and believe the stories. He wants you to experience a fulfilling life in Jesus Christ. Believe and live.

Read: Open your Bible and read John 1:12.

Reflect: Prayerfully consider the following: If John's purpose was to help people believe in Jesus as Savior and Messiah, how can I do the same?

Respond: As a result of these truths, what might need to change in my attitude, beliefs, and actions? What steps do I need to take outwardly?

Empty Nets

"After this Jesus revealed himself again to the disciples by the Sea of Tiberias, and he revealed himself in this way. Simon Peter, Thomas (called the Twin), Nathanael of Cana in Galilee, the sons of Zebedee, and two others of his disciples were together. Simon Peter said to them, 'I am going fishing.' They said to him, 'We will go with you.' They went out and got into the boat, but that night they caught nothing" (John 21:1-3).

Our comfort level increases as we master a particular skill. For musicians, it's the natural expression of what they feel deep within their soul. For athletes, it's the confidence that takes their agility and strength to another level. For the artist, it's mastering a technique or the recognition of how certain color combinations change the overall perception of their creation. In every area where mastery is achieved, the quality is extraordinary.

When Peter and the gang decided to return to the art of fishing, it pointed back to a spiritual milestone in the life of Peter. In Luke 5:1-11, Jesus found Peter as He was delivering His sermon to the crowds. Peter provided Jesus with a boat to finish His sermon. When finished, Jesus told Peter to go further into the deep and let his nets down for a catch. Peter must have thought, "Is He kidding me? I'm a professional fisherman and He is only a teacher. He can teach me about God, but I should be the one teaching Him about fishing." Peter diplomatically responded, *"Master, we toiled all night and took nothing! But at your word I will let down the nets"* (Luke 5:5).

Peter and his team pulled in such a great catch that he had to call other boats over to help him bring in the large number of fish. Peter was beyond belief. It was nothing less than a miracle. Peter knew that Jesus was the one responsible for this abundant catch. That day was not about Peter or his great fishing skills. It was about Jesus and God's unlimited power. Jesus promised Peter, *"Do not be afraid; from now on you will be catching men." And when they had brought their boats to land, they left everything and followed him"* (Luke 5:10-11). Peter left everything to follow Jesus. He found himself back at the place where Jesus found him—fishing. This may or may not have been a spiritual detour. When we take steps in the wrong direction, the results are the same—empty nets. God is the one who fills all of your nets. Leave the fish alone if they distract you and follow Jesus.

Read: Open your Bible and read Luke 5:1-11.

Reflect: Prayerfully consider the following: Am I picking up something again that Jesus has asked me to leave behind? Why am I doing this?

Respond: As a result of these truths, what might need to change in my attitude, beliefs, and actions? What steps do I need to take outwardly?

Do You Have Any Fish?

"Just as day was breaking, Jesus stood on the shore; yet the disciples did not know that it was Jesus. Jesus said to them, 'Children, do you have any fish?' They answered him, 'No.' He said to them, 'Cast the net on the right side of the boat, and you will find some.' So they cast it, and now they were not able to haul it in, because of the quantity of fish. That disciple whom Jesus loved therefore said to Peter, 'It is the Lord!' When Simon Peter heard that it was the Lord, he put on his outer garment, for he was stripped for work, and threw himself into the sea. The other disciples came in the boat, dragging the net full of fish, for they were not far from the land, but about a hundred yards off" (John 21:4-8).

Great technology gives us the ability to record an amazing event on our phones and watch it repeatedly. These events can be uploaded to social media and shared with the entire world in a matter of minutes. Depending on the number of views received, you can get paid well for capturing these great events and being the catalyst for generating large social media traffic.

Peter and his team returned to a very familiar activity—fishing. Like the last time they had gone fishing, they caught absolutely nothing. Their nets were empty once again. Jesus asks a very direct question, *"Children, do you have any fish?"* They respond with a painful, *"No."* Jesus asks them to try again. He confidently tells them to cast their nets on the right side of the boat. The promise was that they would find the fish they were looking for. Jesus changed an unproductive decision into a miraculous adventure.

Consider the major pursuits of your life for a moment. What exactly are you trying to find? How are you measuring your success? For example, is your identity determined by what you do in the marketplace rather than by who you are in Christ Jesus? Are you driven to achieve out of a desire for personal recognition or wealth? Are you leveraging what you have to advance God's purposes through your life? Are your nets filled spiritually?

For a Christian, success is determined by who you are rather than by what you do. Who you are determines what you do. Don't fish in the wrong ocean by focusing on temporary gains. Because you are God's child, the need to "prove yourself" is over. Be who God created you to be. Since people will live forever, focus on reaching people for God's Kingdom.

Read: Open your Bible and read Acts 16:10.

Reflect: Prayerfully consider the following: Am I passionate about bringing lost souls into God's Kingdom? How can I be more intentional?

Respond: As a result of these truths, what might need to change in my attitude, beliefs, and actions? What steps do I need to take outwardly?

Breakfast

"When they got out on land, they saw a charcoal fire in place, with fish laid out on it, and bread. Jesus said to them, 'Bring some of the fish that you have just caught.' So Simon Peter went aboard and hauled the net ashore, full of large fish, 153 of them. And although there were so many, the net was not torn. Jesus said to them, 'Come and have breakfast.' Now none of the disciples dared ask him, 'Who are you?' They knew it was the Lord. Jesus came and took the bread and gave it to them, and so with the fish. This was now the third time that Jesus was revealed to the disciples after he was raised from the dead" (John 21:9-14).

There is nothing like a hot breakfast after an early morning of hard work. Although neglected by many, breakfast has been proven to be an important part of a healthy lifestyle. It is considered essential to maintaining good concentration and maximum strength throughout the day. When you have breakfast with friends, the food and the coffee is even more enjoyable. The disciples were tired and hungry. Jesus was waiting for them to arrive on the shore and share a special meal. The fire was ready. Hot fish and bread were the key items on the menu. Jesus was both cook and server. As Lord, He knew their needs. As Savior, He provided what was needed.

The scene may have reminded the disciples of when Jesus met the needs of more than 5,000 people with fish and bread (John 6:1-13). The needs were overwhelming and the quantities of fish and bread were much greater. The Provider was still the same—Jesus. Jesus delivered the fish into the nets and kept the nets from tearing apart, even with such a large catch. Now things were much more personal for the disciples. It must have been like having a private picnic at the beach. Surely the disciples felt awkward. Everyone knew it was Jesus, but no one dared to ask Him a single question.

Do you find this scene somewhat comical? Jesus is taking the disciples back down memory lane. In a very personal way, He is illustrating the power of His presence. He is showing them firsthand how God provides for all of their needs (Philippians 4:19). You too may have needs, but God has a solution before you even encounter them. Since God is sovereign, He prepares in advance to meet your every need. As with the disciples, Jesus wants to reveal Himself to you. He wants to encourage your heart. Are you ready to follow His plan for your life? Are you ready for breakfast?

Read: Open your Bible and read Matthew 6:25-33.

Reflect: Prayerfully consider the following: How have I seen God provide for the needs of my family? Do I share a part of my day with Jesus?

Respond: As a result of these truths, what might need to change in my attitude, beliefs, and actions? What steps do I need to take outwardly?

Radical

"When they had finished breakfast, Jesus said to Simon Peter, 'Simon, son of John, do you love me more than these?' He said to him, 'Yes, Lord; you know that I love you.' He said to him, 'Feed my lambs.' He said to him a second time, 'Simon, son of John, do you love me?' He said to him, 'Yes, Lord; you know that I love you.' He said to him, 'Tend my sheep'" (John 21:15-16).

It's one of the most popular, but misunderstood words in history—love. It is not uncommon to hear people say, "I really love that car." "I love eating chocolate." "I love watching a good movie." Do these familiar expressions do justice to the word "love?" Does the word love get so overused that we have lost its true meaning? What does it really mean to love someone?

How you define love is very important. There were at least four words people used in Jesus' day to define the word love. *Philia* describes the kind of love you have for a good friend; *storge* describes the kind of love that one has for their family; *eros* describes physical love, more specifically, the sexual form of love. Today, *eros* is the word most commonly used; *agape* describes a love that is unique, self-sacrificing, and giving in nature.

Earlier in His ministry, Jesus defined the characteristics of true love, *"This is My commandment, that you love one another as I have loved you. Greater love has no one than this, than to lay down one's life for his friends"* (John 15:12-13). Jesus connected the word love with sacrifice. If you love someone you will intentionally make personal sacrifices for their benefit. This is the essence of *agape* love. Jesus asked Peter if he was willing to love Him in this way.

Peter understood the commitment, but responded with the word *philia*. This described where Peter was at spiritually. Peter loved Jesus. He loved spending time with Him and serving in His ministry. *Agape* love was not the average kind of love being practiced. It was completely counter cultural. It was not taught at the local fishing school or even in the synagogue. Jesus continued to press Peter for a greater commitment. Jesus wanted Peter to leave the fish alone and begin taking personal responsibility for teaching and leading God's people. This was no small commitment. It was a huge sacrifice and a significant lifestyle change for Peter to consider. Is God asking you to make a radical commitment to serve His people better?

Read: Open your Bible and read 1 Corinthians 13:1-13.

Reflect: Prayerfully consider the following: How does this chapter describe love? Which of these characteristics am I not practicing enough?

Respond: As a result of these truths, what might need to change in my attitude, beliefs, and actions? What steps do I need to take outwardly?

Shepherd

"He said to him the third time, 'Simon, son of John, do you love me?' Peter was grieved because he said to him the third time, 'Do you love me?' and he said to him, 'Lord, you know everything; you know that I love you.' Jesus said to him, 'Feed my sheep. Truly, truly, I say to you, when you were young, you used to dress yourself and walk wherever you wanted, but when you are old, you will stretch out your hands, and another will dress you and carry you where you do not want to go.' (This he said to show by what kind of death he was to glorify God.) And after saying this he said to him, 'Follow me'" (John 21:17-19).

When a baby begins to walk for the first time, parents clap their hands and celebrate. Parents lean down to come alongside their baby and begin walking with them. They want to encourage and connect with their child at their level. A parent might get very close or hold the child's hand to make sure they do not crash into any furniture or fall on his face. They don't expect perfection in one day. Parents know this is a learning process and make adjustments to teach their baby with great love, patience, and care.

Peter was unable to commit to *agape* love. His spiritual maturity was still a work in progress. He had just denied his Savior three consecutive times. He may have been thinking about this incident as he responded to Jesus. Jesus meets Peter right where he is at spiritually. The third time around, Jesus asked Peter if he loved Him with a *phileo* kind of love instead of the *agape* form of love. Like a good parent, Jesus made the adjustments to come alongside Peter and meet him right where he was at spiritually.

Although Peter did not have the confidence to rise up to the uncommon *agape* commitment, he still loved Jesus as a good friend. And as a good friend, Jesus encouraged Peter. Peter was challenged to serve as a shepherd. Peter was still responsible for loving God's people, feeding them spiritually, and protecting them from spiritual wolves. Jesus gave Peter the grace he needed to grow in this agape love as he shepherded the church.

Today, would you respond to Jesus in the same way that Peter responded? Is loving God and serving His people through *agape* love still a tough challenge for you? Don't be discouraged. God meets you where you are. He wants to encourage you as you shepherd His people. When you make the commitment to serve others, God will teach you how to love them.

Read: Open your Bible and read I Peter 5:1-4.

Reflect: Prayerfully consider the following: Am I shepherding others as I grow in my *agape* love? What next steps will help me grow in this area?

Respond: As a result of these truths, what might need to change in my attitude, beliefs, and actions? What steps do I need to take outwardly?

Loved by Jesus

"Peter turned and saw the disciple whom Jesus loved following them, the one who also had leaned back against him during the supper and had said, 'Lord, who is it that is going to betray you?' When Peter saw him, he said to Jesus, 'Lord, what about this man?' Jesus said to him, 'If it is my will that he remain until I come, what is that to you? You follow me!' So the saying spread abroad among the brothers that this disciple was not to die; yet Jesus did not say to him that he was not to die, but, 'If it is my will that he remain until I come, what is that to you?' "
(John 21:20-23).

It is one thing to participate in a special celebration as a distant spectator and another to attend as an honored guest. The distant spectator has a limited perspective. What they see and experience is exciting, but restricted and impersonal. The number on their ticket keeps them far away from the action. The special guest has a totally different experience; what they observe and experience is personal, emotional, and unrestricted.

The Apostle John was invited as a special guest to follow Jesus. He was asked to be part of the inner circle of the disciples along with Peter and James. John's personal observation of Jesus' ministry was exceptional. John was no distant spectator. He describes himself as *"The disciple whom Jesus loved."* John did not find his identity in his native country. He was not trying to climb the corporate ladder. When Jesus said, *"Follow me"*, John accepted the offer of spiritual friendship. John's most precious identity was being loved and accepted by Jesus. His perspective was nothing short of an overflow of this extraordinary relationship. Is that how you want to be remembered? Have you accepted Jesus' offer of spiritual friendship?

Your fruitfulness as a believer is determined by your love and obedience to your Savior. Jesus loved John and John loved Jesus. This relationship was personal. John was constantly in Jesus' presence. It is not surprising that they developed an amazing friendship. John remained very close to Jesus. Imagine how your life would change if your main priority each day was to be in the presence of Jesus? Instead of "checking-off-the-box" of your to-do list, your relationship would be much more intimate and personal. It would be alive and exciting rather than boring, impersonal, or distant.

Read: Open your Bible and read John 15:1-11.

Reflect: Prayerfully consider the following: Is being in God's presence my number one priority each day? Today, am I following Jesus closely?

Respond: As a result of these truths, what might need to change in my attitude, beliefs, and actions? What steps do I need to take outwardly?

The Disciple

"This is the disciple who is bearing witness about these things, and who has written these things, and we know that his testimony is true. Now there are also many other things that Jesus did. Were every one of them to be written, I suppose that the world itself could not contain the books that would be written"
(John 21:24-25).

Committed sports fans are easy to identify. On game day, you can find them wearing their team colors. Some fans paint their faces in unusual ways or color their hair to make their loyalty known to all. They place flags on their cars and banners on their trucks. Die-hard fans adjust their schedules and make special arrangements to make sure they don't miss any games. Identifying the marks of committed sports fans is relatively easy.

How do you identify the marks of a true disciple? How do you know if someone is following Jesus? As John concludes his book, he provides a few clues. First, a disciple is a witness for Jesus. John writes his account from first-hand experience. John was more than a casual observer. He was an eyewitness to Jesus' ministry. A disciple is one who shares his personal experience with Jesus to others. You tell others about Jesus in everyday conversation. You may write down your walk of faith to encourage others.

Second, a disciple is one who has a real God-story. In other words, you have a personal report of God's work through your life. What you speak is the truth. It means that you are a true and faithful witness. There is no deceit or ulterior motives when you share your story with others. You are not trying to astonish people with special effects when you speak. Instead, you faithfully share the truth about the Savior and His work through you.

Third, a disciple is one who has proven God faithful. Notice that John had many more stories to share, but not enough time to write them all down. John regularly experienced God's love, power, and faithfulness. His personal testimony was remarkable. Think through these three marks of a disciple. Are you a faithful witness? Do you regularly share your faith with others? Has God transformed your life and written a new chapter in your story with Him? Have you proven God faithful? Do you trust Him with your children, with your finances and with your career? Are you a disciple?

Read: Open your Bible and read I John 1:1-4.

Reflect: Prayerfully consider the following: Am I growing as a disciple? Which area of spiritual maturity requires more intentionality on my part?

Respond: As a result of these truths, what might need to change in my attitude, beliefs, and actions? What steps do I need to take outwardly?

What's Next?

"But also for this very reason, giving all diligence, add to your faith virtue, to virtue knowledge, to knowledge self-control, to self-control perseverance, to perseverance godliness, to godliness brotherly kindness, and to brotherly kindness love. For if these things are yours and abound, you will be neither barren nor unfruitful in the knowledge of our Lord Jesus Christ" (2 Peter 1:5-8).

What's next for you? The answer may surprise you. You don't have to digest two to three Christian books per week, listen to Christian radio 24/7, or add several new activities to your schedule. The next step is to simply build on the foundation already laid over this last year: read, reflect, and respond. Your daily spiritual nourishment will vary, but the source will remain the same. The vinedresser will work through the vine to shape your life for greater impact. Get ready for God to work in you!

Branches don't change what they're doing to grow and bear fruit. They do however change certain characteristics about themselves as new nutrients are introduced from the vine. Now is the time for you to know the Lord more intimately by adding to this way of life, the abiding life, rather than replacing it with a totally new one. Your old nature was designed to die and be replaced, but your new nature was designed to live and grow generously. How can you continue growing in your faith? Remember the main goal. You were designed to glorify God by bearing much fruit.

You grow in your faith by bearing fruit. As you grow spiritually, you will bear more fruit. Here are some questions for you to consider as you build on the foundation of an abiding life: What changes are still pending for me to make to wholeheartedly follow God's Word? What spiritual deliveries to others are on hold? What changes to my schedule need to happen to help me spend more time in prayer, outreach, Bible study, and fellowship?

Here are some additional questions for you to consider: What other books of the Bible would be best for me to study next and who can coach me along the way? What class or small group do I need to attend to help increase my love for God, His word, His people, and others? Make daily sacrifices to grow your faith. Remember the words of Jesus, *"And anyone who does not carry his cross and follow me cannot be my disciple"* (Luke 14:27).

Read: Open your Bible and read through the entire Gospel of John.

Reflect: Prayerfully consider the following: What truth has changed my thinking and my behavior the most? Which truth is my favorite? Why?

Respond: As a result of these truths, what might need to change in my attitude, beliefs, and actions? What steps do I need to take outwardly?